EMBODIED PERFORMANCE

FRONTISPIECE *Okina* (Old man) dance at a gathering of the Four Schools, from *Hōkoku saireizu byōbu* screen by Iwasa Matabei

Courtesy of Tokugawa Art Museum

EMBODIED PERFORMANCE

WARRIORS, DANCERS, AND THE ORIGINS OF NOH THEATER

MATSUOKA SHINPEI

TRANSLATED BY
JANET GOFF

FOREWORD BY
HARUO SHIRANE

Columbia University Press *New York*

Columbia University Press
Publishers Since 1893
New York   Chichester, West Sussex
cup.columbia.edu

Translation copyright © 2024 Columbia University Press

UTAGE NO SHINTAI: BASARA KARA ZEAMI E by Shinpei Matsuoka
© 1991, 2004 by Shinpei Matsuoka
Originally published in 1991 by Iwanami Shoten, Publishers, Tokyo. This English edition published 2024 by Columbia University Press, New York, by arrangement with Iwanami Shoten, Publishers, Tokyo
All rights reserved

Library of Congress Cataloging-in-Publication Data
Names: Matsuoka, Shinpei, author. | Goff, Janet Emily, translator. | Shirane, Haruo, 1951– writer of foreword.
Title: Embodied performance : warriors, dancers, and the origins of noh theater / Shinpei Matsuoka ; translated by Janet Goff ; foreword by Haruo Shirane.
Other titles: Utage no shintai. English
Description: New York : Columbia University Press, 2024. | Includes bibliographical references and index.
Identifiers: LCCN 2023054685 (print) | LCCN 2023054686 (ebook) | ISBN 9780231212267 (hardback) | ISBN 9780231212274 (trade paperback) | ISBN 9780231559294 (ebook)
Subjects: LCSH: Nō—History.
Classification: LCC PN2924.5.N6 M413 2024 (print) | LCC PN2924.5.N6 (ebook) | DDC 792.0952—dc23/eng/20231213
LC record available at https://lccn.loc.gov/2023054685
LC ebook record available at https://lccn.loc.gov/2023054686

Cover design: Elliott S. Cairns
Cover image: *Okina* (Old man) dance at a gathering of the Four Schools, from *Hōkoku saireizu byōbu* screen by Iwasa Matabei. Courtesy of Tokugawa Art Museum

*This book is dedicated to Janet Goff (1946–2022),
who spent many years of her life on this translation.*

*Many thanks to Matsuoka Shinpei, Okimoto Yukiko,
Phyllis Birnbaum, Christine Dunbar, and the graduate
student assistants Hana Lethen and Yamayoshi Shohei.*

CONTENTS

Illustrations   ix
Foreword by Haruo Shirane   xi
Translator's Introduction   xiii

1 Religion as Theater: The Jishū Sect   1

2 The Archaeology of Performance in an Age of Extravagance   19

3 The Art of Collaboration   45

4 The Genesis of Phantasmal Noh Plays   75

5 Beautiful Temple Boys and the Emperor System   111

6 Zeami and the Graceful Aura of a Boy's Figure   143

7 The Poetics of Space in Noh   171

8 Zeami's Vision of the Actor's Body as a Medium   191

9 The Actor's Basic Posture and the Roof-Covered Noh Stage   215

Notes   231
Glossary   253
Bibliography   259
Suggested Readings   269
Index   277

ILLUSTRATIONS

FRONTISPIECE
Okina (Old man) dance at a gathering of the Four Schools,
from *Hōkoku saireizu byōbu* screen by Iwasa Matabei.
Courtesy of Tokugawa Art Museum. (in color)   ii

ILLUSTRATIONS
2.1. Dengaku performance with drummer at the Gion *goryō-e*
(Gion festival for venerable spirits), from *Nenjū gyōji emaki*
(Picture scroll of annual observances), copied by Tani
Bunch. Courtesy of National Diet Library.   25
4.1. *Odori nenbutsu* (Dancing nenbutsu) at Ichiya in Kyoto,
from *Ippen Hijiri e* (Illustrated life of the holy man Ippen)
by En'i. Courtesy of Tokyo National Museum.   84
5.1. Portrait of Kōbō daishi (Kūkai) as a child/*chigo*, from *Chigo
daishi zō*, Courtesy of Kōsetsu Museum of Art   115
6.1. A *chigo* (young boy) dancing, from *Nikyoku santai ningyō zu*
in Omote Akira and Katō Shūichi, eds., *Zeami, Zenchiku,
Nihon shisō taikei* (Iwanami shoten, 1974), 123.   145
8.1. Woman's *o-omote* noh mask, attributed to Echi, Courtesy
of Tessenkai.   199

9.1. Frontal view of naked man in pose, from *Hachijō-bon kadensho*, in Hayashi Tatsusaburō, ed., *Kodai chūsei geijutsuron*, Nihon shisō taikei, vol. 23 (Iwanami shoten, 1973), 597.   228

FOREWORD

Matsuoka Shinpei, a leading scholar of noh theater in Japan, has written an epoch-making book that goes far beyond noh and performance studies to give us a multilayered understanding of medieval Japanese culture. Noh theater, patronized by samurai elite, has hitherto been associated with *yūgen* (mystery), *wabi-sabi* (understatement), and other subdued aesthetics. But Matsuoka shows us that noh was surrounded by and linked to a wider, more varied popular culture that embraced *odori-nembutsu* (ecstatic dance prayer), the *basara* (extravagance and excess) of Sasaki Dōyo, linked verse, *dengaku* (field music-dance), and *chigo* (beautiful temple-boy) culture. These wild, colorful influences, among other developments, created a new public space that cut across social hierarchies, mixing commoners and courtiers. One of the most influential aspects of the book is the examination of the cultural role of the *chigo*; Matsuoka, who argues that Zeami Motokiyo was himself once a chigo, describes the chigo's impact on gender representation and his connection to the imperial system.

A major contribution of this book is the focus on the body, especially acrobatic and ecstatic corporeal movement, which Matsuoka sees underlying the popular culture of odori-nenbutsu, *dengaku*, and other music-dance performances. He also sees the influence of such movement in the language and dynamics of linked verse, especially popular linked verse, a major passion for many. Matsuoka shows how medieval culture, particularly the work of Zeami, emerged from the intersection of this wild acrobatic body and the restrained body (represented in noh by the motionless mask). This dynamic interaction, operating in an open social space, gave birth to Zeami's noh theater, Sen no Rikyū's tea ceremony, and Ikenobō Sen'ō's art of flower arranging.

With such startling insights, this book provides a deep and nuanced view into one of the most exciting ages in Japanese history and will ignite further enthusiasm for Japanese aesthetics and performance culture. Janet Goff's superb translation of this classic gives English readers the opportunity to explore this exciting world for the first time.

Haruo Shirane
Shincho Professor of Japanese Literature and Culture
Columbia University, New York City

TRANSLATOR'S INTRODUCTION

The fourteenth century was a turbulent period in Japan, a time plagued by political upheaval and radical social and economic change. The chaos contributed to an outpouring of creative energy that gave rise to new forms of artistic expression and new participants at all levels of society. The fruits of all this activity included today's cultural icons such as the art of flower arranging and the tea ceremony. The period also saw the transformation of *renga*, or linked verse, from an aristocratic pastime into a national craze whose modern iteration is familiar to us in the form of haiku. Above all, this period was a catalyst for the development of noh theater, whose chief architect, Zeami Motokiyo, was born in 1363.

The dynamism of the age is vividly captured in *Utage no shintai: basara kara Zeami e* [lit., The body of the feast: from excess to Zeami]. The author, Matsuoka Shinpei, is a specialist on medieval Japanese literature who recently retired from the University of Tokyo. From his early days as a student and throughout his career, he has possessed an interdisciplinary outlook that incorporates a historical perspective and a devotion to noh. These interests are clearly manifested in *Utage no shintai*, as forecasted by the evocative title, *Embodied Performance: Warriors, Dancers, and the Origins of Noh Theater*, given to the English translation of this book. The first part of the book enlists an array of literary, historical, and Buddhist texts, as well as illustrated scrolls, to evoke the world into which Zeami was born. The second part of the book covers Zeami's early training and the theories on noh dramaturgy and performance he developed later in life. Matsuoka's discussion is informed by extensive research on the history and performance of noh in Japan's middle ages (*chūsei*) and in modern times, combined with his long association with the world of the noh stage.

Matsuoka subscribes to the view that chūsei began during the decades prior to 1192, when retired emperors wielded power after ceding the throne to a young male heir. This perspective represents a departure from a common tendency to consider the founding of the first shogunate in Kamakura in 1192 as the start of Japan's medieval era. His stance reflects a belief that the period of cloister rule by retired emperors was a foreshadowing of new trends rather than simply the end of a historical era.

The decades of cloister rule were distinguished by the enthronement of child emperors, a practice that continued until the fourteenth century. This development coincided with the emergence of phenomena such as homosexuality in court circles, the representation of adult historical and literary figures as boys, and the practice of cross-dressing in the performing arts, trends linked to the worship of beautiful temple boys, or *chigo*, in Japan's middle ages, which forms the focus of chapter 5.

Matsuoka's approach is also shaped by a belief that medieval Japanese culture was essentially a physically oriented performance culture with deep roots at the popular level, a trend foreshadowed by the outbreak of *dengaku* (music-dance performance) events in Kyoto in 1096. In other words, the advent of the chūsei is perceived within the framework of radical social and economic changes from below rather than being viewed in terms of systemic change from above.

Chapter 1, "Religion as Theater: The Jishū Sect," opens with a discussion of the practice of dancing ecstatically while intoning the name of Amida Buddha, the ruler of the Western Paradise. Led by the holy man Ippen and his followers, the dance spread like wildfire around the country in the late thirteenth century. Drawing on the illustrated account of Ippen's life compiled by a disciple, Matsuoka stresses the theatrical foundations of the group, whose successors formed the Jishū sect of Pure Land Buddhism. Much of the chapter focuses on the sect's Training Center in the Fourth Ward of Kyoto, which served as a hub of artistic activity, attracting individuals on the margins of society who were involved in a variety of fields including renga and noh.

One prominent supporter, Sasaki Dōyo, was a military governor with outlandish tastes and behavior that earned him a reputation as the epitome of *basara*, or extravagance and excess. Matsuoka argues that the brilliant world created by Zeami was indebted to the culture forged by Dōyo and the Training Center. Dōyo figures prominently in the early chapters of *Utage no shintai*, assisted by colorful anecdotes from the *Taiheiki* (Chronicle of great peace), a fourteenth-century narrative that covers the demise of the Kamakura shogunate in 1333, a fleeting attempt at an imperial restoration, and the founding of a new shogunate in 1336, followed by decades of conflict known as the Age of the Northern and Southern Courts.

Chapter 2, "The Archaeology of Performance in the Age of Extravagance," offers concrete examples attesting to the breakdown in social norms during the Kamakura period, such as the proliferation of outlaw warrior bands and the passion for gambling, dissolute parties, and extravagance (i.e., *basara*).

The temper of the times is epitomized by the energy and excitement generated by the raucous music, dancing, and acrobatics of *dengaku*, which was blamed for the downfall of the Kamakura government. Two highly embellished accounts from the *Taiheiki* capture the spirit of the times: the famous dengaku performance in 1349 when exuberant spectators caused the grandstands to collapse, and Dōyo's grandiose tea party staged beneath the cherry blossoms on the outskirts of Kyoto.

Chapter 3 begins with a discussion of the custom of composing renga beneath *shidare zakura* (weeping cherry trees) in spring, a pastime popular in the Kyoto area during the decades around 1300. The sessions consisted of ten or so unaffiliated monks and holy men; after the first round, all comers (including emperors) were eligible to participate incognito. Renga fever reached a peak with the compilation of the first written anthology of renga in 1356, with help from Dōyo, who served behind the scenes as a mediator between commoners and courtiers. The practice of performing renga incognito was inherited by sessions in which onlookers donned a deep-brimmed woven hat, or *kasa*, as a sign of having freed themselves from society's bonds. The fictive equality maintained by renga sessions was reiterated when military leagues or alliances known as *ikki* emerged in the fourteenth century, forging solidarity among warriors from different backgrounds and ranks by means of special ritual practices. The chapter ends with a discussion of *kaisho*, or gathering places, rooms or independent structures designed for special functions such as flower arranging, renga, and poetry competitions, which allowed individuals on the margins of society to participate in, or oversee, activities of the elite.

Utage no shintai takes its name from Matsuoka's title for chapter 3, which I have translated as "The Art of Collaboration."

Together, *utage* (parties or banquets) and *shintai* (the human body) suggest the activities of performers or actors in social (public) settings where entertainments such as renga, songs and dances, poetry contests, and flower arranging competitions were offered. The account in chapter 6 of the party where a young dengaku player provided entertainment for an elite audience conveys a sense of this kind of venue.

Matsuoka's expansive view of performance affords an opportunity to treat subjects as varied as dengaku and *sarugaku*, initiation rites conducted by militant leagues, and group renga sessions performed incognito. Intriguingly from today's vantage point, chapter 5 also includes an analysis of chigo who underwent special training that anticipated female impersonators (*onnagata*) in kabuki. Matsuoka's observations about the various types of performance cited above are echoed in the chapters on noh that follow. As a complex art form consisting of role playing (dramatic imitation) and oral narratives (*katari*), vocal and instrumental music, and physical movements and gestures including dance, noh reflects its development as a genre that was receptive to existing art forms such as dengaku, *nenbutsu* dances, Buddhist chanting, oral recitations of the *Tale of Heike*, and *etoki* (visual explanations of the origins of shrines and temples).

Chapter 4, "The Genesis of Phantasmal Noh Plays," covers the early development of noh, beginning with the ritual to exorcise evil spirits performed by temple monks at the New Year. The ritual, including the practice of wearing demon masks, was later taken over by sarugaku players. By the early fourteenth century, sarugaku troupes had begun to appear at events that were held to raise funds for temple and shrine projects and other public works. Their plays about demons in hell were in keeping with the pronounced religious aura of the events; organizers were descended from evangelists who traveled around the country encouraging the performance of good deeds to atone for the sins of the departed and promote the salvation of donors.

The discovery of Zeami and his father Kan'ami by the third shogun, Ashikaga Yoshimitsu, at a performance in 1374 or 1375, was a pivotal event in the history of noh. Matsuoka's discussion of Zeami and his writings in the second part of the book begins by addressing an important question regarding Zeami's early life: How did he manage to acquire substantial knowledge about court culture despite his lowly background as a sarugaku player? The answer involves a letter written by the former regent Nijō Yoshimoto to an unnamed Buddhist official thanking him for bringing Fujiwaka (Zeami's childhood name) for a visit in 1375. Rather than attributing Zeami's early education to Yoshimoto or the shogun, as is usually the case, Matsuoka focuses his attention on the recipient of the letter, the head of a major subtemple in Nara, whom he identifies as Zeami's mentor.

In support of this argument, Matsuoka devotes an entire chapter to the phenomenon of chigo, who were cultivated as beautiful creatures to satisfy the tastes of amorous monks. The most widely cited part of the book is chapter 5, "Beautiful Temple Boys and the Emperor System." It describes the strict training of chigo, which encompassed everything from scriptural studies to personal grooming and flower arranging. The discussion throws light on the pedagogical function of major temples as a repository for surplus offspring of military and aristocratic houses that also served as a conduit for classical culture. The chapter title draws attention to the qualities that chigo shared with child emperors, who existed in a vacuum at the center of the body politic. Above all, the chapter expatiates on the nexus between the secret chigo initiation rite on Mount Hiei and an imperial accession protocol that drew on Buddhist doctrines.

Chapter 6, "Zeami and the Graceful Aura of a Boy's Figure," explores evidence in Yoshimoto's letter supporting Matsuoka's argument that Zeami was himself a chigo. The chapter is a revised translation of the original chapters 6 and 7 from *Utage no shintai*, a change designed to compensate for their brevity and overlapping subject matter. (Subsequent chapters have accordingly been renumbered.) After introducing the text of Yoshimoto's letter, Matsuoka identifies the Buddhist official and his connection with Yoshimoto's cultural circle, followed by a discussion of the similarities between Yoshimoto's effusive praise of Zeami and the depiction of chigo in medieval fiction, and a comparison of Yoshimoto's and Zeami's aesthetics.

Chapter 7, "The Poetics of Space in Noh," centers on *enken*, or distant view, a term coined by Zeami that highlights important aspects of noh as a theater form, such as the central role of the principal actor, or *shite*; the relationship between dramatic and performance texts; and the treatment of space in noh. Zeami's advice to incorporate well-known poetic places (*meisho*), in the initial encounter between the shite and the secondary actor, or *waki*, is particularly instructive given the efficacy of time-honored *meisho* in evoking settings on an open-sided outdoor stage. In a similar vein, his recommendation to incorporate language in the shite's entrance speech that was conducive to gazing into the distance (such as longing for a loved one) is couched in terms of expanding the sense of space and building up interest musically. When enken is associated with the figure of the shite dancing, it evokes a vision of the actor merging with the surrounding space. In a few instances, quotations from elsewhere in Zeami's treatises and comments by modern Japanese theater critics and actors are enlisted to suggest enken's meaning, a strategy that offers insight into the appreciation of noh dances today.

Chapter 8, "Zeami's Vision of the Actor's Body as a Medium," explores the shift in Zeami's thinking about role types, acting styles, and playwriting when new types of masks emerged that restricted the actor's ability to see. These chapters covering Zeami's theories challenge readers to think about aspects of noh performance such as the aura emanating from or surrounding the shite, the relationship between actor and audience, and the movements of the actor's body simultaneously through time and space. The discussion about the trancelike physiological and psychological effects of performance represents a recurring motif, echoing earlier observations in the book about the circling of the stage to the beat of a gong by Jishū dancers, and the trancelike state achieved in successful renga where poets serve as both performer and audience.

Chapter 9 brings the translation to an end with a discussion of two unique aspects of noh: the actor's basic posture (the *kamae*) and the roof-covered noh stage. It also includes a translation of chapter 10 of *Utage no shintai* combined with a more recent piece by Matsuoka on the history of the noh stage: "Nō no kūkan: Yane no aru butai" (Noh space: The roof-covered stage), in *Chūsei no tachi to toshi micro no kū*, volume 7 of Asahi Hyakka Nihon no rekishi: Rekishi o yominaosu (1994).

This revision was prompted by the brevity of chapter 10 and the dearth of material in English on the development of the noh stage, whose basic configuration was perfected around 1600. In addition to providing more information about performance aspects of noh discussed in the book, chapter 9 sheds further light on the connection between Jishū dance huts and roof-covered noh stages discussed in chapter 1.

Utage no shintai was written in the 1980s when Matsuoka was closely involved with Hashi no Kai, a noh research association headquartered in Tokyo. The association aimed to bridge the gap in understanding how noh was performed during the Muromachi period and in the modern world. The group sought to look past performance practices and assumptions from the premodern period onward, prior to the discovery of Zeami's writings in the early twentieth century. Members of Hashi no Kai researched early primary and secondary sources, the revival of long dormant plays and performance strategies, and the staging of plays in nontraditional sites in Japan and abroad. In addition, they provided opportunities for noh performers and theater experts to interact with their European counterparts. These goals reflect the achievements of the late noh actor Kanze Hisao, whose lasting influence on noh is reflected in the careers and outlook of Matsuoka and his noh teacher Nagashima Tadashi.

The book's exploration of the relationship between the medieval performing arts and underlying religious beliefs and practices manifests a fundamental human desire to explain the inexplicable, the causes of diseases and natural disasters, and the nature of the afterlife. The composition of renga beneath weeping cherry trees in the thirteenth and fourteenth century is an excellent example. Matsuoka puts a new twist on the enduring Japanese passion for cherry blossoms beyond aesthetic or hedonistic concerns. In addition to noting that the scattering petals were thought to represent the raging of deities that cause disease, requiring the performance of special rituals to subdue them, he points out that trees were regarded as a passageway between this world and the underworld.

The fear of going to hell was especially acute among warriors, whose occupation violated the Buddhist proscription against the taking of life. Early sarugaku (noh) plays, for instance, depict the vengeful ghosts of warriors as demons in hell, while the oral recitation of the *Tale of Heike* by blind raconteurs represented a requiem for the souls of the vanquished Taira clan. The example of peripatetic Heian-period evangelists has already been pointed to as a model for *mugen* noh plays, in which ghosts seeking salvation appear before a priest and then return in their lifetime form and recount events from the past.

Conversely, the longing to escape the endless cycle of rebirth and attain salvation fostered the spread of Pure Land Buddhism, which extolled Amida Buddha's power to save all sentient beings. The belief that merely chanting the deity's name would lead to salvation was instantiated in the ecstatic dance performed by Jishū sect believers while chanting the *nembutsu*. Amida Buddha's attendant Kannon was also widely revered, a fact reflected in the frequency with which the bodhisattva is mentioned in *Utage no shintai*. The most remarkable example of Kannon's vow to alleviate the suffering of all living creatures is the account of the initiation discussed in detail in chapter 5, in which chigo who had been violated by monks are transformed into a Kannon whereby they are able to suffer for the monks' transgressions.

In Matsuoka's discussion of Zeami's work, he presents his own views about time and space, focusing on events and actions from a multiple angles or layers and showing the interrelatedness of past and present, time and space.

A consummate actor's dancing is expressed in terms of nonduality, of transcending distinctions between the self and the other. The term *riken* (detached viewing) that Zeami employs can also refer to the view of the actor from the audience's perspective. Some of his mentions of enken (the distant view) show how an actor directs the gaze of spectators. Of particular interest is the effect produced by wearing a noh mask that limits the actor's ability to see, forcing him to rely on other senses.

The book calls into question assumptions about the world, including social and cultural conventions, that govern what one sees and does, with topics ranging from "appropriate" attire to hairstyles and behavior. The subject of chigo raises interesting questions in this regard. For one, it underscores the nature of gender as an artificial construct shaped by social norms and power relations. The problem of rendering the term in English highlighted the lack of precision—socially, legally, and historically—regarding terms such as boy, youth, and adult.

The above remarks suggest just some of the ways that the book is bound to appeal to audiences in different cultures, with different interests, and create a dialogue including readers interested in medieval Japanese culture as well as students of noh and theater in general.

My own interest in *Utage no shintai* originally sprang from an appreciation of noh plays as literary texts. My doctoral research on the use of *The Tale of Genji* as a source of the noh led to questions about how the tale was understood and appreciated in the Muromachi period when the plays were composed, an approach that reflected my interdisciplinary background. I first met Professor Matsuoka at the University of Tokyo when his teacher, Professor Koyama Hiroshi, the late expert on kyōgen (comic theater) and noh, asked him to assist me in gathering research materials.

While translating the *Genji* plays in the 1980s, I returned to Tokyo on a Japan Foundation postdoctoral fellowship intending to look into performance aspects of noh. Once again, Matsuoka offered invaluable assistance, first of all by introducing me to his noh teacher, Nagashima-sensei. My original intention to take *utai* (chant) and *shimai* (dance) lessons for two or three years turned into more than a dozen years. This transformative experience not only taught me a great deal about noh and traditional Japanese culture, but it also called into question deeply ingrained assumptions about the world, especially regarding the concept of space, which are manifested in everything from theater conventions to daily life.

I was initially drawn to *Utage no shintai* by Matsuoka's discussion of enken, which resonated with what I had learned about how actors evoke a setting on the noh stage. I was also intrigued by his article on the historical development of the noh stage. The idea of translating the book was first raised by an editor at the Institute of Eastern Culture (Tōhō Gakkai) in Tokyo, where I had translated numerous projects on classical Japanese theater under the supervision of Professor Koyama, including Professor Matsuoka's manuscripts. Among them was a special issue of *Acta Asiatica* that included essays by Professor Koyama and Professor Matsuoka on kyōgen and noh, respectively.

My interest in translating *Utage no shintai* was spurred in part by a desire to express my gratitude to Professors Koyama and Matsuoka, as well as to Nagashima-sensei. Their endless kindness and willingness to share their knowledge have enriched my world beyond what words can express. I have persevered long on this translation because of the fascinating possibilities for further exploration of medieval Japanese culture lurking in these pages.

I hope that my work will be an inspiration to others.

THE TRANSLATION

The translation is based on the text of *Utage no shintai* published by Iwanami Shoten in 1991, supplemented by the emendations in the 2004 paperback edition issued in the Iwanami Gendai Bunko series (Gakujutsu 129). The goal of the translation was to make the contents of the book accessible to as wide an audience as possible while at the same time respecting its scholarly origins. With this in mind, explanations of technical terms and background information have been woven into the translation, and endnotes and a glossary have been provided. In addition to supplementary information, the endnotes give the location of Japanese sources, as well as English translations of literary works where available.

A few terms whose meaning has changed markedly over time, or for which no equivalent word or concept exists in English, have been left in the original. Aesthetic terms are a key example. Another, the word *chigo*, proved to be particularly intractable in translation given the frequency with which it is used and its disparate meanings. The word originally signified a child (irrespective of gender). It later came to refer to pages, young attendants in aristocratic and temple circles. It also acquired sexual connotations, which are not necessarily clear in Zeami's treatises. Translation of the term is complicated by cultural, legal, and historical differences governing the gap between childhood and manhood.

Regarding historical figures, the placement of family names before personal names follows Japanese practice. The addition of the particle *no* reflects the custom regarding historical figures from the Heian and early Kamakura periods: for example, Minamoto no Yoritomo (meaning Yoritomo of the Minamoto clan), as opposed to Ashikaga Yoshimitsu.

The handling of historical periods poses a problem, especially given the varied academic disciplines and periods covered by *Utage no shintai*. Wherever possible Japanese dates are rendered using the Western calendar. References to parts of historical periods—the early, middle, or late Kamakura period, for instance—are converted into equivalents such as centuries or decades where possible; otherwise, the name of the period, such as the late Kamakura period, is used. Generally speaking, historical subdivisions known as *nengō* (era names) are readily convertible into a Western equivalent when the year, month, and/or day are specified. Japanese diary entries, for instance, are cited using the following format: Japanese era name + year [Western year] / month / day.

A few observations are in order regarding the handling of noh terminology in the translation. The distinction between noh and sarugaku reflects modern practice—that is, referring to the form of sarugaku perfected by Zeami and his father as noh (or *nōgaku*)—in contradistinction to sarugaku, which in fact was commonly used prior to the modern era. Regarding the handling of noh texts and stage directions, dramatis personae are identified by the type of actor that plays the role: for example, *shite* (principal actor), *waki* (secondary actor), and *tsure* (an attendant or attendants of the principal or secondary actor). Noh libretti consist of musical and spoken segments known as *shōdan*. Apart from their semantic import, *shōdan* help to locate and discuss sections within and between plays. In extended quotations from noh texts, the name of the *shōdan* is set in bold type, and the distinction between spoken and sung passages is indicated by indenting sung lines further than spoken ones. The use of Japanese terms in the stage directions is unavoidable given the unique configuration of the noh stage. Definitions of the technical terms regarding *shōdan* and the noh stage directions can be found in the glossary; a diagram of the noh stage has also been provided.

References to Zeami's noh treatises are to *Zeami, Zenchiku*, edited by Katō Shūichi and Omote Akira, in volume 24 of *Nihon shisō taikei* (Iwanami Shoten, 1974). Page numbers are given in parentheses in the text after the title, which is abbreviated as ZZ. For an English translation of Zeami's treatises see Thomas Hare, *Zeami: Performance Notes* (Columbia University Press, 2008). An English translation of *Sarugaku dangi*, Zeami's remarks on noh recorded by his son Motoyoshi, is available in Erika de Poorter, *Zeami's Talks on Sarugaku* (J. C. Gieben, 1986).

I wish to thank Paul Atkins, who kindly read an earlier draft of chapter 5 and provided many useful comments. I would also like to thank Professor Haruo Shirane for his assistance in the publication of the translation, and his student Hana Lethan for compiling the list of reference works and suggested readings. Above all, my heartfelt thanks to Professor Matsuoka who unfailingly agreed to meet me in Tokyo in spite of his busy schedule, and patiently answered my sometimes inane and inexplicable questions. In the end, all mistakes are my own.

EMBODIED PERFORMANCE

1

RELIGION AS THEATER

The Jishū Sect

Japanese emperors in the twelfth century adopted the practice of abdicating the throne in favor of a young male heir, a strategy that enabled them to wield real, rather than symbolic, control over governmental affairs in retirement. These decades of rule by retired emperors can be looked upon as the start of the middle ages in Japan. An examination of medieval culture in light of these circumstances makes the "carnival" that occurred toward the beginning of the period truly emblematic.

The event that I am referring to is the *dengaku* (field music) craze that engulfed Kyoto in 1096. A contemporary account describes the phenomenon thus:

> In the summer of the first year of the Eichō era, dengaku broke out all around the capital. Where it began is unknown. It first surfaced among villagers and then spread to the nobility. Day and night, there was no end to the tall stilts, single stilts, *koshi-tsuzumi* drums, small rattle drums (*furi-tsuzumi*), cymbals, *binzasara* rattles, and singing and dancing of the sort performed by rice-planting and rice-hulling maidens. The din was astonishing. Bureau employees, government officials, and warriors formed groups and visited temples and filled the streets. It was as if

everybody in the capital had gone mad. It was probably the doing of fox spirits. The exquisite costumes were fashioned to perfection. The beautiful clothing was adorned with gold and silver. The wealthy squandered their resources; even the poor strove to imitate them.[1]

Rather than viewing the essence of medieval Japanese culture in linguistic terms, I look upon it as a physically oriented performance culture with deep roots at the popular level. A reexamination of medieval culture from this perspective casts a spotlight on the kind of world represented by the Great Dengaku of 1096—in other words, the world of the festival—as a rudimentary form of medieval culture.

During the final decades of the thirteenth century, this carnivalesque world was reconstituted as a religion under the holy man Ippen (1239–1289); he is regarded as the founder of the Jishū (Time) sect, a branch of Pure Land Buddhism that centered on the invocation of the name of Amida Buddha, the deity who presides over the Western Paradise. (Although the term dates from later centuries, Jishū is used here for the sake of convenience.) When contemplating medieval Japanese culture, one is struck by the extraordinary scope and depth of the issues posed by this sect, because the fertile world of the festival in medieval Japan eventually took a religious form.

Ippen was viewed as a holy man who renounced social ties and worldly possessions. A person of action rather than words, he began to perform dances (*odori*) while invoking Amida Buddha's name (Namu Amida-butsu) and created an organization around this practice known as the *odori-nenbutsu*. In so doing, he invested the religious group with rich physicality. This unusual activity performed by Ippen and his followers is described as follows in a set of picture scrolls called *Tengu sōshi* that date from

1296 and feature mythical creatures called *tengu*: "They wear short horse cloths when they perform the dance. The way they shake their heads and rock their shoulders as they dance resembles wild horses. The racket they make is no different from monkeys living in the mountains. The men and women expose their private parts and eat with their hands. Their fondness for outrageous behavior will surely result in rebirth in the realm of beasts."[2] Although this criticism clearly reflects the jaundiced view of traditional Buddhism, one can readily imagine that Ippen's dance was a lively group performance pulsating with energy.

The location of the first performance in the village of Odagiri in Shinano Province (now Nagano Prefecture) is also suggestive. The depiction of the dance in scroll 4 of *Ippen hijiri-e* (1299), a pictorial account of Ippen's life also known as *Ippen shōnin eden*, includes an earthen mound in the background above the dancers. It has been argued that the mound is the grave of Ippen's uncle who died in exile in that area after a rebellion in 1221. This detail has given rise to the theory that Ippen's dance began as an event to pacify ancestral spirits.[3]

Another theory has it that the dance was first performed elsewhere in the province, at the marketplace in Tomono. In addition to providing a venue for trading goods, markets served as an execution ground. Since holy men called *sanmai-hijiri* and *nenbutsu-hijiri* for centuries had participated in the burial of individuals who had been executed, Ippen's dance—regardless of whether it was first performed at Odagiri or Tomono—can readily be viewed as forming a direct link with Japan's ritual tradition, namely, rites for the dead souls of vengeful spirits, such as flower-pacification ceremonies (*chinka-sai*) and services for the repose of vengeful spirits (*goryō-e*).

According to the illustrated account of Ippen's life, the dance at Odagiri was held on the grounds of a warrior's residence, whereas the one depicted at Katase near Kamakura (not far from modern Tokyo) in scroll 6 was performed on a temporary dance hut at the Jizōdō, a hall dedicated to the bodhisattva Jizō, a deity revered as a savior of beings that have gone to hell. The addition of a bridgeway (*hashigakari*) to a hut would transform it into a noh stage. What concerns us here is neither the configuration of the hut nor the symbolic setting in which the dance was performed, but rather the performers themselves and the radical shift that occurred in the sect during the time that had elapsed between that event and the earlier one at Odagiri.

A dance was also performed inside and outside of the residence of a warrior named Ōi Tarō in Shinano. The picture in scroll 5 is accompanied by an explanation that the dancing of several hundred people caused the floorboards to break. The large number of participants makes it safe to assume, I think, that they included both Jishū members and ordinary lay persons. Likewise, the earlier scene in front of the warrior's residence does not neglect to include among Ippen's followers someone who appears to be a warrior, gazing up at the sky with a half-dazed countenance as he dances. At the Jizōdō hall in Katase, on the other hand, members of the sect are the only ones depicted dancing on the stage. Ordinary folk are merely standing around the platform looking up at Ippen and his followers ecstatically dancing in a clockwise direction as they chant Amida Buddha's name and stamp their feet on the floorboards to the sound of a hand-held gong.

This change signaled the transformation of Ippen and his followers into a kind of religious theater group whose repertoire consisted of only one item: the *nenbutsu* dance. Or, if a theatrical nature had already been gestating in the odd itinerant group as performers watched by an audience, it was a conscious outward expression of the group's latent nature as theater and as spectacle. Whatever the case, after the dance the crowd gathered around the roofed stage to watch the performance received amulets inscribed with Amida Buddha's name, along with a promise of rebirth in paradise. This itinerant group led by Ippen performed the dance and distributed amulets in different places until it eventually took the entire country by storm. The frenzied physical performances of the primitive religious theater group, whose sensibilities were rooted in the world of the festival, enthralled commoners—their audience—and redrew the map of the traditional religious world.

It also radically altered the map of medieval Japanese culture. The extensive involvement of the sect's members in cultural phenomena that epitomize the arts of the middle ages—such as linked verse (*renga*), banquet songs (*sōka*), warrior tales, noh, didactic stories (*sekkyō*), tea, and flower arranging—is incontestable, although the level of involvement varied from field to field.

At issue here, however, is a simple fundamental question: What accounts for the sect's ability to become deeply involved in these varied cultural phenomena? The answer, I would argue, lay ultimately in the unusual physicality of the sect. In other words, the members' engagement in religious activities of a quasitheatrical nature honed their underlying physical nature as actors. This unusual characteristic facilitated their entry into artistic fields that centered on physical types of performance. I would argue that it also enabled them to flourish in those realms.

Given the fact that the sect's doors were open to entertainers at the lowest rung of society such as conjurers, jugglers, acrobats, and sarugaku (early noh) and dengaku performers, it could be argued that such people found their way into the sect, and that performers who joined the sect were a driving force behind medieval culture. Even if that was often the case, however, it should be emphasized that the distinctive theatricality at the heart of the sect would have acted as a magnet that attracted entertainers.

Just as the Great Dengaku of 1096 began in villages (or among villagers) and expanded to include the nobility, the nenbutsu dance performed by Jishū members first took place in the recesses of Shinano Province and eventually spread to Kyoto. The sect established a foothold in several places in the capital, of which the Training Center in the Fourth Ward, namely, the Shijō dōjō, developed as the main location. (Jishū temples were referred to as dōjō.) During the fourteenth century when imperial rule was divided between the Northern Court in Kyoto and the Southern Court in the mountains of Yoshino, this training center reigned in the capital as the place where Jishū culture shone the brightest. The following discussion examines various aspects of this cultural site, which thus far has drawn scant attention.

THE TRAINING CENTER IN THE FOURTH WARD

The Training Center covered an area along Shijō-dōri street slightly west of the bridge over the Kamo River that led to the Gion shrine, an area around today's Daimaru Department Store—what, in terms of location and function, could be called Kyoto's "gut."

The center was founded in 1311 by Jōa (d. 1341), who studied under Ippen's disciple Taa, the head of the main branch of the Jishū sect located in Fujisawa, not far from Kamakura. The latter's statement in a collection of his teachings (*Taa Shōnin hōgo*) that devotees of Jōa abounded in the capital is a frank recognition of

Jōa's renown as a religious figure in Kyoto. It also suggests that the branch of the Jishū sect headquartered in the Fourth Ward occupied a major place in the religious world, which was centered on the capital.

The dance was performed at the Training Center, too, as the earliest text on kyōgen, the comic counterpart of noh, shows.[4] Known as the *Tenshō kyōgen bon* (ca. 1578), the work contains summaries of a large number of plays, including one called *Imo-arai* (Washing potatoes) about a servant who visited Kiyomizu temple and watched nenbutsu dancing at the Training Center while sightseeing in the capital without his master's permission: "A daimyo appears and summons his servant Tarō Kaja. He scolds him for shirking his duties. Tarō Kaja says that he has been to the capital. The daimyo tells him to recount the famous places and historical sites there. 'I went to Kiyomizu,' says Taro Kaja. 'I also went to the Training Center in the Fourth Ward. I watched the dancing and washed potatoes along the bank of the Kamo River.'"

The dance apparently continued to attract commoners inside and outside of the capital. It was not unusual for high-ranking individuals in Kyoto to attend performances, as the following diary entries show. For instance, on the second day of the Fourth Month of 1419, Nakahara Yasutomi, a Confucian scholar at the Imperial Court, mentions watching nenbutsu dancing at the Training Center after visiting the Gion shrine. On the ninth day of the Second Month of 1480, the courtier Nakamikado Nobutane states that he went to the Training Center with a middle counselor to watch nenbutsu dancing. On the second day of the Third Month of 1517, another courtier, Washinoo Takayasu, comments that he visited various temples on the final day of the spring equinox, and then watched the dancing at the Training Center, while Yamashina Tokitsugu, an imperial official, mentions heading to Shijō to watch the dancing at the Training Center on the sixteenth day of the Eighth Month of 1564.

The kind of stage on which nenbutsu dances were performed at Jishū training centers has been likened to noh stages, on the assumption that the main hall, which was constructed with the nenbutsu dance in mind, closely resembled noh stages, particularly ones erected for subscription performances.[5] For instance, spectators (i.e., worshippers) sat on three sides of the protruding dance platform, and a statue of Amida Buddha, the chief image of worship, was placed at the rear of the platform like the mirror boards at the rear of a noh stage (on which a pine tree is painted), beyond which lay the dressing room. In actuality, the main hall where the dances were performed probably more closely resembles the configuration of indoor noh theaters introduced during the Meiji era (1868–1912) in which spectators sat on three sides of the stage. (Spectators' seats are never located behind the chorus in today's noh theaters.)

The nenbutsu dance held in this kind of space was presumably conducted in almost the same manner as Ippen's. The energy, the extraordinary excitement generated by the group dance, which still pulsated with life even after having been somewhat toned down, was surely what attracted old and young, high and low, male and female alike, inside and beyond the boundaries of the capital. The Training Center in the Fourth Ward surely also continued to exist as a foreign site in the capital as long as this extreme physicality survived in the dance.

Ippen's dance was performed with the goal of becoming a living Amida Buddha. In addition, it had the pronounced aura of a ritual to pacify the souls of the dead. As a result, it was commonly performed in settings linked to the world of the dead such as marketplaces and Buddhist temples devoted to the worship of the bodhisattva Jizō.

The Training Center in the Fourth Ward was no exception in the sense that it served as a gateway to the land of the dead. Its predecessor at that location, a temple called Gidarinji, had been famous as a holy site dedicated to Jizō since the mid-Heian period (794–1192). According to the early twelfth-century Buddhist tale collection *Konjaku monogatarishū* (Tales of times now past), Jizō services there seem to have attracted many commoners in Kyoto. Moreover, the hall donated to the Training Center in 1388 by the third Ashikaga shogun Yoshimitsu (1358–1408) was a holy site dedicated to Jizō, as a statue of the bodhisattva was the chief object of worship there. In other words, the grounds of the Training Center in the Fourth Ward at that point in time had two sacred Jizō sites. The text of a pictorial account of the miracles of Jizō (*Jizō bosatsu reigen ekotoba*) dated 1491 lists fourteen sacred Jizō sites in Kyoto including both Gidarinji and the Training Center, a claim that has some validity.

From the outset, the Training Center had the pronounced aura of a literary salon. Its founder Jōa was a poet whose work was included in the twentieth and twenty-first imperial anthologies of thirty-one-syllable *waka* poems. The frequency with which waka competitions and parties were held at the Training Center can be glimpsed from the headnotes to poems in the *Sōanshū* (Grass hut collection), a personal collection of verse compiled by Jōa's student Tonna, a poet-monk hailed as one of the four deva kings of waka.

Linked-verse sessions must also have been frequently held, otherwise it would be difficult to explain the reason behind the large number of renga experts produced by the center. The relationship between the Jishū sect and this literary genre became so firmly established that renga poets in later times were automatically associated with it. The primary factor was the pronounced element of a religious ritual underlying linked verse produced by commoners, that is to say, *jige renga*. Commoners' renga sprang from linked-verse parties held in the springtime when weeping cherry trees (*shidare-zakura*) were in bloom. *Nenbutsu hijiri*—itinerant holy men with close ties to burial rites who traveled around chanting Amida Buddha's name—gathered to hold renga sessions beneath the blossoming cherry trees, which were regarded as a gateway between this world and the land of the dead. After the core group completed one round of stanzas, ordinary people wearing a deep-brimmed woven hat (*kasa*)—a medium for possession by a deity and symbol of otherness—anonymously added stanzas. These events formed the prototype for what was known as *hana no moto renga*, namely linked verse composed beneath the cherry blossoms.

The activity was truly a quiet nenbutsu dance in its function as a verbal rite of spirit pacification at the entrance to the world of the dead, as well as in the sense that it forged a heightened linguistic world through kinesthetic or somatic empathy with other members of a group and took place in front of a large number of spectators. The common ground shared on a deep level by hana no moto renga and the nenbutsu dance was nothing less than the folk tradition represented by flower pacification rites.

It was here that an avenue presented itself for Jishū members to make their way into renga as celebrants officiating at services for the repose of departed souls and as linguistic performers. The deep intrinsic ties between the Jishū sect and renga is epitomized by Zenna, the last great master of hana no moto renga and father of commoners' renga, who emerged from Konkōji, a temple at the Jishū Training Center in the Seventh Ward in Kyoto. The presence later on of famous renga practitioners from the Training Center in the Fourth Ward requires no further explanation.

THE SECOND HEAD OF THE TRAINING CENTER IN THE FOURTH WARD

The Training Center's nature as an artistic site founded on the underworld developed even more dynamically after Jōa's death in 1341, when his disciple Sakua took over as its head and assumed the Jōa name. The sequel to Tonna's poetry collection contains poems that he exchanged with Jōa II lamenting the death of their mentor. In addition to being a waka poet whose work is included in the eighteenth imperial waka anthology of poetry, Jōa II was a renga enthusiast whose compositions are represented in the *Tsukubashū* (1356), a renga collection modeled after imperial anthologies.

Jōa II's true talent lay in opening up the Training Center to the performing arts. The rapport exemplified on a physical level by nenbutsu dances—a world that led to collective religious exaltation during the physical and psychological interaction of the members with each other—lay behind waka and renga gatherings. It also forged a direct link with the performing arts, which are inherently physical. Furthermore, the aspect of a spectacle or show possessed by nenbutsu dances would have attracted various types of performance to the Training Center. Jōa II can be regarded as a catalyst in taking the center's latent nature as a world characterized by physical rapport or spectacle and turning it into reality as a venue for the performing arts.

Banquet songs—a popular medieval genre—were performed at the Training Center in 1343, two years after Jōa II took over as its head. On the thirteenth day of the Ninth Month that year, the diary of the Gion shrine administrator offers the following account of the musical event held at the Training Center that evening: "There were numerous musicians. The performers of banquet songs included the lay-priest Jinbō, Mishima Kōami, Jiami, Mishima Kage-yuzaemon, Endō Gorōzaemon, and Kōa. I attended the event accompanied by Shinano Hōgen's youth with flowing locks (*taregami*)."

At this sort of event, offerings of incense and flowers were placed in front of a pair of hanging scrolls that depict bodhisattvas dancing and playing musical instruments, and the deities Brahma and Indra in the World of Desire. Music was played and popular songs—sacred Shinto songs (*kagura*), ancient ballads (*saibara*), miscellaneous pieces, and regional songs [notably, eastern songs, or *azuma uta*]—were sung. The category of popular songs naturally also included banquet songs, but perhaps it would be more accurate to view these banquet songs as the main fare.[6]

The Gion shrine diary represents one of the earliest references to banquet songs in the historical record. The entry on the twenty-fifth day of the following month, which mentions a visit to the Training Center that morning and an audience with Jōa II, also mentions dances (*mai*), another popular performance mode of the day. The word *mai* here has been taken to be a reference to extended narrative songs called *kusemai* that featured a lively rhythm accompanied by simple dance movements. The assumption is based on a comment about *daigashira* dances at the center in a cloistered prince's diary in the Seventh Month of 1544. Since the Daigashira school specialized in a form of kusemai dance, the comment about dances at the Training Center in 1343 suggests that they were kusemai. Moreover, a writer of kusemai songs—the renga poet Rinna—later emerged from the Training Center. Hence, it seems likely that the dances mentioned in the Gion shrine diary were kusemai. If so, the entry represents the earliest reference to this performance form in historical records.

Two lyrical kusemai songs composed by Rinna—"Tōgoku kudari" (Journey to the eastern provinces) and "Saigoku kudari" (Journey to the western provinces)—had an influence on the noh plays of Zeami Motokiyo. Another poet, Soa, wrote the main part of a lost piece called *Sumiyoshi no sengū no nō* (The noh about moving the Sumiyoshi shrine) that was set to music and performed to great acclaim by Zeami's father Kan'ami. In short, Jishū members from the Training Center played a significant role in the composition of noh texts.

One can imagine that Jōa II quickly took steps to introduce the two new genres, banquet songs and kusemai, at the Training Center. He also had extensive ties with performance forms such as dengaku. For instance, the Gion diary indicates that the shrine's chief administrator Kensen in the Eighth Month of 1352 received a visit from the leader of the lion dancers troupe, a person called Kuniyaki, whom he criticized for not following through on an agreement to perform a lion dance. The main reason for failing to do so, according to the leader of the troupe, was that bloodshed had been spilled during a fight between the lion dancers and the Shinza (New Troupe) of dengaku performers in the Sixth Month, which left a lion dancer dead. The diary notes that somebody suggested asking the holy man in the Fourth Ward to serve as a mediator regarding the knifing by the Shinza troupe in the Sixth Month, a proposal that Kuniyuki did not object to.

Lion dances commonly preceded dengaku at festivals, creating a kind of rivalry that made this sort of trouble possible from time to time. The most noteworthy point in the entry is the remark that Kuniyuki made no fuss when somebody broached the idea of asking the holy man (i.e., Jōa II) to serve as a peacemaker regarding the stabbing incident that embroiled the lion dancers and the dengaku troupe. According to Gion records, the lion dance was performed on the tenth day of the Tenth Month, so Kuniyuki would appear to have agreed to the arbitration. In any event, the fact that Jōa II occurred to somebody as a mediator in a dispute involving lion dancers and dengaku players would seem to indicate that he had close ties with dengaku.

THE FLAMBOYANT DAIMYO SASAKI DŌYO AND THE JISHŪ SECT

The holy man with a pronounced appetite for the performing arts acquired an advocate in the person of Sasaki Dōyo, a *shugo daimyo* (military governor) who even donated land to the sect. Dōyo was a *basara daimyo*, that is, a warrior renowned for his outlandish taste and behavior. The extravagant ornamentation that characterizes *basara* is illustrated by the following passage in the fourteenth-century war tale *Taiheiki* (Chronicle of great peace): "Sasaki Dōyo's kinsmen and young retainers, following current fashion, astonished people with their extreme luxury. Dressing themselves opulently in a manner known as basara, they went falcon hunting in the Nishinooka area and the Eastern Hills, and then headed home."[7]

A concrete image of basara can be found in the legal code issued by the new military government in 1336 which declares: "Recently, there has been an all-consuming love of excess that is referred to as basara. Everything—from the damask and brocade to the beautifully crafted silver swords and fashionable attire—dazzles the eye. It is utter madness."[8]

A detailed examination of Sasaki Dōyo—the epitome of basara tastes—already exists.[9] Here I would like to examine him in terms of his relationship to the Training Center by focusing on the existence of semirecluses known as *tonseisha*, who are thought to have served as intermediaries between Dōyo and the Training Center. The fact that tonseisha tended to belong to the Jishū sect is evident from a treatise called *Gaijashō* (Notes on rectifying heresy; 1335). The document includes a remark by the Buddhist monk Kakunyo, who explained that in those days the term was widespread in the capital and the countryside, and that it seemed to refer largely to followers of Ippen and Taa.

In 1366, Dōyo staged a lavish performance in the form of a cherry-blossom viewing party on the western outskirts of Kyoto. The event not only took the townspeople's breath away but it also humiliated his political rival, who had arranged a party at the shogun's residence for that very same day. Dōyo also astounded the townspeople by choosing a quiet, festive setting in which to stage such an ostentatious event. The individuals who orchestrated this improper use of the festive space were none other than tonseisha.

Chapter 37 of the *Taiheiki* offers another glimpse at Dōyo's relationship to tonseisha. It describes the unusual step taken by Dōyo when the Northern Army withdrew from Kyoto in 1361: he sumptuously decorated his vacated residence, which was about to fall into enemy hands, and left a pair of tonseisha in his employ at this residence with instructions to treat whoever came there hospitably. The first person to turn up was Kusunoki Masanori, a warrior who fought on the side of the Southern Court. The two tonseisha Dōyo had left behind came out and invited the warrior inside, saying that Dōyo had left instructions to serve him refreshments.[10] Touched by Dōyo's gesture, the warrior redecorated the residence before he retreated from the capital, leaving behind a priceless suit of armor and a silver sword, as well as two retainers.

The world ridiculed Kusunoki Masanori for his unsuccessful effort to imitate Dōyo and for losing the pair of treasured objects.

But it seems to me that the world would have also laughed at him for leaving the two retainers at the residence, whereas Dōyo had left two tonseisha. Because tonseisha existed outside of mainstream society, they were perfectly suited to being improperly placed at the head of a festive space. In other words, the warrior's stationing of two retainers—positively regarded individuals—in a space already degraded by the tonseisha represented a grave miscasting. I cannot help thinking that he was disparaged as a yokel by critics in the capital for not realizing that placing two retainers in that space would destroy the aesthetic balance of the festive world as a whole. In any event, Dōyo fully understood that the tonseisha were a reverse image of himself, his negative alter ego. The conjecture that he was the first warrior to employ tonseisha seems to make sense.[11]

A concrete image of tonseisha can be glimpsed from an account of the hostilities between the military governor of Shinano Province and the local gentry in 1400 that paints the following picture of Tonna in the ostentatious *basara* procession celebrating the military governor's arrival at Zenkōji temple:

> The tonseisha Tonna and Rikiami rode at the head of the procession. Despite his ugly countenance and uncouth body, Tonna was renowned in the capital. He learned the old style of renga under Jijū Shūami and mastered two styles of banquet songs: that of Kenna of Suwa and Danjō of Aida. He was trained as a storyteller under Shu'ami of Koyama. His eloquence and quick wit resembled his mentor's. His antic dancing entertained gatherings, and when he sang everybody roared with laughter.
>
> In the procession, he wore a gold brocade hood that came down to the nape of his neck, while his elaborately embroidered kimono with narrow sleeves (*kosode*) extended up to his ears. He nonchalantly rode a half-tamed horse, his favorite kind of mount,

on a saddle made from a sea-lion skin. As he rode along, he sang and struck his saddle with a bat-wing shaped fan. His outlandish taste and appearance were beyond words; they defied criticism. Spectators considered him a model.[12]

Tonna played the role of a basara type of fool to perfection. Like Tonna, Dōyo exhibited bizarre, theatrical behavior and tried to acquire an identity in a more elemental inclusive realm that physically transcended the everyday world. What linked the two men, who on the surface represented the polar opposites of power and marginality, was their extreme theatricality and physicality—the very qualities that formed the essence of the world of the Jishū sect that I have spelled out thus far.

As previously mentioned, Dōyo donated land to the Training Center, a gathering place for Jishū members and individuals like Tonna. From Dōyo's perspective, in a sense the donation, arguably, was property bestowed on a group that represented his negative alter ego, although on the surface his objective was to pacify and pray for the souls of countless individuals, foes and allies alike, who died during the strife that beset the country in the fourteenth century.

The cultural world formed by the likes of Sasaki Dōyo and the Training Center created a fertile matrix for artistic activity in Japan's middle ages. Although not producing any achievements recognized as being of the highest order, it consistently maintained a level just shy of that. In other words, the world was characterized by cultural chaos that abounded with a range of possibilities prior to the narrow ascent to the top. The world of noh realized by Zeami, for instance, formed a brilliant opposing world that only an individual inextricably connected to the chaotic culture of excess forged by Dōyo and the Training Center could have achieved.

2

THE ARCHAEOLOGY OF PERFORMANCE IN AN AGE OF EXTRAVAGANCE

The code of conduct issued by the new military government in 1336 begins by banning the recent passion for excess known as *basara*. It lists damask and brocade, finely crafted silver swords, and fashionable attire as examples of all the things that amazed people. Calling the phenomenon the height of madness, it warns, "The rich increasingly take pride in it, and the poor are ashamed because they cannot emulate it. Nothing is more injurious to the populace than this. It must be strictly regulated."

Following a brief reconciliation with the new government, Emperor Go-Daigo (1288–1339) suddenly fled Kyoto for the mountains of Yoshino in the waning days of 1336. His flight marked the start of a turbulent period known as the Nanbokuchō, or Age of the Northern and Southern Courts, which lasted until 1392 when the Northern Court in Kyoto, backed by the shogunate, won out. As the curtain opened on the age, the basara trend was already so widespread that the new government's first move was to issue a ban against it. Moreover, the phenomenon, far from waning, flourished throughout the period.

The Kemmu code describes basara in terms of excess in the use of gorgeous material, beautifully made silver swords, and fashionable attire, which can be interpreted as extreme, outlandish ornamentation in a person's outer appearance. The extravagance and excess, however, were not limited just to warriors, the immediate target of the code.

Lawless individuals known as *akutō* are one example. Outlaw warrior bands who doubled as gamblers, performers, tradesmen, and craftsmen, they wreaked havoc around the country, particularly in the provinces near Kyoto, as the Kamakura period (1192–1333) drew to a close. For instance, Kusunoki Masashige (d. 1336), a military leader supporting the Southern Court who plays an active role in the first part of the *Taiheiki*, is described as an akutō from Kawachi Province (now Osaka Prefecture).

A topographical history covering a province that was part of present-day Hyōgo Prefecture, west of Osaka, provides a detailed look at akutō around 1300: "Ten or twenty men holed up in a fortress, motivated by treachery, join the attackers or let them inside in complete disregard of prior agreements. They revel in gambling and betting and make stealing and petty thievery their calling."[1]

The history casts akutō as a ragtag lot, a strange, odd-looking and oddly shaped band dressed like outcasts. "They were furtive figures who wore unlined persimmon-colored robes and large conical hats with deep brims rather than regular caps (*eboshi*). They carried motley quivers and swords with frayed hilts and scabbards and had no regular military gear such as armor or corselets, just long staves, clubs, and sticks."

By around 1325, however, the outlaws had emerged as a mounted warrior band glittering with gold and silver, according to the history: "Fifty to one hundred horsemen rode in a single file on fine mounts. Their richly caparisoned horses and Chinese chests, bows and arrows and other weapons were studded with gold and silver, and their armor and corselets glittered."

The outlaw bands became a guerrilla force in wartime armed with rocks, poles, clandestine measures, and the like. They also served as contractual deputies on proprietary estates and seized others' domains, carried out robberies in broad daylight, committed murder and arson, and appropriated rice crops, even as they plundered their own domains. They gradually amassed wealth as they boldly continued on in this manner and began to flamboyantly adorn their dissolute traitorous bodies in garish, glittering attire. The akutō portrayed in the local history of the late Kamakura period (early fourteenth century) were forerunners of the basara daimyo during the Age of the Northern and Southern Courts vividly depicted in the *Taiheiki*.

The prohibition against basara that opens the Kemmu code did not just forbid luxury and extravagance in personal attire. It also unmistakably included a ban against the lawlessness of warriors—namely, dissolute, uncontrollable behavior.

DENGAKU

The unbridled behavior that included violent activity in daily life emerged in a purer physical form in *dengaku*, whose popularity in a sense followed a trajectory similar to that of outlaw bands.

The passion for dengaku as an entertainment form remained undiminished for roughly three centuries from around the time of the Great Dengaku of 1096, which engulfed all of Kyoto in mass hysteria at the dawn of the period when retired emperors wielded power, to the Age of the Northern and Southern Courts. It began to reach an extreme level, however, in the early fourteenth century. In 1311, a high-ranking courtier frankly attributes the phenomenon to demonic forces: "There was a performance of dengaku at the Kitayama villa today," writes Tōin Kinkata in his diary. "Recently, this type of entertainment is all the rage. It could perhaps best be described as the work of evil spirits."[2] A week later, he makes a comment about an epidemic being called the dengaku disease, an offshoot of the dengaku fever.

The craze eventually spread to Kamakura, the seat of the military government. "Dengaku flourished in the capital in those days," says the *Taiheiki* in chapter 5. "Everybody, high and low alike, took great pleasure in watching it. Hearing what was going on, the Sagami Lay Monk summoned the Shinza troupe and Honza (original troupe) to Kamakura and buried himself in dengaku night and day, completely oblivious of everything else."[3] The tale refers to Hōjō Takatoki, the last regent of the Kamakura shogunate. The existence of a letter sent in 1329 by a fellow clansman and advisor, Kanazawa (Hōjō) Sadaaki, which states that the regent was oblivious to everything but dengaku, is a possible indication that his obsession with it dated from around that time.

According to the *Taiheiki*, he was so besotted with dengaku that he assigned a dengaku performer to each of the leading daimyo and had them dress the players in gorgeous attire. This is lord so-and-so's performer, that is lord so-and-so's performer, it was said of the players, who wore damask and brocade and glittered with gold, silver, and precious gems. The war tale would go on to describe Takatoki's passion for commanding brocade-covered fighting dogs with gold- and silver-studded leashes to attack each other in packs of two hundred at a time.

The graffiti posted on the Nijō riverbank in Kyoto in 1335 lists *renga*, dengaku, tea, and incense as types of entertainment that were popular in the capital.[4] Known as the Nijō-gawara lampoons, the writing attributes the downfall of the Kamakura government to the regent's obsession with fighting dogs and dengaku while at the same time acknowledging the ongoing popularity of dengaku. In fact, the craze increased even further during the Age of the Northern and Southern Courts. It was a basara type of entertainment whose performers, like outlaw bands (*akutō*), wore a profusion of gold, silver, and precious gems, and were covered in damask and brocade.

An account of New Year's rites performed by monks at the Imperial Palace on the thirteenth day of the First Month of 1141 describes a dengaku event: "Several dozen dengaku dancers moving in a frenzied, intoxicated manner emerged from the building in broad daylight. The spectators roared with laughter at the antic movements of the dancers weaving in and out." The unusual dancing is described, without mincing words, using the expression *kyōran basa* (translated here as "frenzied, intoxicated"). An ancient Chinese mimetic term employed in reference to actions such as dancing and walking in an inebriated manner, in Japan *basa* described the dances of shrine maidens possessed by a deity. The dance performed in a circular or linear formation by several dozen dengaku players was clearly a licentious uninhibited sight that made spectators roar with laughter.

The frenzied, intoxicated nature of dengaku group dances was heavily indebted to the raucousness, extemporaneity, and constantly changing rhythm of the music. This aspect is captured in the following account of a dengaku performance at the Uji Rikyū festival in 1133: "The show put on by the dengaku players was extraordinarily exciting. The flute music was played randomly without any fixed melody. The drums were struck freely without any fixed pattern. Everybody was astounded by the din created by the drums and the flute music."[5]

One must not overlook the fact that these impressions of dengaku sounds and rhythms were recorded by a high-ranking nobleman, Fujiwara no Munetada, whose ears were accustomed to court music. Even so, it can be inferred that the dengaku was raucous and highly improvisational and possessed a free rhythm. Binzasara rattles, a folk percussion instrument, would certainly have been employed in the performance as well, although the instrument apparently went unmentioned in the diary owing to the limitations imposed by the nobleman's use of parallel Chinese prose. Binzasara consist of flat wooden slats strung together with a cord that make a sharp sound when the instrument is waved from side to side. Their dry, sharp sounds accompanying the dancers' steps clearly intermingled with and reinforced the raucous music produced by the drums and flute music.

The comment about the beating of drums without a fixed rhythm presumably referred to the two types employed in dengaku: *kotsuzumi* (shoulder drums); and *koshi-tsuzumi* (drums fastened at the waist or hung from the neck). There was a strong tendency, especially, to perform acrobatic feats with the former. For instance, *Chōjū jinbutsu giga* (Scrolls of frolicking animals and humans) contains a picture of a drummer kicking his left leg up in the air and striking the shoulder drum under his knee. *Nenjū gyōji emaki* (Picture scrolls of annual ceremonies and events) depicts a player tossing his shoulder drum up in the air while the dengaku performers around him play their instruments. The drummer presumably struck the drum as it came down. *Daisenji engi emaki* (Illustrated scroll of the legendary origins of Daisenji Temple) and *Urashima Myōjin engi* (Legendary origins of the deity Urashima Myōjin) depict a performer striking a kotsuzumi held in his left hand above his head.[6] The latter scroll also depicts a koshi-tsuzumi drummer beating his instrument with his arms crossed. The acrobatic beating of drums in this manner would have intensified the rhythmical variety and improvisational quality of dengaku.

The shoulder drum was struck in an acrobatic manner in group dances in which all of the dengaku players—the full

FIGURE 2.1 Dengaku performance with drummer at the Gion *goryō-e* (Gion festival for venerable spirits), from *Nenjū gyōji emaki* (Picture scroll of annual observances), copied by Tani Bunch

Courtesy of National Diet Library

ensemble—performed. The repertoire also possessed as side entertainment many stunts that belonged to the tradition of *sangaku*—miscellaneous arts imported from China that included acrobatics, magic, and comic elements. Although of later vintage, an account of dengaku dance patterns and musical notations from 1518 describes the performers sitting on the ground and removing their broad-brimmed hats, which they placed in front of them. The koshi-tsuzumi players untied their drums and set them down. A circular dance and acts featuring ball juggling, knife juggling, diabolo (*ryūgo*), stilts, and the like were performed to the beating of the drums at a rapid tempo. After performing together as an ensemble, the players removed their hats and sat down. Five such acts were performed while the koshi-tsuzumi played at a rapid tempo.

In the *Taiheiki*, the frenzied dancing and stunts of dengaku players performed to a jazz-like rhythm are compared to the movements of birds. At a party one night the Sagami lay monk Hōjō Takatoki stood up and danced while in his cups. A dozen or more dengaku performers suddenly appeared and sang and danced. A waiting woman's curiosity was so aroused by the voices that she peeked through a crack in the sliding door expecting to see the dengaku players from the Shinza and Honza troupes, but none of the performers had the shape of a human being. "Some looked like kites with sharp angular beaks, others like mountain ascetics with wings on their backs," writes the *Taiheiki*. "Strange oddly-shaped apparitions had assumed a human form.... When she raised the alarm, Takatoki's father-in-law came and chased them away. He lifted a taper and, glancing around the banquet chamber,remarked that it seemed as if there had indeed been a gathering of *tengu*, for the tracks of birds and beasts were scattered across the soiled tatami mats."

The dengaku performers are thought of here as apparitions resembling mountain ascetics (*yamabushi*) with heads, feet, and wings like kites—in other words, tengu. In fact, the passage conveys an image of dengaku performers who moved so lightly and agilely that they were capable of taking wing, and had birdlike bodies that abruptly twisted and turned with the angularity of a kite's beak. One could hardly expect Hōjō Takatoki to have acquired an obsession for dengaku below that level given his taste for the bizarre, which had escalated into a passion for fighting dogs, a mania for deranged situations fueled by the energy and speed of feral muscles and the ear-splitting cries of canines attacking each other. According to the *Taiheiki*, four hundred dogs "chased each other around in a wild frenzy, ending up on top of and under one another. Their shrill cries as they bit each other was earth-shattering."

The image evoked by the *Taiheiki*'s description of the dengaku performers' agile, disconnected movements is reinforced by the following remarks in *Sarugaku dangi* (Zeami's talks on *sarugaku*; 1430), a record of Zeami's reflections on noh and other subjects set down in writing by his son Motoyoshi: "In dengaku," says Zeami, "actions and singing are performed separately. The players stand in a line singing in a strong straightforward manner. They quickly change places to the sound of drumbeats (*ya tei tei*), and somersaults and other acrobatics are executed whereupon the performers quickly exit."[7]

The passage indicates that the performers' quick agile bodies rapidly and crisply executed somersaults and other stunts and immediately withdrew. This physicality, we may assume, was closely linked to dengaku singing, which Zeami describes throughout his treatises as well as here using a mimetic expression *kaku kaku* (or an etymologically related word) denoting a quick straightforward tempo broken into short units that are forcefully attacked.

While continuing to maintain its brisk acrobatic physicality, dengaku acquired greater richness as a performing art by expanding its repertoire from traditional dengaku dances and stunts to include sarugaku plays (namely, early noh) that incorporated this physical quality. In the process, it became even more popular. The first reference to a dengaku event that contained plays with a storyline—in other words, sarugaku—can be found in *Enkyō sannen ki*, an account from 1310, the third year of the Enkyō era. The performance of sarugaku plays by dengaku performers around that time exactly coincided with the popularity of dengaku mentioned by Tōin Kinkata in 1311.

The above-mentioned illustration from *Nenjū gyōji emaki* attests to the nature of dengaku as a kind of street performance, a description bolstered by its central role in festival processions, or pageants. During the Age of the Northern and Southern Courts, dengaku came to include a diverse array of entertainments centering on sarugaku plays held in a theater space containing grandstands. The performance of dengaku in this type of setting reached a peak in the famous subscription performance at the dry riverbed at Shijō in Kyoto in 1349 when the grandstands collapsed.

The account of the event in the *Taiheiki* (chapter 27) begins by commenting on the extraordinary popularity of dengaku at the time, saying that the passion for it in the capital stood out among the series of strange happenings that year.[8] Ashikaga Takauji, the founder of the new shogunate, was crazy about it, and the whole world day and night squandered vast sums on it. People said that it was an ill omen, inasmuch as Hōjō Takatoki's passion for dengaku had led to the demise of the Hōjō family at a time when the military government in Kamakura was on the verge of collapse. While criticizing the phenomenon, the *Taiheiki* goes on to offer a detailed, albeit exaggerated, account of the performance, which had been organized by a holy man to raise funds to erect a bridge over the Kamo River at Shijō:

> An extraordinary number of men and women, nobility and commoners alike, gathered in the expectation of witnessing a rare spectacle. Given the fondness for dengaku on the part of the regent [Nijō Yoshimoto], the Kajii Abbot [Cloistered Prince Son'in],

and the shogun, it goes without saying that those of lesser rank among courtiers, military retainers, and Shinto shrine officials and Buddhist monks outdid each other outfitting the spectators' boxes in the stands set up along the riverbank.

Holes were bored in wood of high quality to make multitiered stands measuring roughly 150 meters in circumference that were covered with a vast quantity of personal items. When the performance was about to begin, the area around the stands was thrown into a commotion by the arrival of the nobility. The anonymous author writes that swift vehicles and carriages made of aromatic wood vied for space, and aristocrats wearing light fur had no place to tie up their well-fed horses.

> In the stands, curtains fluttered in the breeze, and incense filled the air. The boys and men in the Shinza and Honza troupes erected temporary enclosures on the eastern and western sides for the dressing rooms and connected them to the stage by means of a bridge. The dressing rooms were surrounded by tie-dyed curtains. The silk canopies over them, which served as a sunshade, had designs created with gold thread. When the edges fluttered in the breeze, it was exactly as though flames were rising in the air. Low curved-back chairs and rope chairs were arranged on the stage, and red and green carpets were spread out and covered with leopard and tiger skins.

The dazzling scene boasted an array of Chinese objects on the stage and gold-brocade and tie-dyed curtains that emitted a fragrance as they fluttered in the breeze along the riverbank.

> The spellbound spectators' eyes glowed with excitement. The clear notes of the elegant tuning could faintly be heard like the

whispering of a breeze, whereupon the drums began to play the introductory piece in time to the melody of the flutes in the dressing rooms.

Eight beautiful boys wearing finely scented costumes, white makeup, and rouge filed out of the eastern dressing room attired alike in luxurious gold-brocade cloaks with wide sleeves (*suikan*). Eight handsome men filed out of the western dressing room, their woven rush hats at an angle, as they kept time. The men wore pale makeup and teeth blacking and had on colorful wide-sleeved cloaks covered with a gaily woven pattern of flowers and birds, over trousers decorated with a silver scattered-figure pattern. The lower part of the trousers was dyed a deeper hue and the hems were drawn tight at the ankle.

The boys and men displayed the height of extravagance and beauty as they made their way across the eastern and western bridges onto the stage. Ako of the Honza troupe was the lead binzasara player; the *ranbyōshi* foot-stamping to the beat of a drum was performed by Hiko Yasha of the Shinza troupe, the knife juggling by Dōichi. The spectators' eyes and ears were dazzled by the marvelous skill of each performer. The competitive performance, mentioned in *Sarugaku dangi* as a dance performed jointly by eight players (ZZ 272), was followed by a play, the climax of the day's program:

> The dengaku players launched into the unforgettable performance of a felicitous sarugaku play about a miracle realized by the deity of the Hie shrine. An eight- or nine-year-old boy wearing a monkey mask emerged from the Shinza dressing room holding up a wand with white paper streamers (*gohei*). He wore an outer robe (*uchikake*) over a gold brocade robe with a red background, and

had on tiger-skin shoes. To a quick tempo, he crossed the arched red and green bridge at an angle and jumped up onto the railing. He circled to the left and then to the right, jumped off of and onto the railing. He did not seem like a creature from this world. The spectators were overcome with emotion, wondering if the deity had suddenly descended and revealed this miracle before their very eyes.

The spectators filling the one hundred or so sections of the stands could not contain themselves. Unable to sit still, they screamed and shouted, "How thrilling! I can't bear it!" The excited voices overflowing the stands did not soon quiet down. A lovely lady could be seen in the vicinity of the shogun's box holding up the hem of her silk robe as she lifted a curtain with her fan. Suddenly, the scaffolding erected with five- or six-inch-thick beams tilted and before anybody could say a word, roughly 450 meters of the upper and lower stands collapsed like dominoes.

The multitiered stands suddenly gave way because the spectators were whipped into such a frenzy by the play. Their wild enthusiasm was in no way aimed at the overall story, but rather was directed at the boy's acrobatic performance itself, which, like an improvised cadenza, was incorporated into the story yet boldly departed from it. Crossing the red and green arched bridge at an angle in time to the rhythmical beats of the music, he struck different poses in the air from one moment to the next as he sprang up onto the railing, turned to the left, rotated to the right, and repeatedly jumped on and off the railing. His powerful figure cutting poses in the air with a series of sudden leaps in different directions perfectly accorded with the mixture of bright colors: the white paper strips attached to the *gohei* wand, red and gold of the outer robe, yellow and black of the tiger skins, and red and green of the arched bridge. As he relentlessly etched lingering images in the air with one bounding leap after another in all directions, he kept up the visual deceptions until he had swept the spectators into a feverish pitch.

The war tale goes on to describe what transpired from the perspective of mountain ascetics (*tengu*), saying that the destruction of the stands was due to the enormous power of *tengu*. This attribution, however, was clearly another way of saying that the stands collapsed because of the enormous effect on spectators of the energy generated by the dengaku performer's body, which constantly redefined the space around it.

What should not be overlooked here is the fact that the kineticism of the acrobatic dengaku body was first captured linguistically by the *Taiheiki* author's vivid prose. The description of the boy's movements closely resembles the tale's narration of battle scenes and the discussion of guerrilla tactics employed by small forces against larger ones. A case in point is the following passage from chapter 10 describing the fierce fighting during the final battle of Nagasaki Takashige, when the Kamakura shogunate was about to fall:[9]

> [Takashige] drew the 150 mounted warriors close together. Letting out a war cry with one voice, they charged past, charged into, and mingled with more than three thousand enemy on horseback. Appearing here, disappearing there, they sent sparks flying as they fought. They instantaneously assembled and scattered, separated and regrouped. Just when they seemed to be in front, they were suddenly behind; in place of an apparent ally suddenly loomed the enemy. Since they all fought the same way, they seemed to multiply in all directions, making it appear that there were ten thousand of them.

Another example can be found in chapter 15 when Nitta Yoshisada, a supporter of Emperor Go-Daigo and the Southern Court, instructs his men on the use of guerrilla tactics during an attack on Ashikaga Takauji's forces in Kyoto. His remarks were made just before the men under him descended from Kachōzan in the eastern hills to do battle against Takauji's large force in the city. "After infiltrating the capital, hold your banners aloft in front of and behind, to the left and right of, the enemy. Without slowing down your horses, make your way to the rear when you appear to be in front. When you appear to be on the left, circle around to the right. If you confuse the enemy, they will think you are an ally, which will leave Takauji with only one of two choices: to do battle against confederates or retreat."

Just as the dengaku performance caused the grandstands to collapse as a result of the repeated visual deception generated by the boy's acrobatics, a small military unit vanquished a large force using a strategy that consisted of surprise attacks from all directions, like "the sudden appearance of a deity or disappearance of a demon into thin air." The narrative style employed by the *Taiheiki* illustrates the common ground shared by these actions. Dengaku transfers the physical nature of guerrilla warfare (a specialty of outlaw bands) into the physicality of an acrobat on a performative level. In the process dengaku refines that physicality while seeming to embody the war tale's dynamic language itself.

LINKED VERSE

Renga was a group-performance verse form centering on acrobatics of a linguistic kind, a collaborative art whose sessions contained a hidden dengaku-like physicality. The lampoons posted on the Nijō riverbank placed renga at the head of the list of entertainments popular at the time in the capital. Bemoaning the production of pseudo-renga in which Kyoto and Kamakura poets intermingled indiscriminately at renga gatherings, the lampoons lament the fact that anybody could serve as a judge at waka and renga sessions. They also characterize linked verse as a free, uninhibited (*jiyū rōzeki*) world that ignored distinctions between veteran poets and novices.

Renga, the most popular type of performance in Kyoto in those days, is characterized here as a free, uninhibited art like dengaku. But that label did not necessarily refer only to the dissipation characterizing renga parties as sites of revelry and prodigious gambling, behavior banned by the Kemmu code. And it did not necessarily concern just the unbridled conduct at the party beneath the cherry blossoms at Washinoo in the eastern hills of Kyoto, as described in the renga treatise *Kokon rendanshū* (Conversations past and present on linked verse; 1444–1448): at that party Zenna, the great master of commoners' renga who presided over the event, escaped censure for his drunken behavior after he slightly lifted the screen of the carriage in which the retired emperor had secretly traveled to the event. What is key here is the uninhibitedness inherent in the art of renga itself.[10]

The designation of the *Tsukubashū* as a quasi-imperial anthology marked the high point in the surging renga fever during the Age of the Northern and Southern Courts. The collection consists of renga links and seventeen-syllable verses that open a session (*hokku*).[11] The technique of linking verses is illustrated in the following example by a poet called Dōshō:

sugi no ita-buki	Cedar shingles on the roof:
tsuki zo morikuru	moonlight streams through.

His verse was attached to one on the subject of love:

awanu ma o	During the gap without meeting
nado hitosuji ni	why did I so single-mindedly
uramikemu	feel resentment?

In other words, during the interval when we did not meet, why did I bear such resentment even though there were probably various reasons that prevented us from being able to do so? The poet reinterprets the first line of the previous composition—*awanu ma* ("gap without meeting")—as "gaps where the cedar (*sugi*) shingles on the roof do not meet." Taken together, the two stanzas now mean: "Until now, I had single-mindedly lamented that the cedar boards on the roof did not meet; but, seeing the moonlight streaming through the gaps, it puzzles me why I regretted it so much." The verse brilliantly transforms the earlier expression of love into an aesthetic statement about the natural world. The notion of a rundown dwelling covered with cedar slats that do not tightly meet adds a humorous note.

Of course renga sessions did not proceed in a free, uninhibited manner solely by means of sudden twists such as the one displayed by this splendid example. But, as Yamaguchi Masao has observed, renga sessions are not fixed in spatial terms. "Instead, they move in a new direction from one moment to the next in accordance with the latent deictics. Renga sessions form an extremely fluid subjective world in which the new situation is always destroyed as soon as it has been realized."[12] As these remarks suggest, the unanticipated element of chance comes into play to a greater or lesser extent in renga because the next verse is always composed by a different person. The accumulated sense of surprise generated by the element of chance whips the group as a whole into a state of excitement.

"Thus, awareness of whether a particular person's verse is good or not disappears by the end of a sequence," says the modern-day renga poet and linguist Yamada Yoshio. "A sequence is considered first-rate when the sole impression is one of exhilaration or pleasure and the participants are so caught up in the performance that they forget themselves."[13] In short, renga produces a trance based on the same principle as dengaku.

When successful, the process of linking verses has the capacity to put the participants in a trance by the end of a session. Moreover, this magical power, which differs from the primitive force of waka, is precisely why commoners' renga early on was performed as a flower-pacification ceremony to appease the vengeful spirits of human beings who had died in a state of anger. It was also a factor connecting renga with militant leagues (*ikki*).

Linked-verse parties and militant leagues shared common ground as social groups defined both by a lack of connection between the participants and a sense of equality; this brought ordinary people together to form a group in tension with the world beyond. Their overlapping nature has been demonstrated by a detailed study of the renga society at the Someda Tenjin shrine in Yamato Province. The study demonstrates that the administrators of the society's annual renga party lived within the eastern highlands of the province. Their rice payments to the powerful Kōfukuji temple complex in Nara placed the society within the sphere of influence of the Southern Court in the mountains of Yoshino.[14] The study also points out that the language used when the society's rules were formulated in 1434 coincided with terminology used in the covenant of a militant league that was created amid the social turmoil in the preceding century. This evidence led the author of the study, Yasuda Jirō, to conclude that the linked-verse society formed not long after the league was none other than the militant league in the guise of renga. In this instance, bodies that participated in renga gatherings were a

THE CULTURAL ROLE OF SASAKI DŌYO

Sasaki Dōyo, the flamboyant daimyo, was famous for his outrageous akutō-like behavior, which included burning down the Myōhōin, a temple in the eastern hills of Kyoto headed by a cloistered prince, and the theft of the military governorship of Ōmi Province east of Kyoto. He was also an ardent renga enthusiast.

Renga reached a peak during the Age of the Northern and Southern Courts when the gap closed between the court style represented by the regent Nijō Yoshimoto (1320–1388) and the style practiced by commoners (*jige*) led by Gusai. The completion of the *Tsukubashū* (1356) marked the first time that renga had been preserved in writing. A key role in its creation was played behind the scenes by Dōyo in his capacity as a warrior mediating between the nobility and commoners. His passion for linked verse peaked in the years leading up to the completion of the collection, which contains eighty-one of his verses. The *Taiheiki* (chapter 32) tells how a warrior named Yamana Morouji went to Dōyo's residence repeatedly around 1351 seeking a reward for his valor on the battlefield but was always turned away with excuses such as that Dōyo, then a senior official in the shogunate's Administrative Bureau, was participating in a renga party that day, or attending a tea gathering. Morouji was so incensed that he even launched an insurrection.[15]

The passion displayed by Dōyo for both linked-verse parties and tea gatherings was no fluke, as the art critic and scholar Kurita Isamu has shown. Kurita demonstrates the ties between the two arts using remarks by the renga master Sōchō in a treatise called *Renga hikyōshū* (A collection of analogies to renga;

1532). In response to a question about composing a hundred-verse renga sequence, Sōchō replies:[16]

> It is like hanging paintings next to each other. Doing so randomly without any association between them would be visually displeasing. One should, so to speak, place a buddha next to a bodhisattva, or pair a sage with a saint. A painting of a famous poetic place with withered trees on a mountain should be hung with one of a waterfall so as to create the effect of water streaming down the mountainside.

Kurita points out that this advice is couched almost entirely in terms of three-dimensional sensibilities: "It is as though seeing before our very eyes lessons on how to decorate alcoves, choose sets of three hanging scrolls and landscape paintings, and construct gardens. For Sōchō and his contemporaries, renga represented the creation of a spatial drama that was akin to knowing how to decorate alcoves and select utensils in the tea ceremony (*chanoyu*)."

As noted in the Kemmu code, linked-verse sessions and tea gatherings were parties that involved drinking and revelry where gambling took place on a vast scale. In addition, they were venues for cultivating a sense of how to combine things. Therein lay another reason for Dōyō's simultaneous enthusiasm for both types of collaborative performances.

Overall, the verses that he produced emphasize the visual and lack subtle overtones. His output includes the following unusual example from the *Tsukubashū* (no. 405):

sora wa tsuki	In the sky the moon;
yamamoto wa nao	in the hills below,
yūbe nite	evening, still.

His verse was composed in response to the following one:

| ukigumo ni koso | It is in the drifting clouds |
| kaze wa miekere | that the breeze is visible. |

Sora wa tsuki (literally, "as for the sky, the moon") can presumably be taken to mean "the moon in the sky above." If so, his verse creates a picture in which nature is divided into three planes, with the image of clouds drifting in the breeze in the preceding verse (*maeku*) serving as a middle ground between two still pictures: the moon in the sky above and the evening landscape beneath the hills. The overall scene has been created by placing the scene in the preceding verse squarely in the one depicted in his own composition. Here he has nonchalantly cut and pasted nature to form a pattern.

Dōyo's interest in renga apparently subsided once the collection was finished, for he seems to have focused his entire attention thereafter on the staging of decorative spaces. According to the *Taiheiki* (chapter 36), when the Northern Army retreated from Kyoto in 1361, he took the unusual step of lavishly decorating his lodgings, which were about to fall into enemy hands:[17]

> He spread mats with large crests in the six-bay meeting place (*kaisho*) and fully appointed it with everything from the main object of worship and two flanking paintings to a flower vase, incense burner, kettle for boiling water, and tray. He installed a Buddhist verse (*gāthā*) written in cursive script by the famous calligrapher Wang Xizhi in the *shoin* study along with a prose anthology by Han Yü, and placed an aloeswood pillow and damask bedding in the sleeping chamber. In the twelve-bay guardsmen's room, he hung birds, rabbits, pheasants, and swans from three poles and filled a three-*koku* cask with sake.

Following Dōyo's instructions, the two *tonseisha* that he left behind at his residence handsomely treated the first person who showed up: Kusunoki Masanori, a warrior who fought on the side of the Southern Army. Masanori was impressed by Dōyo's gesture and, far from burning down the place, "did not harm so much as a tree in the garden. Nor did a single mat in the guest chamber disappear. He even stocked the guardsmen's room with finer sake and provisions. Not only that, but he put treasured armor and a silver sword in the sleeping chamber and left two retainers at the residence" before trading places with Dōyo and leaving the capital once more when the tides of war turned. Ever the wily old gambler in the words of the *Taiheiki*, Dōyo performed an astonishing act and won the bet, enabling him to effortlessly recover the decorated space in better shape than he had left it.

That year he also deliberately scheduled a banquet for the seventh day of the Seventh Month, fully aware that his political rival Hosokawa Kiyouji had already invited the new shogun, Ashikaga Yoshiakira (1330–1367), to a poetry contest in seven hundred rounds that same evening to celebrate the Tanabata festival. This festival marked the meeting in heaven between the stars Altair (Ox Herder) and Vega (Weaver Maiden) on that day each year. Dōyo enticed the shogun with his plan to offer "decorations in seven places, prepare seven kinds of delicacies, assemble seven hundred prizes, and arrange to have guests drink seventy rounds of genuine tea (*honcha*) and tea from elsewhere (*hicha*)."[18] The shogun cancelled the earlier invitation, thinking that decorations in seven places would be a rare treat. Although Dōyo succeeded in luring the shogun to his mansion, his action earned him the enmity of his rival.

This sort of production by Dōyo of basara spaces magnificently adorned with Chinese objects (*karamono*) took the form of a flower (tea) party that incorporated the natural world, including the theatrical use of time. The event was held on the western outskirts of Kyoto in the Third Month of 1366, the same day as a banquet beneath the blossoms at the shogun's palace that had been arranged by another political rival, the deputy shogun Shiba Takatsune.

The *Taiheiki* (chapter 39) casts Dōyo's unparalleled flower-viewing party as a theatrical space resembling a kind of pilgrimage:

> He headed for Mount Oshio in Ōharano accompanied by members of noble houses who wore light fur attire and rode on well-fed horses. Leaving their carriages at the foot of mountain, they climbed the steep slope, clinging to vines as they went. The winding path led to a quiet place overrun with flowering trees. They passed through the temple gate near a meandering brook. The path twisted like a sheep's intestines, and the crosspieces of the bridge, which resembled a formation of flying geese or a set of teeth, looked precarious. The railings were wrapped in gold brocade, and the jewel-shaped knobs crowning the posts were covered with gold leaf. Chinese carpets and colorful Wujun damask and Shujiang brocade were spread on the planks. Flowers had fallen on them, like snow on a bridge in the dark recesses of a valley that the rays of the morning sun did not reach.
>
> The feet treading the petals were chilly, and shoes became fragrant as they walked along. When they ascended the endless stone steps in the breeze, tea water from delicious spring water that flowed through a bamboo pipe was bubbling in a stone kettle. The tea party in the open air was an enchanted realm where the wind in the pine trees intermingled with the bubbling water in the kettle. Moreover, Chinese cords were hung high up on every gnarled branch of wisteria. The incense in the dragon-headed

censers suspended from the cords filled the spring breeze with a warm fragrance. It was like having entered a fragrant grove of sandalwood.

Gazing a thousand leagues into the distance afforded a panoramic view of the mountains in all directions. The mountains and streams rose steeply amid layers of mist. The spirit of painstakingly taking ten days to paint a river converged there without any need to apply a paint brush. A view of the four seas and five lakes seemed to have been obtained right then and there without moving a step.[19]

It was as if a view of all the famous places in China had been reenacted there. While arranging each scene during the ascent, like the exquisite flow of linked verses, Dōyo devised a scheme that briefly ignored the guests' rapture. In so doing, he led them onward to a more ecstatic state.

After climbing a long way marveling anew at every step, they came to the main hall of the temple. In front of it were four huge flowering trees to which brass vases more than three meters high were attached, creating a pair of flower arrangements. Two large censers lit with a *kin* of precious incense were set on low tables between them, wafting scented air in every direction. It was as if they were in the Realm of Wafting Fragrance.

The brass flower vases attached to the large cherry trees (presumably weeping cherry trees) created a pair of flower arrangements, and a large quantity of precious incense (about six-hundred grams) was burned simultaneously in the two large censers placed between them. It was the consummate performance of Dōyo's lifetime.

A sumptuous repast unfolded in this incense-filled paradise: "Curtains had been installed in the shadows of the blossoming trees, and a row of low chairs with curved backs had been set up. Innumerable delicacies were prepared, and a competition was held with a hundred cups of tea. Prizes were piled high."

Dōyo, however, did not simply create a gigantic flower arrangement by attaching brass flower vases to large cherry trees, just as one might link a renga stanza to a previous one. Linked verse beneath the blossoms presumably played a prominent role at the banquet beneath the blossoms held by his rival Shiba Takatsune. The performance beneath the blossoms was a pacification ceremony, a banquet, conducted in a sacred space delimited by cosmic trees, namely, weeping cherry trees, which mediated between hell and this world. The act of attaching a flower vase to these trees severed their roots, which descended down to the land of the dead. Dōyo stripped them of the sanctity extracted from the profound darkness and presented cherry blossoms merely as superficial forms.

Dōyo performed the act here of cutting out and detaching nature which he had already practiced in renga. Furthermore, in contrast to Shiba Takatsune's renga party beneath the blossoms at the shogun's palace, he sought through an impersonal nonverbal performance—the extravagant use of precious incense—to mock the party as child's play. In this way, the dynamic religious setting in which renga parties were held was forcibly twisted into a dynamic manmade site.

After severing nature here precisely in the manner of a diamond, the root meaning of basara (Skt = *vajra*), Dōyo vanishes from the world of the *Taiheiki*. In the end, no complete picture of him is presented in the work. He invariably appears simply as an anecdote protruding from the subplot. In each scene, something is momentarily created and then shattered, whereupon he retreats once more into the background. His presence has the powerful kineticism of the dengaku boy performer. While etching a vivid image that lingers on the surface of the tale, he disappears from its pages as a character whose meaning remains elusive.

3

THE ART OF COLLABORATION

In the early middle ages, *renga* was composed every spring beneath blossoming cherry trees on the outskirts of Kyoto. This custom was a prototype of the sessions that flourished on a national scale at all levels of society in the later middle ages. The issues surrounding the practice of composing poetry beneath the blossoms, however, are not limited just to renga, a unique medieval genre that supplanted waka as the dominant literary form. The unusual collaborative nature of the poetry sessions brings into focus another shared world in Japan's medieval era: the leagues, or *ikki*, which displayed a new approach to interpersonal relationships.

Inherently collaborative, *Hana no moto renga* was composed "beneath the blossoms," that is, under cherry trees. Since antiquity, Japanese people have displayed special reverence for cherry trees. It was believed that the scattering of the petals represented the raging of the vengeful spirits of human beings known as *goryō*, those who died in a state of anger. As a result, rituals were performed to pacify the vengeful spirits residing beneath cherry trees. The events became a state ritual in the early Heian period, when the wrath of malevolent spirits called goryō caused tremendous fear and trembling.

The section on divinities in *Ryō no gige*, a ninth-century commentary on the Yōrō civil code (718 CE) states, "In spring, flower pacification rites: ceremonies held at Ōmiwa and Sai. In the spring when blossoms fall, the gods of epidemics scatter, causing epidemics to occur. These rites are held without fail in order to pacify the deities."

According to the commentary, the gods of epidemics (*ekijin*) scatter, spreading disease, when cherry blossoms fall in the springtime. To placate them and make them desist, flower-pacification rites were conducted at the Ōmiwa and Sai shrines in Yamato, where the deity Ōmononushi and the deity's raging spirit (*ara-mitama*), respectively, were enshrined. The term *ekijin* also refers to a vengeful spirit, or goryō. Flower-pacification rites were performed at those two sites because Ōmononushi, the primordial vengeful spirit of the entire country, controlled the vengeful spirits of individuals who died in a state of anger, such as Prince Sawara (d. 785) and the poet-statesman Sugawara no Michizane (845–903), who were forced to go into exile.[1]

The Yasurai Hana festival in Kyoto can be viewed as a variant form of a flower-pacification rite. The festival first surfaced at the Imamiya shrine in Murasakino in the twelfth century and continues to be held there today. ("Imamiya" refers to a new vengeful spirit.) The following description of the festival can be found in a collection of secret teachings on popular songs of the day known as *imayō*: "Recently, [ca. 1154], men and women from around the capital flocked to the Murasakino shrine to take part in a colorful spectacle featuring singing and the playing of flutes, drums, and hand-held gongs, an event described as 'entertaining the gods.' The songs and musical accompaniment resembled neither *imayō*, nor unorthodox dances or the fast tempo of rapid songs. The frenetic energy produced by the sounds was unreal." As is clear from this account, the aim of the festival was to exorcise vengeful spirits through frenzied singing and dancing.[2]

The composition of renga beneath the cherry blossoms, on the other hand, was a flower-pacification ceremony driven by linguistic fervor that flourished for about a hundred years beginning in the mid-thirteenth century. Although dating from later times, a Zen monk's eighteenth-century travel diary called *Angya zuihitsu* (Random notes of a pilgrim traveling on foot) vividly demonstrates the nature of hana no moto renga as a rite to pacify the souls of the dead. An entry about a temple in what is now Gumma Prefecture transmits the following legend handed down by local villagers:

> Jigenji is an old temple belonging to the Mount Kōya branch of the Shingon sect. It is the sect's local government-liaison temple. Long ago in the Third Month of 1350, the shogun Ashikaga Takauji instructed the deputy shogun to hold a Hungry Ghost Service on behalf of dead warriors, whereupon the spirits of hungry ghosts appeared. Even now there is a place called the Hungry Ghost Slope. I was also told that a bottomless pit suddenly opened up in the garden, and hungry ghosts with burning faces emerged from the hole, which is known today as the Crimson Spring Pit. At the sight of the bizarre spirits, Takauji's faith deepened even further, and he donated a thousand stupas. There was a cherry tree with hanging, thread-like branches in the garden. The shogun, I am told, composed the opening stanza of a renga sequence while gazing at the flowering blossoms. Place-names such as Shogun Mound and Shogun Moat still exist today.

According to local lore, Ashikaga Takauji ordered the deputy shogun, Uesugi Noriaki, to hold a Hungry Ghost service at Jigenji to pray for the souls of subordinates who had landed in the realm of hungry ghosts after they died in battle. When the service was held, souls of the dead that had become hungry ghosts appeared on the slope. In addition, a chasm suddenly appeared in the temple garden, out of which hungry ghosts with burning faces emerged. "Crimson Spring" is a translation of *kōsen*, a homophone for the word for Yellow Spring (in other words, the Land of the Dead), so the hole seems to have extended as far as the underworld. At the sight of the bizarre spirits, Takauji's faith deepened even further, and he donated a thousand stupas. Moreover, the sight of the blossoming cherry tree with drooping branches in the garden inspired him to hold a renga party. Later, a ghost emerged from the Crimson Spring Pit and transmitted the following message from King Enma in hell: If you do not come to see the bodhisattva Kannon's cherry tree at Jigenji, you will go to hell and suffer torments inflicted by demons.

Cherry trees with pendulous thread-like branches (*tare-ito*)—namely, *shidare zakura*, or weeping cherry trees—transmit signals to this world from the land of the dead. When the ghost emerged from the Crimson Spring Pit and conveyed King Enma's message, it was, to put it briefly, an order to conduct a flower-pacification ceremony. The renga party held by Takauji, together with the donation of stupas mentioned in local village lore, was clearly a performance beneath the blossoms that served as a flower-pacification rite to appease the souls of the warriors under his command who had died.

What is also intriguing is that the shogun's renga party was held beneath a cherry tree with drooping branches, in other words, a weeping cherry tree. After Yanagita Kunio drew attention to weeping cherry trees as a place visited by the spirits of the dead, the scholar Okami Masao linked the famed ethnologist's observation to the composition of renga beneath the blossoms at sites in and around Kyoto, using the *Tsukubashū* renga anthology as a source. His analysis of verses composed at *hana no moto renga* parties revealed that such events took place beneath weeping cherry trees that were considered sacred.[3] For instance, the following opening verse by Zeshō (no. 2060) bears a headnote stating that it was composed beneath the blossoms at Jishu Gongen, the guardian shrine of Kiyomizu temple in the eastern hills, which was famous for hana no moto renga:

haru zo miru	A sign of spring!
shiroki wa taki no	white is the cascade
ito zakura	of cherry blossom threads.

Ito zakura (literally, "thread cherry [tree]") is another name for a weeping cherry tree. Since opening verses (hokku) by convention were the only ones in a renga sequence that referred directly to the scene before the poet's eyes, it is reasonable to assume that the party took place in spring beneath a weeping cherry tree that had a profusion of blossom-laden branches resembling the cascading white "threads" of nearby Otowa Waterfall (Otowa no taki) alluded to in the second line.

The anthology also contains the following opening verse (no. 2044) by Zenna, the great master of commoners' renga:

eda nokoru	The blossoms remaining
hana wa oiki no	on the ancient tree:
kazashi kana	decoration on an aged head?

The accompanying headnote states that it was composed at Washinoo in the eastern hills during a party beneath the blossoms, at which half of the two thousand verses were composed according to the new rules for composing renga, and half the traditional rules. From ancient times, Washinoo had been a burial ground as well a settlement inhabited by *nenbutsu hijiri*, itinerant holy men who extolled the benefits of invoking Amida Buddha's name. (In later times, the area was mainly populated by Jishū members.) Renga parties were apparently conducted there beneath an aged weeping cherry tree.

During the first half of the fourteenth century, linked-verse parties beneath the blossoms took place mostly at Jishū Gongen and Washinoo. In the 1240s, when the phenomenon first began, however, they tended to be held at two other sites in Kyoto: Bishamondō and Hosshōji. The following example (no. 67) was composed by the poet Dōshō at a hana no moto renga party at Bishamondō in the Third Month of 1248:

uchinabiku	On a tranquil spring day
yanagi ga eda no	long as the fronds
nagaki hi ni	on the pliant willow tree

The poet linked the verse to *hana mo sakinu ya / katsuragi no yama* (Have the flowers also bloomed / on Mount Katsuragi?). Although it was not an opening verse, Okami argues that the weeping cherry tree at Bishamondō lay behind it. "The flowers and willows are linked more by the association with weeping cherry blossoms," he says, "than by the notion of adorning one's hair with a willow frond (*yanagi o sasu*) elicited by the pun on *katsura* (vine / tresses) in the place-name Katsuragi."

Cherry blossoms in full bloom at Bishamondō are also mentioned in *Saigyō-zakura* (Saigyō's cherry tree), a noh play by Zeami:[4]

unro ya	A path through clouds
yuki ni nokoruran	that linger like snow:
bishamondō no	Bishamondō's
hana zakari	flowers in full bloom.

Bishamondō was located on the former site of a temple called Shimo Izumo-dera. Known as Izumoji (the Izumo Road), the area was a place for pacifying the raging spirits of aristocrats who had died in a state of anger in the early Heian period.

The weeping cherry trees (*ito zakura*) at Hosshōji, a temple in the northeastern part of Kyoto, were also famous, as demonstrated by the following poem (no. 177) in the seventeenth imperial anthology of waka titled *Fūgawakashū* (Collection of elegant poems; ca. 1345). According to the headnote, the poem was composed by a former regent on going past Hosshōji when the cherry trees were in full bloom:

tachiyorade	I passed by
suginu to omoedo	without drawing near,
ito zakura	but the ito zakura
kokoro ni kakaru	is still on my mind
haru no ko no moto	beneath the spring tree.

The following anonymous linked verse (no. 1973) was composed on seeing somebody lingering in the shadows of the blossoms at Hosshōji until nighttime:

itozakura	Ito zakura:
yoru made miru wa	who is gazing at them until nighttime
tare yaran	I wonder.

The composition of renga beneath the blossoms at Bishamondō and Hosshōji is further attested by the observation of Nijō Yoshimoto in his renga treatise *Tsukuba mondō* (Questions and answers on renga) about renga poets such as Dōshō, Jakunin, and Mushō gathering together throngs of people from all strata of society every spring to compose renga beneath the blossoms at these two sites.

In short, hana no moto renga sessions were events conducted beneath blossoming cherry trees on the grounds of specific shrines and temples in Kyoto—a liminal space under a cosmic tree that mediated between this world and the underworld. The management of the sessions by individuals who appear to have been holy men with no formal social ties, including nenbutsu hijiri—such as the above-mentioned Zeshō, Zenna, and Dōshō as well as Jakunin and Mushō—shows that this sacred liminal space was a setting transcending the everyday world that was also linked to hell.

The sessions were conducted chiefly by a core group of ten or so poets referred to as *renju*, led by one of those holy men, at a place where throngs of people from all levels of society, high and low alike, congregated. It should be noted that the right to submit verses was opened up to all comers after the core group had completed one round. In other words, hana no moto renga were sessions in which the audience took part.

A collection of Buddhist tales called *Shasekishū* (Collection of sand and pebbles; 1283) contains the following account of a session at Bishamondō:

> While composing linked verse at Bishamondō in Izumoji, nobody was able to add a verse to
>
> | | |
> |---|---|
> | usukurenai ni | The sky has turned |
> | nareru sora kana | a rosy hue! |
>
> After more than thirty verses had been rejected, casting a pall over the proceedings, the lay monk Tō no Nyūdō, a secret onlooker, offered the following link:
>
> | | |
> |---|---|
> | ama tobu ya | Are they soaring in heaven? |
> | ina ōsedori no | The shapes of wagtails |
> | kage miete | are visible. |

It was deemed to be suitable, given the circumstances. One of those present at the session was Hana no Moto Jūnenbō. When he heard the first line, he exclaimed that the lay monk had done it. He knew straightaway.[5]

This passage shows that rejection by the renga master of more than thirty verses was beginning to dampen enthusiasm, but a verse was successfully offered by a secret onlooker, the lay monk Tō no Nyūdō, who prior to taking vows had been a warrior serving as an advisor and waka teacher under the third Kamakura shogun. Jūnenbō knew as soon as he heard the words *ama tobu ya* (soaring in heaven) that the lay monk had done the trick.

Jūnenbō is believed to have been one of the core participants at the session. As a layman, he had been hailed for his ability to link Chinese verses and for his humor. While living in Nara in his later years, he made his way every spring to Shirakawa in the capital where his daughter lived, and he participated in hana no moto renga. The sobriquet Hana no Moto reflects his status as a core member at annual linked-verse events beneath the cherry blossoms. In any case, it was one of the onlookers, Tō no Nyūdō, secretly sitting in on the session, who broke the impasse created by a difficult verse that not even the skilled core participants were able to handle.

A little later, the above-mentioned collection of Buddhist tales describes a renga party beneath the blossoms secretly attended by a court chamberlain named Fujiwara no Takasuke who succeeded in attaching a verse to a very difficult one. The son of a leading waka poet during the age of the eighth imperial waka anthology, the *Shinkokinshū*, he seems to have been more proficient at renga than waka. Like Tō no Nyūdō, he secretly participated in renga parties as an ordinary onlooker and successfully handled difficult verses.

The category of all comers (*yorozu no mono*) secretly listening in on the proceedings even included a retired emperor. The *Tsukubashū* contains an opening verse (no. 2053) by Zenna bearing a headnote stating that it had been composed during a renga party on the day that the retired emperor set down his carriage in disguise beneath the blossoms at Washinoo:

asu mo tate	Alight once more on the morrow
usuhana-some no	spring cloud on the mountain peak
haru no kumo	the color of lightly tinted blossoms.

The unidentified retired emperor, a renga enthusiast, traveled incognito to the hana no moto renga party in his carriage. Zenna's opening verse concomitantly serves as a greeting: please come again tomorrow and set your carriage down here.

Although renga conducted beneath weeping cherry trees was open to all comers, it was necessary to attend incognito—that is, they had to conceal their social rank and name. The linked-verse master who presided over the session and the core poets—for instance, Zenna and Hana no Moto Jūnenbō—were mainly nenbutsu hijiri. They were semireclusive *tonseisha*—outcasts, individuals unhindered by social norms. In order to participate in linked-verse parties presided over by these holy men who lived on the fringes of society, regular members of society had to render themselves unconnected to others, if only temporarily, by hiding their rank and name. The setting of linked poetry beneath the blossoms, with its lack of connection among participants, was at the same time a space where rigid social constraints were set aside.

The fifteenth-century professional renga master Sōzei offers the following description of the renga party at Washinoo along with an interpretation of Zenna's opening verse:

After the poetry and music ended, everybody made merry beneath the blossoms. The sight of the retired emperor setting down his carriage created as much excitement as the composition of linked verse beneath the blossoms. During the pilgrimage to Sumiyoshi by [Hikaru Genji], the carriages were lined up in the shadows of the multihued autumn foliage between the pine trees. Feeling blessed to have the good fortune of living during a splendid reign, Zenna declared,

asu mo tate	Alight once more on the morrow
usuhana-zome no	clouds on the mountain peak
mine no kumo	the color of lightly tinted blossoms.

I think that this ostensibly simple verse has a deep meaning. Zenna uses the blossoms as a metaphor to express a desire to see the imperial carriage again on the following day, feeling that the opportunity to practice the unworthy art of renga in a reign such as this would never happen again.[6]

The anecdote also tells how the inebriated Zenna slightly lifted the screen on the retired emperor's carriage, prompting the emperor to remark, "Long ago Li Bo did not take off his shoes; today Zenna behaved playfully in my presence." Sōzei explains that the famous Tang poet Li Bo (701–762) presented himself at the imperial court in Chang'an in an inebriated state after receiving an imperial summons, but because of his great renown he was not censured when he mounted the steps of the throne wearing his shoes. Sōzei also notes that Zenna had been lauded by the regent as the Li Bo of Japan. In other words, the retired emperor forgave Zenna for his transgression by likening the relationship between himself and Zenna to that of the Chinese emperor and Li Bo.

Sōzei speaks enviously of the great honor accorded Zenna by the retired emperor's willingness to forgive him. He takes this episode to be a concrete example of the special merit enjoyed by renga, which permitted commoners to interact with persons of exalted rank Seen as a fringe activity, the composition of hana no moto renga could dispense with formalities, allowing Zenna's breach of etiquette to be forgiven and permitting high and low to freely intermingle.

The development of these sites over time seems to have been accompanied by the emergence of country bumpkins who are thus described around 1330 by Yoshida Kenkō in *Essays in Idleness* (*Tsurezuregusa*; section 137): "They twist and turn to get near the trees and stare endlessly at the blossoms while drinking rice wine and composing renga. In the end, they heartlessly break off large branches and carry them away."

In a similar vein, *Taregami ōrai*, a thirteenth-century epistolary-style textbook for boys, disparages a breed called *hana no moto no kushi* (aesthetes beneath the blossoms) who engaged in heated discussions about the quality of linked verses despite composing none of any value themselves: "Recently, a species of fellows known as *hana no moto no kushi* delight in nitpicking, they reject ordinary verses and dispute matters for hours on end."[7]

Although both works criticize this trend, such censure is wide off the mark: In actuality, the practice of linking verses beneath the blossoms originated in the tradition of the Yasurai Hana festival, in which vengeful spirits were pacified by means of feverish singing and dancing. The frenzied atmosphere was an important element in pacifying the souls of the dead.

The social nonattachment (*muen*) characterizing renga beneath the blossoms continued in sessions known as *kasagi* renga in which the participants linked verses while wearing a *kasa*, a deep straw hat that hid much of the face. The phenomenon is illustrated by the following anecdote in *Daijingū sankeiki* (Account of a pilgrimage to the Grand Shrine of Ise; 1342) by the hana no moto renga poet Saka Jūbutsu, describing his reluctant participation in a votive renga gathering performed to entertain the gods: "A desire was expressed to follow up the evening session by composing renga every day. I ignored my embarrassing lack of ability and joined the proceedings, which demanded great skill. More than ten poets took part along with a throng of people wearing *kasa*. A youth with flowing locks offered a splendid verse that muddled my aged brain even more. To the previous verse

wasuru na to	So as not to forget,
kakioku fumi no	I set it down writing
hitofude ni	with the stroke of a brush

he offered the following link

| hito no namida o | it brings back memories |
| omoi-idekeri | of his tears. |

Everybody was amazed when they heard it. The entire gathering was deeply moved.... The youth simply wrote the Chinese character for 'night' on the sheet of renga paper and vanished."[8]

An eighteenth-century commentary on the account by a Shinto scholar defines *kasagi* ("hat wearing) renga as sessions that were not limited to the core participants: anyone could drop by and compose a verse wearing a kasa. In other words, ordinary people (*yorozu no mono*) who wanted to jump in and participate first had to perform the symbolic act of donning a hat to obscure their identity and acquire socially unattached status (muen). One such person who came to the gathering as an onlooker, donned a kasa to participate, and composed a splendid verse that everybody marveled at—someone who bewitched Jūbutsu—was a *chigo*, a beautiful boy—literally, *taregami* ("[boy with] flowing locks")—who simply wrote down the Chinese character for "night" and left. The use of the word "night" as a pseudonym indicates that the principle of social non-attachment was maintained even regarding the sheets of paper on which renga verses were recorded.

The tradition of performing renga wearing a kasa continued until the Edo period (1603–1867). Sessions were held every month at the Kitano shrine in Kyoto. The following passage from shrine records offers a glimpse of the manner in which these sessions were conducted:[9]

> At the monthly sessions at the Kitano Renga Hall, even now shrine visitors sit on the verandah and link verses. The voice of the scribe reading aloud the verses inside the hall can be heard beyond the reed blinds. The session's members, consisting of priests, low-ranking shrine attendants, and the like, sit inside and link verses. It has long been the custom for the audience to add verses while wearing a broad-brimmed hat, so the monthly sessions are known as *kasagi* renga.

These gatherings on the twenty-fifth day of each month were dedicated to the vengeful spirit of Sugawara no Michizane, whose death occurred on that day of the month. A seventeenth-century topography called *Dekisai Kyō miyage* (Dekisai's Kyoto souvenirs) offers the following account of the service:

> Monthly renga again. Visitors to the shrine anonymously offered links while hiding their faces and disguising their voices. The

scribe applied brush to paper and read the verses aloud all day long until he was hoarse. Most of the verses composed by passersby outside the hall were rejected as being unsuitable, and people moaned and groaned. Verses offered by novices were laughed at by the assembled group because of their inferior quality. This will surely help to pacify the deity.

In the writer's words, the composition of renga in a rather tumultuous atmosphere with groans and snickers would help to propitiate the deity (the spirit of Michizane).

A description of the practice of composing renga wearing a kasa at a crossroads can be found in a chronicle of the life of Katō Kiyomasa, a prominent daimyo in the late sixteenth and early seventeenth centuries:

> The term *kasagi* refers to the practice of lighting a torch at night at a crossroads and erecting a curtain enclosure about six feet on each side. The scribe sitting behind it composes the opening verse and recites it aloud. Anybody who wishes to do so may put on a woven hat to hide his face and come forward and add a stanza. If it is flawed, the scribe promptly rejects it. If it is a good verse, he writes it down and asks the person's name. The versifiers disguise their voices and have him inscribe a pseudonym. People stay there as long as they wish, whether it is for one verse, two verses, or an entire sequence. The session begins in the early evening; by around two or three o'clock in the morning, a hundred-verse sequence is completed. The sessions generally take place nightly in the Seventh Month and Eighth Month. This sort of event, too, is indebted to the peace that prevails throughout the province. No untoward incidents have occurred at sites where the events are held; one-hundred verse sequences are performed without incident every time.[10]

The statues of the bodhisattva Jizō, a savior of the dead in hell, at many crossroads bespeaks their direct connection to hell. The crossroads were nondescript places where executions were carried out and passersby were cut down by samurai; where spectacles such as sumo and street entertainment as well as roadside noh were performed; where prostitutes hung out and fortune-telling was available. Kasagi renga was composed in this kind of setting with participants disguising their voices and wearing hats to hide their faces.

LINKED POETRY AND MILITANT LEAGUES

The collaborative nature of renga beneath the blossoms, the origin of kasagi renga, was characterized by the equality of all the participants, symbolized by wearing a deep-brimmed woven hat, and by the enjoyment they shared as a group in an artificially constructed setting—a site where everyday rules governing rank and status were cast aside. This communal setting governed by fictive equality was obtainable only through opposition to the transcendent darkness of vengeful spirits and the netherworld, for which weeping cherry trees served as a medium. It could even be argued that large weeping cherry trees with their branches stretching out in all directions were themselves a giant kasa, or canopy, that stood above the entrance to the realm of the dead. Just as individuals freed themselves from society's bonds by donning a kasa, renga parties beneath the blossoms created a fictive community under a large kasa—that is, a weeping cherry tree—cut off from the everyday world and its conventional social relationships and constraints.

Renga beneath the blossoms can be viewed as a shared world based on social nonattachment and equality—a realm in tense contrast to the world beyond—that brought together the general public using the symbolism of the kasa. Viewed in this light, renga parties point toward the militant leagues or alliances known as *ikki*, a uniquely medieval form of social cohesion that flourished during the middle ages, particularly from the Age of the Northern and Southern Courts onward.

The leagues forged solidarity by means of a ritual called *ichimi shinsui* in which all of the members, as a pledge of unity, inscribed their names on a written oath and then burned it and mixed the ashes with consecrated water (*shinsui*), which was then passed around and drunk by all of the members (*ichimi*). Hence the term *ichimi shinsui*. These groups began to surface among monks, peasants, and warriors very early on in medieval times, but they became conspicuous across a wide area under the name *ikki* starting in the Age of the Northern and Southern Courts. The *Taiheiki* announced the dawn of the age of ikki as military fighting units formed on the battlefield, and in chapter 25 it tells how a military commander serving the Northern Court sought to organize the forces under him into ikki prior to attacking the enemy at the battle of Sumiyoshi in the Eleventh Month of 1347:

> Summoning the warriors from Shikoku, Hosokawa Akiuji whipped up their fighting spirit, saying, "If we return from this battle like we did the previous one, we will become the laughingstock of the world. We must fight without any regard for our lives and erase the shame from the previous battle." The Bandō, Banzei, Tō, Kitsu, and Ban fighters formed ikki, each of which consisted of five hundred mounted warriors. The men were

divided into three units under three standards: large banners, small banners, and banners dyed deeper along the lower edge. They drank consecrated water and set out vowing to fight to the death without retreating a single step. They displayed fierce resolve in the face of extreme adversity.

The historian Katsumata Shizuo has made the following observation regarding this episode: "Warriors united under names such as Banzei and Bandō [were] samurai and peasants, whereas warrior bands with surnames such as Tō were united to some extent by kinship ties. They included a multitude of warriors on the fringes who became independent after the collapse of the traditional system of lordship and inheritance, as well as land-based samurai who had advanced themselves using local villages as a power base."[11] In other words, ikki represented a new type of organizational network that was first forged among people whose social identity was destabilized as traditional communities broke down. It was common practice to forge a written covenant when a military league was established. The circular configuration of the signatures on those documents would later inspire the name *karakasa renban*, or joint Chinese-umbrella seals, owing to the resemblance between the signatures, or seals, and the ribs of an open umbrella when the signatures were viewed from above. This shape was clearly a visual representation of the equality of all the members of the league.

The leagues were founded on the concept that individual feudal leaders were equal when in fact their actual social level was different, says Katsumata. Moreover, one could argue that the symbolism of the equality of all the league's members beneath an umbrella lay behind the term *karakasa renban*, like the practice of wearing a hat in linked-verse sessions beneath the blossoms. During the following Edo period, the customary attire of peasants who drew up Chinese-umbrella compacts and launched uprisings consisted of straw raincoats and woven hats.

Katsumata culled information from the medieval epic *Heike monogatari* (Tales of the Heike) depicting the civil war between the Taira and Minamoto clans in the 1180s, as well as other sources, to create a composite picture of assemblies at which all of the monks at Enryakuji temple on Mount Hiei hammered out the unanimous will of the temple prior to submitting collective appeals to the authorities:

> All three thousand monks belonging to the temple assembled in front of the Great Lecture Hall at Enryakuji. They were oddly attired with torn surplices wrapped around their heads and carried three-foot-long monk's staves. Brushing aside the dew on the grass with their staves, they sat in rows on stones that each person had brought. The monk sponsoring the petition covered his nose and altered his voice so that neither his disciples nor his associates knew his identity, as he shouted, "Has everyone on the mountain assembled?" He explained each item in the petition and asked for approval or disapproval regarding it. After a discussion, the view of each person was sought. If the response was affirmative, the person would shout that he agreed; if not, he would shout that the item was without merit. The conclusion arrived at in that manner was a consensus formed by the assembly described above. The majority decision that was orally arrived at became the unanimous will of the assembled monks. As in the case of Hakusan in Kaga Province, a bell was probably rung at that point. A pledge regarding the decision—that is, the ritual known as *ichimi shinsui* in which holy water was passed around and drunk by the entire congregation—would presumably have been conducted, and a petition drawn up representing the collective will of the three thousand monks at the temple.

Katsumata also argues that the protocol about wearing strange attire and disguising one's voice at such meetings was essential in a place where the unanimous will was forged:

> The circumstances surrounding the formation of the unanimous will of the temple inevitably entailed altering the participants' actual state. Their collective transformation through a complete metamorphosis provided the means.... League members were known for covering their faces. The eccentric appearance that resulted from shrouding one's face and head and the unusual manner of speaking could be said to have derived from this concept of transformation.

The militant leagues cut all social ties by performing the water-drinking ritual in the presence of a deity, and creating an autonomous, socially unattached community governed by equality that was organized around some sort of symbol. It follows, then, that general assemblies of monks constituted an ikki type of setting, although the term had yet to come into use. Kasagi renga sessions, which shared with the assemblies the practice of hiding one's face (i.e., wearing a large hat) and disguising one's voice, were clearly ikki-like settings in the realm of the arts, as was their precursor, the composition of linked verse beneath the cherry blossoms. (Although no ceremony was conducted in which everybody drank holy water, renga constituted a kind of linguistic passing around of a cup.) Both types of activities were conducted in a state of tension with the transcendent darkness formed by vengeful spirits and the netherworld. These circumstances and the creation of a socially unattached community governed by fictive equality leave no doubt that the sessions represented a kind of ikki setting in the realm of the arts.

After first surfacing in the fourteenth century as fighting units made up of local proprietors, ikki continued to evolve throughout the middle ages. Samurai leagues based more on local ties than belonging to the same social stratum were known as *kokujin ikki*, while landed and debt-cancellation leagues (*tsuchi ikki*) also rallied peasants in an effort to gain tax relief, and *ikkō ikki* (literally, "single-minded leagues") boasted fierce religious cohesion and power.

What should be noted here is that the emergence of the earliest ikki, namely military units, was in line with the popularity of renga beneath the blossoms in the first half of the fourteenth century. At the time, hana no moto renga was spreading widely among local warriors. In 1320, ten thousand verses were composed in a single day beneath the blossoms at a huge gathering in Kamakura, and the *Taiheiki* tells how hana no moto renga masters were summoned to take part in a ten-thousand verse session in 1333. This was a way to alleviate the boredom of the attacking forces during the prolonged siege of Chihaya Castle, which was defended by Kusunoki Masashige and his men. The two events attest to the many warriors during that period who were renga enthusiasts. Moreover, the Nijō riverside graffiti preserved in a 1335 document mentions the indiscriminate mixing of Kyoto and Kamakura poets at renga gatherings, and waka and renga sessions at which anyone could serve as a judge, while the Kemmu code the following year called for the strict regulation of group drinking and carousing, citing the vast sums spent on gambling in the name of tea-tasting competitions and renga parties. These remarks convey an idea of the enormous popularity of renga in both the capital and the countryside around that time.

Of particular interest are the direct ties between militant leagues and renga parties that could already be seen in the fourteenth century, as Yasuda Jirō has demonstrated in his study of the militant league in the eastern highlands of Yamato Province. Evidence of the direct link between the Someda Tenjin renga society and local land-based samurai uncovered by Yasuda has already been introduced in chapter 2.[12] The society, which remained in existence until the latter half of the sixteenth century when the process of national political unification began, centered on an image of Sugawara no Michizane that had been acquired by a devotee in the 1360s. The society's members held an annual thousand-verse renga session using income from rice land that they had acquired. The person in charge of that year's event brought the image of Michizane (Tenjin) to his own residence or a nearby temple and made the arrangements for the renga party, which was held in front of the image.

Yasuda's research confirms that the administrators came from the eastern highlands area, which fell under the Southern Court's sphere of influence owing to the circumstances surrounding payments of rice taxes to Kōfukuji temple in Nara. Similarities between the society's rules drawn up in 1434 and the league's contract include the use of the term *ikki* and expressions corresponding to the concept of majority rule in the contract such as "majority decision" and "administrator's decision." Moreover, the rule governing the expulsion of individuals whose participation in one-thousand verse sequences and payment of fees existed in name only echoed the language in the contract regarding the expulsion of league members. These similarities led Yasuda to conclude that the Tenjin renga society established soon after the formation of the league in the eastern highlands area amid the unrest in the fourteenth century was none other than the league dressed up in the guise of renga.

As an artistic form, renga served two important functions that had a bearing on the establishment and maintenance of the leagues as a group. One was its conciliatory aspect. The composition of competent verses in renga required an understanding of others and a sufficient grasp of the preceding verse. Undistinguished verses sparked no interest, while obtrusive ones destroyed the overall atmosphere. In other words, careful consideration was required throughout a renga session to gauge the overall mood of the group and offer verses that suited the flow. This function is related to the care taken to foster unity in ikki. The second function concerned the excitement generated by the act of linking verses. With a different person creating the next verse, an unexpected element of chance was brought into play each time. The elements of chance and surprise stimulated interest and transported all of the participants onto another plane.

Renga involves a departure into unfamiliar linguistic territory, a verbal adventure undertaken by a group. The modern-day renga poet Yamada Yoshio offers the following definition of superior renga: "All awareness of whether someone's verse is good or outstanding vanishes by the end of a sequence, and a state [is reached] in which one is lost in a trance and simply experiences a feeling of pleasure."[13] This situation dovetails perfectly with the physical and psychological boost offered by ikki leagues.

The accessibility of a collaborative art form that provided entertainment at drinking parties and banquets—a world where social ties were forgotten and complete unanimity was possible—must have meant a great deal to local warriors. In an age of social fluidity and instability, local warriors would have actively sought out and enjoyed renga settings as a new shared venue. In any event, the bodies that enjoyed renga parties governed by collaboration imbued with the spirit of social nonattachment and equality were readily transposed into bodies that participated in militant leagues.

RENGA MEETING PLACES

Linked poetry flourished at the Kitano shrine in Kyoto, replacing renga beneath the cherry blossoms, which waned in the last part of the fourteenth century. Still, the Kitano shrine was always a marginal site unfettered by ordinary social ties and status, and its renga *kaisho* ("meeting place") participants composed *kasagi* renga wearing a deep-brimmed hat that hid the person's face. Although that *kaisho* does not survive, a renga hall still exists at Kumata shrine in Osaka. The room startles visitors with its symmetrical interior, a rarity in Japanese architecture. Overall, the room is roughly twelve feet wide and eighteen feet deep, a space equivalent to twelve tatami mats. Opposite the entrance is a low wooden platform, roughly six feet wide, a forerunner of decorative *tokonoma* alcoves. The beautiful, very simple, symmetrical space is empty except for pictures of the thirty-six immortals of poetry on the upper half of the walls.[14] Four pictures are installed in each bay, except for the central bay above the wooden platform, which is bare. Images of two deities are apparently hung there during renga sessions. One depicts the deity Gozu Tennō (Ox-Headed King of Heaven) worshipped at the Gion shrine in Kyoto, which is famous for its goryō-e festival. The other image—the avatar of a Buddhist deity at the Kumano shrine complex in southern Wakayama Prefecture, a site of darkness—is said to be the local manifestation of an Indian prince whose mother had continued to breast-feed him after being beheaded.

The image of Tenjin acquired by a devotee is thought to have been kept permanently in the renga hall at the Someda Tenjin shrine. The interior of this hall, too, is an empty symmetrical space. The startling manner in which the shrine sanctuary juts out into the room, however, creates a space that more vividly suggests the presence of a transcendent being than would a flat wall containing just a hanging scroll depicting the deity's image. As a result of the protruding shrine and the flat horizontal space in front of it, the Someda Tenjin renga hall seems to embody the tension and equality of the medieval renga participants— land-based samurai who formed a militant league. The space beneath weeping cherry trees that exalted social nonattachment and equality in this way entered renga meeting places, where it was architecturally defined as an empty symmetrical space in front of the chief object of worship.

The term *kaisho* began to appear in works such as the poetry treatise *Mumyōshō* (ca. 1200) and the Buddhist tale collection *Shasekishū* as a place where Japanese poets met to compose Chinese verses and waka. The room in Sasaki Dōyo's residence described in the *Taiheiki* is an intriguing harbinger, in various senses, of the kaisho that developed later on. The episode, quoted in chapter 2 of this book, relates how he lavishly appointed his quarters by spreading mats with large crests in the room and installing a central object of worship and two adjoining paintings, along with a flower vase, incense burner, kettle for boiling water, and tray, before retreating from Kyoto in 1361.

Like the *kaisho* at Kumata shrine where renga was composed, Dōyo's meeting place was a six-bay room (the equivalent of twelve tatami mats). A set of three scrolls was hung on the wall facing the entrance, and three articles (*mitsu gusoku*) were placed below them. This configuration resembles the waka gathering depicted in *Boki ekotoba* (1351), a pictorial account of the monk Kakunyo's life, which features a hanging scroll of the great *Man'yōshū* poet Kakinomoto no Hitomaro as the chief object of worship. The difference is that the tatami mats depicted in the scroll are arranged to form three sides of a rectangle, whereas in Dōyo's room they covered the entire floor, a radical innovation at the time. Renga parties and tea gatherings hosted there by Dōyo on mats covering the entire room were enjoyed in a more relaxed manner, such as one finds in *Sairei zōshi*, a fifteenth-century picture scroll depicting festival scenes.[15]

Moreover, Dōyo left behind two *tonseisha* to greet whatever military commander showed up at his lodgings with the *kaisho*. Their status as neutral unaffiliated individuals meant that they would not be killed if they remained behind. Dōyo's action suggests the existence of special ties between tonseisha and kaisho. He was probably the first military leader to employ such individuals. Tonseisha would eventually gain official positions in the shogunate. Known as companions (*dōbōshū*) or companions of the meeting hall (*go-kaisho no dōbō*), their main responsibility was to oversee the interior of the kaisho erected as independent structures built by Ashikaga shoguns, beginning with the third shogun Yoshimitsu. The tonseisha overseeing Dōyo's residence with its meeting place were forerunners.

Kaisho were gathering places supervised by individuals who lived on the fringes of society as well as a space free of society's rules governing rank and status. This point is illustrated by the following description of a New Year's ceremony celebrating the first reading of the year in the kaisho at the Hōshin'in, a temple with ties to the imperial house that stood next to the palace in Kyoto:

> The process by which this ceremony came to be held in the kaisho was as follows. The original plan was to arrange seating for the elders and officials in the nine-bay room in the Small Audience Hall and hold the ceremony there, but it was unsuitable because the monks in charge of such rituals who would be sitting in the officials' section included persons whose low rank precluded their entering the room. As a result, the ceremony was

moved to the nine-bay kaisho. In other words, the use of kaisho meant more freedom since it did not have rules regarding rank and status. Conversely, restrictions since ancient times regarding social rank seem to have existed in the minds of the users of the Small Audience Hall. Restrictions could also be found regarding the living quarters at the palace and aristocratic mansions (*tsune-no-gosho*).

No evidence of the existence of a room under the eaves (*hisashi-no-ma*) or room built a step lower (*ochima*) than the main room can be found either in the kaisho at the villa belonging to the eighth-shogun Ashikaga Yoshimasa or in kaisho that were set aside for special use (*sen'yō kaisho*). In other words, kaisho contained no architectural elements denoting differences in rank. In addition, they played no part at all in the development of chambers with a raised platform area, a distinctive feature of shoin architecture in the early-modern period."[16]

The fifteenth-century diary *Kanmon nikki* (Diary of things seen and heard) kept by Prince Sadafusa (1372–1456) offers a detailed description of a banquet in his kaisho on the seventh day of the Seventh Month of 1432 that featured a Tanabata flower competition.[17] Seven scroll paintings were hung from two sets of screens set up in the kaisho. A variety of objects were arrayed on a shelf, and low tables and incense burners were also set out. The tables were covered with more than four dozen Chinese vases brought by the participants, creating a sea of flowers. When the prince retired to take a bath, a throng of lay people and monks came to view the flower-filled room. In other words, the kaisho was a site open to commoners as well as aristocrats. After the prince returned, waka was read aloud, and the first sheet of a renga sequence was composed. At night, musical entertainment was offered. The prince seems to have been rather done in, for he mentions resting after the day's activities.

Whereas the noh stage is an empty space possessing powerful directionality in a cosmic sense, kaisho were flat empty spaces that were appropriate for use as decorative places in which to display objects. Prince Sadafusa's kaisho containing several dozen vases and a sea of flowers could be characterized as a *basara* space permeated with undirected energy.

Kaisho served as a matrix for the development of arts such as flower arranging, tea, and linked verse. But once these arts became refined as aesthetic pursuits, as in the Way of the Flower or the Way of Tea, kaisho gave way to asymmetrical spaces: *chashitsu* (literally, "tea rooms") are a case in point.

In medieval Japan, kaisho were erected as a space free from conventional rules governing social relationships, even in the mansions of the powerful. Although kaisho disappeared in the Edo period, even then they are thought to have remained in existence underground as versatile, socially neutral spaces. "During the late Edo period," writes Yamaguchi Masao, "kaisho-like elements were eradicated on the surface, but it seems to me that they continued to exist in a different form. For instance, an opposition movement from the lower ranks of society emerged from there, as did hidden Christians in Kyushu. Pure Land Buddhists also secretly gathered in Kyushu to form Buddhist associations where samurai, merchants, and farmers came together. What originated in the middle ages as a sanctuary free of rules governing social status and rank disappeared from view as a result of the creation of uniform, standardized political spaces. However, kaisho manifested themselves under other guises."[18]

Indeed, this phenomenon seems to have carried over into the modern world. Research on a peasant rebellion near Tokyo in 1884, for instance, has shown that the political party behind the rebellion, and the area from which the party's members were mobilized, closely overlapped with a network of poets who practiced *haikai*, an informal form of linked verse popular in the Edo period. Accordingly, the range of issues generated by linked verse, militant leagues, and meeting places in the middle ages seem to have extended down to the modern world and our own time.

4

THE GENESIS OF PHANTASMAL NOH PLAYS

The most popular type of noh play today is a two-act drama in which a monk traveling around the country comes to a place that reminds him of a story associated with it, whereupon a stranger appears and tells him about the site. Upon revealing that he or she is in fact the subject of the story, the stranger disappears. While praying on this person's behalf, the monk falls asleep, hoping to witness a miracle. The person reappears in a dream, displaying his or her lifetime form, and recounts what had happened in the past. After performing a dance, the person asks the monk to conduct a memorial service and then vanishes, whereupon the dream comes to an end, leaving the monk alone at the site.

As Paul Claudel famously observed about this type of play, "Le drama, c'est quelque chose qui arrive, le Nō, c'est quelqu'un qui arrive (in drama, something happens; in noh, somebody arrives)."[1] That "somebody" is almost always a ghost. The question is, how did this unusual type of play, which casts a ghost as the protagonist, come into existence, and how did it come to occupy the heart of the noh repertoire?

Of course Japanese theater did not possess such dramas from the very start. The description of *sarugaku* in an eleventh-century work *Shin sarugaku ki* (A new sarugaku record) indicates that it did not rise above the level of comic skits. But by the time of Zeami's father Kan'ami in the mid-fourteenth century, sarugaku had made the leap to dream plays (*mugen nō*) in which ghosts appear. The foundations of today's noh were solidified by the revisions and refinements made by Zeami. An exploration of how dream plays featuring ghosts took shape at midcentury before Zeami came on the scene simultaneously paints a picture of the dawn of Japanese theater history.

NARRATIVE TALES WITH A DREAM STRUCTURE

The genre of Japanese anecdotal tales known as *setsuwa* includes a group of stories that closely resemble the contents of two-act dream plays. The following example from *A Collection of Tales of Times Now Past* (*Konjaku monogatari shū*) provides some hints about the genesis of this type of play. The tale is set in Tachiyama (now pronounced Tateyama) in the mountains of present-day Toyama Prefecture, a place with "sulphurous fumes and bubbling pools" resembling hell where, it was said, many Japanese who had committed sins landed after death.[2]

The story concerns a monk from Miidera temple at the foot of Mount Hiei who practiced the way of the Buddha by performing austerities at various sacred sites. When he came to Tachiyama, he encountered a young woman while he was walking around the fields of hell there. Since it was not a place where one would expect to encounter any human beings, he was frightened, thinking that she must be an evil spirit. When he started to flee, she called out, "Don't be afraid. I am not an evil spirit. It is just that there is something I wish to say."

The monk stopped and listened as she explained, "I am from the district of Gamō in Ōmi Province. My parents still live there. My father is a man of weak faith who earned a living carving wooden Buddhist images. I went to hell and suffer unbearable torments as a result of profiting from the Buddha for food and clothing during my lifetime. Please take pity on me and tell my parents to copy the Lotus Sutra in my memory to release me from my suffering. I have appeared here now to tell you this."

The monk was suspicious and asked why she was able to freely appear there in spite of undergoing punishment in hell.

"'Today is the eighteenth day of the month, Kannon's special day,' she explained. 'Although I intended to serve the bodhisattva and recite the Kannon chapter of the Lotus Sutra during my lifetime, I merely thought about it and ended up dying without doing so. On one occasion, however, I devoted myself to praying to the deity on the eighteenth. As a result, the deity appears every month on that day and undergoes the torments of hell on my behalf. During that time, I am free to leave hell and enjoy myself. That is why I was able to come here like this."

After telling him this, she vanished from sight. The monk immediately went to Gamō in Ōmi Province to ascertain whether her story was really true. When he repeated to her father and mother everything that she had said, their tears and sorrow knew no bounds. After he left, they immediately copied the Lotus Sutra on behalf of her soul. Later she appeared before her father in a dream dressed in beautiful attire and told him that the Lotus Sutra memorial service and Kannon's divine intervention had enabled her to leave the Tachiyama hell and attain rebirth in the Trāyastriṃśa realm of heaven. She also appeared in a dream before the monk. When he went back to her parents' home to tell them, he discovered that her father had had the very same dream. The monk delightedly returned home and told the world what had happened.

Although the contents of the service and the time and setting in which it takes place may be different, the underlying structure—an apparition's appearance before a traveling monk, a tale of past sins, a memorial service, and the reappearance in a dream (attainment of enlightenment)—closely resembles two-part dream plays. The ending of this story is also important: although casting a character as the source of the story could be viewed as a fictional device invented by the creator of the tale, in this particular instance it is entirely possible that a monk from Miidera who traveled around the country following the teachings of Buddha actually spread word of his own personal experience, for the story has the makings of a fine sermon encouraging ordinary folk to perform meritorious acts such as holding a memorial service on the Lotus Sutra.

The second example of a story with a dream structure comes from an early ninth-century collection of Buddhist tales called *A Record of Miraculous Events in Japan* (*Nihon ryōiki*). The story concerns the harsh retribution suffered by a lustful woman who had neglected to breastfeed her children.[3] The protagonist is a dharma master named Jakurin, a native of Kii Province who was now residing in the Kaga district of Echizen Province after having traveled around the country practicing austerities.

One night he had a dream about encountering an obese woman while he was walking near Ikaruga Palace in Yamato Province. She was crouching naked in agony in the shadows of the trees and grass beside the road and pus was oozing from her swollen breasts. When he asked who she was, she told him that she was the mother of Yokoe no omi Narihito in Uneda village in Ōno in Kaga district. She explained that in her younger days she had been very licentious and slept with many men, ignoring her children who were starving for milk. Narihito was the hungriest of all. She said that her punishment was in retribution for not giving her children milk.

When Jakurin asked if there was anything he could do to help, she replied that her son Narihito would probably forgive her if he knew about her suffering. At that point, the dream ended. Jakurin doubted whether it was true, so he went to the village where her son lived and told him about it. Narihito and his siblings were saddened by Jakurin's account, and they made Buddhist images and copied sutras to enable their beloved mother to end her suffering and eradicate her sin. Later she appeared in a dream by Jakurin's pillow and announced that she had been absolved of her sin.

This story differs from the previous one in that the monk's encounter with the apparition takes place in a dream. Nevertheless, it can be viewed as following almost the same pattern because the protagonist is a monk traveling on foot when he encounters the apparition. An interesting observation has been made about the background behind the story: "The promotion by holy men of good deeds that entail economic expenditures conveys the idea that the sins committed by the departed during their lifetime, and the sufferings inflicted on them as a punishment in the afterworld, require the performance of good deeds of a religious kind, such as making Buddhist images or copying sutras. The story provides concrete evidence of the homilies employed by holy men as a means of evangelism."[14] This kind of dream story was disseminated around the country by *kanjin hijiri*—evangelistic holy men—as a didactic tale to encourage the living to perform good deeds to alleviate the sins of dead relatives. Holy men regularly traveled on foot telling stories about dreams that involved memorial services for the dead, and these kanjin hijiri played a decisive role in the creation of noh during its formative years. As a result, the narrative form of dream tales could be said to have left an enduring mark on noh.

THE TRANSFORMATION OF EVANGELISM INTO A PERFORMING ART

The above tales indicate that evangelistic activities promoting the accumulation of merit among the common people date from early times. During Japan's middle ages, however, the term *kanjin* came to refer chiefly to fundraising efforts, and holy men who specialized in such work also emerged. Economic factors lay behind this development, as the land estates (*shōen*) that many temples and shrines depended on financially were lost or eroded in this period owing to the expansion of local power. As a result, it became necessary to rely on fundraising activities to collect donations to defray the enormous ad hoc cost of repairing and restoring temple and shrine buildings. The campaign conducted by the monk Chōgen at the end of the twelfth century to raise funds to restore the Great Buddha Hall at Tōdaiji in Nara, which had been destroyed during the civil war between the Minamoto and the Taira clans in the 1180s, epitomizes this kind of activity in the early part of the middle ages.

Fundraising events involving cash were made possible by the development of a monetary economy. As time went on, such events flourished, prompting a contemporary observer to exclaim in 1255 that evangelism permeated the entire country. The success of the fundraising activities altered the mode of soliciting donations as well. Nakanodō Kazunobu's study on the development of medieval fundraising activities in the thirteenth century sheds light on the rising use and types of entertainment in religious services, sermons, the viewing of Buddhist statues, and so forth. The admission fee charged for those events provided a way to collect funds beyond traditional methods such as touring the country with a subscription list, charging a fee at toll gates, and levying a tax on households. The practice of traveling around the country with a subscription list is illustrated by the famous legend about how the warrior-monk Benkei saved the life of his master, Minamoto no Yoshitsune, by passing himself off as a holy man (i.e., *yamabushi*) raising funds to rebuild the Great Buddha Hall at Tōdaiji.[5]

Around 1300, a new phenomenon arose in which the holy men who organized events to raise funds turned into entertainers themselves. The lay monk Jinen Koji is a representative example. His role is clear from his depiction in an eponymous early noh play that casts him as someone gathering donations through the distribution of amulets. At the start of the play, he urges listeners to obtain amulets to rebuild Ungoji temple in Kyoto.[6] In fact, a contemporary record in 1310 shows that he went to Nara and conducted a *hisashi* sermon at Shin-Yakushiji temple to raise funds. This reference is intriguing because a *hisashi*, the wide aisle surrounding the core part of a building, was exactly where he preached and sang and danced.

"Crazy Zen figures" such as the lay monk Jinen Koji are subjected to harsh criticism in the *Tengu sōshi* picture scrolls: "Known as Zen entertainers, they wear laymen's caps (*eboshi*) and do not shave their heads. They ignore the seat of meditation and perform sermons in public while striking bamboo sticks together (*sasara-suri*). They leave the window of contemplation and entertain in an antic manner in public."[7] This censure is accompanied by a picture of Jinen Koji performing on a temple verandah (*hisashi*) in front of a cluster of spectators. He is depicted as a handsome youth wearing a beard and mustache and has shoulder-length black hair covered by a hood. He is holding a pair of bamboo sticks in his hands as he dances and sings, "Sasara Tarō who has appeared out of nowhere is a natural beggar who emerged from the void when born, like the natural lay-monk Jinen Koji."

A history of Japanese Buddhism by the Zen patriarch Kokan Shiren dating from 1322 decried the recent state of preaching, which had seen the emergence of preachers who appeared in various guises and wept in an effort to move people. The true path has been swept aside by fraudulent actors, he laments.[8] Jinen Koji's preaching, however, was more radical; rather than merely interjecting performance elements into the traditional framework of preaching, he descended from the raised platform, the proper place for a preacher, and stood on the same level as commoners as he mixed orthodox preaching with popular songs and dances accompanied by the striking of bamboo sticks.

Another play, *Tōgan Koji* (The lay monk Tōgan), contains the following announcement by the eponymous main character, a disciple of Jinen Koji: "This is the bridge that my teacher Jinen Koji erected through Buddha's desire to save all beings." The remark suggests that Jinen Koji was also involved in the construction of a bridge over the Kamo River at Shirakawa in Kyoto. Moreover, a sixteenth-century history of Rozanji temple in Kyoto depicts Jinen Koji himself as a carpenter, saying that he applied himself assiduously to the construction of the hall by gathering materials of high quality and drawing the inking lines like a carpenter. Medieval *kanjin* holy men are described as performing the roles of what today would be called a director and manager, for they served as intermediaries between donor, temple, and craftsmen in negotiating agreements and procuring goods and services.[9] Rozanji's ties with the father of *sekkyō* preachers, the fourth-century monk Hui-yuan of Mount Lushan (Rozan) in China, raises the possibility that Jinen Koji may have been actively involved in other carpentry projects at Rozanji.

The preface to a fifteenth-century hand-scroll depicting a poetry competition in thirty-two rounds among representatives of different occupations reveals that the poems were transcribed on a scroll and, seeking his approval, were taken to a kanjin holy man's hermitage.[10] The holy man's role as a judge of the competition was an indication of the position of kanjin holy men as mobilizers and supervisors of tradesmen and artisans.

Jinen Koji sought to enlighten the common people with a combination of preaching and singing and dancing that projected a folklorish physicality. One could argue that this activity represented the fruits of the kind of sensibilities honed by kanjin holy men traveling around the country coordinating and integrating various occupations.

Whereas Jinen Koji was a preacher who sang and danced, Ippen was a *nenbutsu* performer who danced while chanting Amida Buddha's name. Like Jinen Koji, he was the subject of scathing criticism in *Tengu sōshi*, which attacked the outrageous behavior of his followers and him, saying that it would result in their rebirth in the realm of beasts (see chapter 1).

Ippen was not a professional kanjin preacher like Jinen Koji; rather, his principle as a holy man was not to seek funds for material things. That said, although he may not have conducted fundraising activities such as collecting donations for building projects, he did erect temporary dance huts as training centers around the country, where he used the nenbutsu dance as a magnet to gather people together and distribute slips of paper bearing Amida Buddha's name. In so doing, he established early on the style of kanjin entertainment that characterized later times.

For instance, the temporary structure where the dance was performed for forty-eight days at Ichiya in Kyoto was much higher than elsewhere, indicating that it was intended for a large audience.[11] It is the only venue in which viewing stands are depicted on three sides of the stage. At a time when stands were

FIGURE 4.1 *Odori nenbutsu* (Dancing nenbutsu) at Ichiya in Kyoto, from *Ippen Hijiri e* (Illustrated life of the holy man Ippen) by En'i

Courtesy of Tokyo National Museum

usually erected along both sides of a road to view festivals, it must have been a remarkable sight. The temporary elevated stage with its gable roof can clearly be regarded as a prototype of the noh stages of later times. Moreover, the Ichiya site surrounded on three sides by two-tier grandstands was a true forerunner of the performance space employed at the famous *dengaku* subscription event in 1349 described in the *Taiheiki*.

THE ADVENT OF SUBSCRIPTION PLAYS

Around 1300, fundraising activities began to take on the pronounced aura of public entertainment owing to the emergence of a new type of kanjin holy man in the person of Ippen, Jinen Koji, and others like them. The ideology legitimizing such activities was expressed by the phrase *kyōgen kigyo* ("wild words and specious phrases"), which transformed such activities from a sin into a means of extolling Buddhist law. The participation of the performing arts themselves in fundraising activities was a predictable development that became a reality at a surprisingly early point.

The first mention of subscription sarugaku in historical records occurred just seven years after Jinen Koji's fundraising sermon in Nara. The event appears in an entry for the sixth day of the Eleventh Month of 1317 in *Kagenki*, the annals of Hōryūji temple in Nara. The entry states that a subscription event featuring eight lectures on the Lotus Sutra was held to collect donations to build (or repair) a shrine attached to the temple. The lectures were followed by entertainment provided by Kesa Tayū, who received slightly less than one *koku* of rice from the temple as a remuneration. The person who conducted the lectures and the kanjin holy man who organized the event were also listed.[12]

The entertainer named here was the same person as the performer mentioned in a Hōryūji account of annual events down through the ages in 1511, which states: "The post of substitute musical director for dengaku was granted to Kesa Tayū of Sakato by a unanimous decision of the temple monks. He came for the first time on the fourth day of the Sixth Month of 1320. The temple gave him one koku as a special payment. However, it was limited to just that year." The passage is preceded by a statement that dengaku had been released from its obligation to perform at the Sixth Month ceremonies.

The account states that Kesa Tayū, a sarugaku performer linked to the founding of the Kongō noh school, had been chosen to serve as substitute head of music after the dengaku performers abandoned the post of musical director. The account also says that he began serving at the Sixth Month ceremonies in 1320 in a temporary capacity in place of dengaku rather than as the music director of sarugaku. According to the account, performers from the Sakato troupe served for generations as musical director of sarugaku at the Sixth Month ceremonies at the temple. For some reason, a sarugaku group affiliated with Hasedera temple in Nara held that post around 1320, so Kesa Tayū was installed instead as music director of dengaku. But his appointment to the position by a unanimous decision of the monks at Hōryūji suggests that his performance following the lectures on the Lotus Sutra in 1317 had been well received.

Of importance here is that the Hōryūji fundraising event in the Eleventh Month of 1317 centered on a series of sermons on the Lotus Sutra and that sarugaku was merely appended to it. The status of sarugaku can also be surmised from Kesa Tayū's remuneration that day, which amounted to less than one koku of rice. According to the 1511 account, his nephew, who succeeded him as substitute head of dengaku at the sixth-month ceremonies, received less than two koku for the event. A later entry for the twelfth day of the Tenth Month of 1320 in the Hōryūji annals indicates that the dengaku and sarugaku troupes each earned five koku for performing at a ceremony at the Tatsuta shrine that day to give thanks for rain, while an entry for the fifth day of the Sixth Month of 1359 states that the Sakato troupe received three koku at a performance of sarugaku in front of the Hōryūji Sutra Hall that was modeled after market festivals.

The sum of less than one koku that Kesa Tayū received for the subscription event in 1317 pales in comparison to these amounts. There was also a world of difference between his remuneration and the fee of more than twelve koku presented to the sarugaku players who performed in 1339 at the fundraising sarugaku event at Hatagawa-dera temple (Zenrinji) in Kii Province. The first full-fledged subscription sarugaku mentioned in historical records, the event at Hatagawa, attests to the early spread of this kind of activity in outlying provinces.

The 1317 record—the earliest documented evidence of subscription sarugaku—indicates that in the beginning sarugaku quietly entered the religious setting of subscription events as a performance attached to a sermon. Another kind of performance emerged at subscription events around the same time as sarugaku and dengaku: musical narratives consisting of oral recitations of the *Heike* accompanied by a *biwa* (a lute-like instrument), a genre known as *heikyoku*. Here, too, early events consisted of a combination of sermons and musical recitations of the tale. Three noteworthy entries can be found in the diary of the official Nakahara Moromori. The first one, dated the twenty-first day of the Second Month of 1347, mentions visiting the Yata Jizōdō hall that day to listen to a sermon and the recitation of the tale by the famous blind storyteller Kakuichi. On the following day Moromori remarks that he accompanied the head of the house in the latter's carriage to listen to the sermon and Kakuichi's recitation of the *Heike* at Yata. On the eighth day of the following month, he states that they went as usual by carriage to a temple, along with an instructor from the imperial academy, after which they went to Yata and listened to Kakuichi's *Heike*.

Kakuichi's narration of the *Heike* was in all likelihood a subscription performance. Moreover, it probably consisted of a recitation of the entire work, what was referred to as *ichibu Heike*, a conjecture reinforced by two entries regarding subscription events in the diary of Nakahara Yasutomi, a bureaucrat, a century later. The first one, dated the seventh day of the Fourth Month of 1444, states: "Went to Kajūji Uhyōe Gonza's residence. He said that he was setting out for the subscription event at

Seiganji temple to listen to the *Heike*, and told me to come along, so I went with him. . . . The blind performers Chin'ichi and Jūichi started reciting the *Heike* on the third." The second entry, on the fifth day of the following month, states: "Listened to *Heike* at Seiganji. Subscription performance of entire tale ended today. Performers included Chin'ichi, Jūichi, etcetera."

The performance at Seiganji, which lasted about a month, consisted of a recitation of the entire work. Since performances of the tale in its entirety are presumed to be subscription events, the information that Kakuichi recited it from at least the twenty-first day of the Second Month to the eighth day of the following month at the Yata Jizōdō hall in 1347 makes it likely that it, too, was a subscription event covering the entire *Heike* that took place over the span of about a month. The entries for the twenty-first and twenty-second days of the Second Month indicate that the program took the form of a sermon and an oral recitation of the *Heike*.

A seventeenth-century work on the musical narration of the *Heike* called *Saikai yoteki shū* (Remnants from the western sea) describes the ritual connected with the recitation of the whole work like this: "A monk enters and lights incense. After bowing three times and paying reverence to the Shinto and Buddhist deities, he chants the Heart Sutra. After that, the performer, dressed in formal attire, mounts the platform and performs a segment on the biwa. . . . The 120 sections are recited in thirty days." This passage reinforces the impression that the pronounced religious nature of the format, consisting of a sermon with an oral narration of the complete tale, persisted in later times.[13]

When the entire *Heike* was recited at fundraising events, however, the section performed in one day was fixed, so the sermon could conceivably have been adjusted to suit the contents of the tale, meaning that the choice of the scripture and the lecture reflected the part recited that day. In any event, on a formal level the recitation of the *Heike* rendered the preceding sermon more accessible.

Before performing arts such as sarugaku, dengaku, and oral recitations of the *Heike* found their way into fundraising events, activities such as religious services, preaching, and public viewings of Buddhist statues were held at the venues, which were completely religious in nature. Although the emergence of Jinen Koji and Ippen marked the rise of fundraising holy men as entertainers, the former conducted sermons with songs and dances. In the latter's case, even though his performances were referred to as a dance, they were in essence a religious ritual featuring the invocation of Amida Buddha's name. At the very beginning, the performing arts probably did not gain entrance into this type of venue solely as entertainment. One can imagine the use of a mixed format at first, such as a sermon and sarugaku (or dengaku), or a sermon and recitation of the *Heike*. Moreover, the contents of sarugaku or oral *Heike* narratives probably recast the preceding sermon in a way that was easier to understand, so that the performances retained a pronounced didactic tone while possessing an element of entertainment.

The advancement of musical performances of the *Heike* in subscription settings was facilitated by the war tale's close ties on multiple levels with *shōdō* preaching and its underlying aim of pacifying the souls of the Heike clan. Whereas the *Heike* attained a more or less complete form as a type of musical performance in the thirteenth century, the establishment of sarugaku and dengaku as theater occurred during the following century. This timing coincided exactly with the advancement of sarugaku and dengaku into subscription events. It is my belief that their becoming a new theatrical form sprang from their exposure to the intensely religious setting of subscription events.

MEMORIAL SERVICES FOR THE DEAD

The nature of the religious force field, the subscription venue, which spurred the creation of a new type of theater, can be seen in the depiction of the sermon by the lay preacher and fundraiser Jinen Koji at Ungoji temple in Kyoto in the eponymous noh play. As he enters, Jinen Koji exhorts spectators to buy amulets to restore the temple. He advances from the bridgeway onto the main stage and begins preaching on the raised platform at center stage.[14] After invoking Shakyamuni (the Historical Buddha) and the Buddhas of the Past, Present, and Future, along with the bodhisattvas throughout the universe, and the gods of heaven and earth protecting Buddhism, he announces the recitation of the Heart of Perfect Wisdom Sutra. As he does so, he notices a beautiful robe. Picking up the petition attached to it, he reads: "I reverently submit a petition with an offering of alms for the Three Treasures and the assembly of monks. I wish to donate a rain cloak to the Three Jewels so as to enable the souls of my parents to immediately attain salvation."

The petitioner turns out to be a girl who had sold herself into slavery to obtain the means to conduct a memorial service on behalf of her late father and mother. Jinen Koji continues reading:

> The cloak I obtained in exchange for my freedom is lined
>   with sorrow.
> I wish to quickly leave this wretched world
> and be reborn on the same lotus seat
> as my late father and mother.

Her words express a desire to quickly escape from this unhappy world in which she had to resort to selling herself to a slave trader in order to obtain a robe to use as an offering. In response to her moving request, which even contains an intimation of suicide,

Jinen Koji dampened his dark sleeves and none of the spectators' gaily colored sleeves were dry.

The girl went to the sermon with a robe and a petition seeking prayers on behalf of her late parents. Her decision to do so clearly demonstrates the attitude of ordinary people who attended subscription events, namely, that services for the dead were a key motivation. The slave trader's entrance speech reinforces this interpretation: "The girl said yesterday that she wanted to hold a service on behalf of her parents, so she must be at a place where a sermon takes place. Since Jinen Koji is at Ungoji, I think I'll go there and take a look." His decision, as well as the assumption upon which it rests, sprang from common knowledge that sermons connected with fundraising were venues where services for the dead were held.

The nenbutsu dance that Ippen performed while chanting the name of Amida Buddha began as a ritual to pacify the souls of the dead. The historian Ōhashi Shunnō points out that memorial stupas and funerary urns were also accepted on those occasions. As evidence, he cites the scene at Sekidera temple in Ōmi Province depicted in Ippen's illustrated biography:[15] "A temporary hut roughly eighteen feet (three *ken*) by six feet (one *ken*) in size has been erected next to the temple gate. The roof is covered with wooden slates. Four tall, five-ringed wooden stupas have been erected outside the hut, and two monks inside the hut are receiving a funerary urn in a lantern-shaped decorative box." Ōhashi also draws our attention to the dance scene at Yodo, which includes the depiction of a stupa being offered at a temporary hut under a large willow tree where nine tall five-ringed stupas have already been erected.

People who gathered to watch nenbutsu dances did not do so just to promote their own rebirth in paradise but also on behalf of the souls of the departed. A study of medieval fundraising events at local temples and shrines has thrown light on the kinds of religious expectations with which people responded to fundraising activities.[16] The study offers a wide range of examples, beginning with inscriptions on the back of a thousand amulets inside a 1268 statue of Prince Shōtoku at Gangōji temple in Nara. One amulet was offered "on behalf of my beloved late father and to eradicate sins in this life and generate merit in the future world for my mother who is still alive." Another one was offered to expiate the donor's sins and ensure complete faith at the hour of death, as well as to deepen the benefits available to all in the realm of the law. A third was donated by a daughter seeking to enable her late parents to attain rebirth in paradise.

A list of donations to construct a pagoda at Nagahama Hachiman shrine in Ōmi in 1435 begins with an offering of two hundred *kanmon* for a woman's thirty-third-year memorial service. Prince Sadafusa's diary *Kanmon nikki* mentions a fundraising effort in 1421 to rebuild the Mandala Hall at Jōkongō-in temple on the western outskirts of Kyoto, a project that was set to begin the following day. The prince offers the following explanation for the motive behind the campaign: "Hōsen, a major donor, solicited funds for the construction work from relatives to generate merit for his mother who died seven years ago."

Jinson, the head of the Daijō'in temple complex at Kōfukuji in Nara, contributed to a campaign by a holy man from Mount Kōya to defray the cost of rethatching the roof of a Jizōdō hall. Temple records in 1497 state that he issued instructions to donate twelve kanmon for services on behalf of his late father (the former regent Ichijō Kanera), his mother, and others, major anniversaries of whose deaths fell during that year.

Based on this evidence the author of the study, Sasaki Kōshō, concluded that donations were inspired in general by a desire to perform memorial services for the dead and eradicate sins and attain rebirth in paradise for oneself and others.

RELIGIOUS PLAYS ABOUT HELL[17]

If people made donations primarily for services for the dead, and if the fundraising events themselves had the pronounced aura of a memorial service on behalf of the deceased, we can expect these factors to have also influenced the choice of settings where fundraising were held during the Age of the Northern and Southern Courts onward into the fifteenth century.

The tendency to choose locations with deep ties to the netherworld is obvious in the case of riverbeds, which served as execution grounds and places for seeing off the dead. It is evident, too, regarding religious sites frequently mentioned in records pertaining to subscription events: for example, the Yata Jizōdō hall in Nara, which is linked to the story of the monk Manmai Shōnin's tour of hell; and the Rokudō Chinnoji temple and Senbon Enmadō hall in Kyoto, which figure in tales about the ninth-century courtier Ono no Takamura's descent into hell. In addition, the Jishū Training Center in the Fourth Ward is mentioned in an account of the miracles performed by the bodhisattva Jizō, while *Kitano Tenjin engi emaki* (A pictorial account of the origins of Kitano shrine) includes a story about a visit to hell by the tenth-century monk Nichizō.[18]

Research by Tokuda Kazuo on the link between kanjin holy men and temple and shrine histories offers a detailed picture of tales about hell collected and disseminated by holy men as they traveled around the country promoting the creation of religious merit to expiate the sins of the dead. Along with legends about Manmai and Nichizō, the material includes the scholar-monk Jishinbō's summons to the palace of King Enma, the ruler of hell, recounted in chapter 6 of the *Heike*; the story of the historical Buddha Shakyamuni's disciple Moggallana in the Ullambana sutra; and tales that depict the ninth-century courtier Minamoto no Tōru and the eleventh-century warrior Minamoto no Yoshiie in hell.

Tales about Minamoto no Tōru, the Kawara (Riverside) Minister of the Left, are especially noteworthy because of the connection with noh. The possession of Retired Emperor Uda by Tōru's ghost at the Kawara-no-in, the late minister's former home, is well known from works such as *Gōdanshō* (Ōe no Masafusa's conversations; early twelfth century) and *A Collection of Tales of Times Now Past*.

The late minister is portrayed as having gone to hell in the preaching (*shōdō*) of kanjin holy men. The following example is a fundraising petition offered by a monk named Kyōkō in 1199 seeking donations to defray the cost of casting a new bell at Daianji temple in Nara:

> I humbly present a petition to recast the bronze bell at Daianji temple which has stopped ringing. The bell is a vessel of the Dharma that announces to monks the truth about impermanence. It is an instrument that eradicates suffering and bestows happiness.... Recently, in our country, the ghost of the Kawara Minister of the Left revealed to Retired Emperor Uda, "As a result of the sin of taking life, I have gone to hell, where I undergo terrible sufferings and am unable to speak. I wish to have prayers conducted at seven temples. The sound of the hammer striking the bell will bring to an end the suffering that my tongue has endured. Despite practicing countless good deeds, I have accumulated no merit from them. By means of this [the sound of the bell], the power to absolve sins will be manifested."
>
> The sound of the bell at the Gion monastery preaches the impermanence of all things. When those who are ill hear it, they are immediately reborn in paradise. Sinners shatter the cauldron of hell, and giant elephants mend their raging spirits. In this way, infinite good karma will ensue.

The bell is extolled as an object that eliminates suffering and bestows happiness. As proof, the petition cites the confession of Tōru's ghost to Retired Emperor Uda that he has gone to hell because of killing living creatures and suffers from an inability to speak (a bit of a contradiction). He asks to have prayers read at the seven Nara temples. The sound of the temple bells, he says, will enable his tongue to move again, demonstrating the vast power of the bell to eradicate sins. The text goes on to list three benefits bestowed by the bells at the Gion monastery in India.

The essay by Tokuda cited above points out the similarities between this petition and the language and narrative approach in two thirteenth-century tales about Tōru. These tales, he says, are the only ones that mention the business about composing a prayer petition and conducting a memorial service for the Kawara Minister of the Left who had gone to hell. Tokuda believes that the composition of the stories in all likelihood was influenced by a kanjin holy man associated with Daianji temple who preached about the virtues of the bell ("sinners leave the cauldron of hell") in conjunction with a memorial service for the dead and the salvation of people who had gone to hell. The influence of a brief Chinese text in the mid-eleventh-century anthology *Honchō monzui* (Choice literature of this realm) also needs to be taken into consideration. Titled "Composed for a Prayer Petition Offered by Retired Emperor Uda on Behalf of the Late Kawara Minister of the Left," the text cites Tōru's confession that he killed living creatures during his lifetime, in punishment for which he was condemned to suffer in hell. Nevertheless, tales about Tōru going to hell were unquestionably spread by kanjin holy men preaching at events to raise funds for temple bells and the like.

These circumstances served as a backdrop to the creation of the play about Tōru the Minister performed by Zeami's father. A passage in *Sarugaku dangi* about Kan'ami's acting style in fierce roles gives as an example his expansive, vigorous movements as the demon in *Tōru the Minister* (ZZ 265), indicating that the play by Zeami called *Tōru* in today's repertoire was a demon piece before being extensively reworked by him.[19]

Further evidence can be found a little later in a passage from *Sarugaku dangi* regarding *Ukai* (Cormorant fishing), a play about the punishments in hell suffered by a fisherman, which states that the demon in the second act was transferred from the second part of the play about Tōru the Minister (ZZ 266). The casting of a deity in hell (Gushōjin or Kushōjin) as the principal actor in the second act indicates that the drama about Tōru masterfully performed by Kan'ami was one in which a demon assailed Tōru in hell. Numerous references to performances by Kan'ami at subscription noh events can be found in fourteenth-century records; his hit play about Tōru would no doubt have been indispensable on such occasions.

RITUAL SARUGAKU AND PLAYS ABOUT DEMONS

The character of the demon in hell in *Ukai*, apparently transferred as is from the play about Tōru the Minister, was a good kind of deity that assigns sinners to heaven. The notion of good demons in hell is not strange, inasmuch as the belief that the bodhisattva Jizō was an avatar of Enma, the King of Hell, dates back to ancient times. More importantly, the appearance of good demons in hell was inevitable, given the history of sarugaku itself. According to *Sarugaku dangi* (ZZ 302), Zeami played the role of the demon in the second part of *Ukai* wearing a *ko-beshimi* mask. This type of mask was a smaller version of ones with bulging eyes and tightly pursed lips that evolved from the masks used by performers of ritual *shushi* (or *jushi*) sarugaku, a precursor of noh, when playing the role of demons in rituals to exorcise devils.

In the late thirteen century, sarugaku centered on performances of *Okina* (Old man). The earliest reference to the play can be found in a record about a Kasuga shrine festival in Nara in 1283 that mentions sarugaku and the monks' names and the roles they played. The parts include a youth and three felicitous old men: the white-masked Okina; black-masked Sanba Sarugaku (now known as Sanbasō); and Chichi no jō (old man). These roles refer to *Shiki sanban* (Three ritual pieces), another name for *Okina* (see frontispiece). A few years later in 1297, a work on preaching refers to the white hair of the Okina mask, followed by a comment about the singing of sixteen songs.

The custom of referring to *Okina* as *shushi-bashiri* at torchlit sarugaku performances at Kōfukuji temple in Nara reflects the play's roots as a ritual conducted with rapid movements (*hashiri-bashiri*) by *shushi* players to dispel evil spirits. The sarugaku of Kan'ami and Zeami, who made *Okina* the centerpiece of their art, is a descendant of shushi sarugaku.

Rituals to exorcise demons (i.e., *hashiri*) were conducted on the final day of the New Year's Buddhist services in the First Month (*Shushō-e*) and Second Month (*Shuni-e*) when shushi sarugaku players performed. The rituals consisted of three roles: a pair of pursuing demons called Ryūten and Bishamonten, and a demon that was driven away. An important event with a pronounced religious character, the rituals were performed by temple monks known as *hozushi*. But the roles were eventually taken over by shushi sarugaku players. Evidence as to when that may have occurred can be found in an entry in an aristocrat's diary in the First Month of 1141 which identifies two sarugaku players as shushi performers at the ceremony at Hosshōji. Three days later the diary states that they played Ryūten on the last day of the First Month services at another temple, a role that should have been assigned to hozushi. This information suggests that the ritual was transferred to sarugaku around that time.

The demon masks such as Ryūten and Bishamonten worn by shushi sarugaku performers in devil-quelling rites (*tsuina*) evolved into *tobide* and *beshimi* masks. The process by which this occurred has been described thus:

> The exorcism rituals were also performed as a shushi art during the First Month services at Buddhist temples. Ryūten and Bishamonten—one with an open mouth, the other a closed mouth—enter and drive away a devil (or devils). Sarugaku actors raised in this environment would have been fully aware of this pair of demon masks. The nature of these two kinds of demons was the same as that of the lion-like *koma inu* statues in front of Shinto shrines and the fierce Deva Kings (Niō) at temple gates which guard the enshrined Shinto and Buddhist deities against evil spirits. Nurtured by Japanese culture and sensibilities, the two masks gradually gave rise to tobide masks with a wide-open mouth and beshimi masks with a tightly clenched mouth. The use of the masks today in felicitous noh plays depicting the subjugation of evil spirits can be viewed as a legacy.... The basic elements of these two types of masks, which form a unique aspect of the medieval performing arts, are thought to be a product of the Kamakura period.[20]

A historical document belonging to the Taka shrine in Yamashiro Province (what is now the southern part of Kyoto Prefecture) indicates that sarugaku performers had already taken the demon-quelling ritual beyond the walls of major temples by the mid-thirteenth century. According to the document, performers wearing demon masks with an open and a closed mouth conducted a ritual in 1271 to exorcise demons at the ground-consecration ceremony when the deity was transferred to the new shrine sanctuary.

By this point, the foundations had presumably been laid enabling sarugaku performers to put on plays about hell. All that was needed in addition was for kanjin holy men and others to provide stories. It is also possible that sarugaku in the early fourteenth century possessed primitive demon plays in which tobide and beshimi masks were used. The possession, or potential possession, of this kind of play allowed sarugaku to work its way into subscription events overseen by kanjin holy men at the beginning of the fourteenth century. It was principally in the setting of subscription performances that sarugaku honed a wide range of demon plays as religious dramas, beginning with works about hell.

SUBSCRIPTION DENGAKU EVENTS AND DEMON PLAYS

To gain a clear picture of the types of plays performed at subscription sarugaku events, one must in fact wait until the three-day program at the dry riverbed at Tadasu in Kyoto in the Fourth Month of 1464. By that point, however, noh had already been perfected as a theater form. Moreover, the subscription program was in essence a public event that enjoyed the full backing of the eighth shogun, Ashikaga Yoshimasa, undermining its value as evidence about the types of plays presented at early fundraising sarugaku events.

That leaves two plays performed at subscription dengaku events as our only source of information. The first one was the sarugaku piece about a miracle revealed by the Mountain King (Sannō

Gongen), the guardian deity of Mount Hiei, which was performed at the famous fundraising event in 1349 when the stands collapsed. The second one was a piece about a demon with four heads and eight legs performed at a subscription dengaku event at Gion in the 1350s that was mentioned in a pair of treatises by Imagawa Ryōshun, a military leader and prominent poet and critic.

The noh scholar Amano Fumio has sought to identify the demon in the latter play using an episode in the *Taiheiki* (chapter 23) that casts Kusunoki Masashige as an attendant of the ruler of the Ashura realm of existence after death.[21] According to the *Taiheiki*, his ghost appeared in a dream and confessed that he was a deeply sinful person who was tempted by evil thoughts when he died, as a result of which he had become a thousand-headed demon king and rode on a seven-headed ox.

Amano linked this passage to the depiction of *asura* (*shura* in Japanese) in a Buddhist sutra that describes them as fire-breathing demons with nine heads, each of which possesses a thousand eyes, and whose bodies have 999 hands and eight legs.[22] He also cites an earlier theory that the play dealt with the fourteen-century warrior Kō no Moronao, and his younger brother, nephew, and son—an assumption based on the variorum text of Ryōshun's treatise *Rakusho roken*, which has "four demons," rather than the currently accepted version of the treatise, which has "demon with four heads and eight legs," as does the testament composed by Ryōshun for his heir (*Ryōshun isshiden*). Based on this evidence, Amano conjectured that the play mentioned by Ryōshun was probably an early warrior piece cast in a demonic mode in which Moronao manifested the form of a multiheaded, multilegged shura in hell. Whether or not the warrior was the main character in the play remains open to question, but it seems certain at least that the protagonist was a shura in the form of a four-headed, eight-legged demon.

THE GENESIS OF PHANTASMAL NOH PLAYS ⌘ 101

The contents of the famous sarugaku performance described in the *Taiheiki* are difficult to imagine inasmuch as the passage covers only the last part when a boy playing the role of a monkey, a messenger of the guardian deity of Mount Hiei, enters with nimble acrobatic steps, triggering such excitement among the spectators that the stands collapsed. The account of the ensuing chaos, however, is noteworthy:

> A dengaku performer wearing a demon mask brandished a crimson rod as he ran after a thief fleeing with stolen costumes. Someone's attendants drew their weapons from their scabbards and chased after a man running off with one of their master's women slung over his shoulder. Some men turned around and engaged in fighting. A wounded person was smeared with red. It was like viewing a shura battle and the punishments of hell before one's very eyes.

In this passage, "punishments of hell before one's very eyes" clearly refers to the remark about the player brandishing a rod as he chased a thief running away with stolen costumes. Likewise, "shura battle" has to do with the business about brandishing swords and slashing at each other while blood flowed. Since an actor would not have gone to the trouble of donning a mask after the stands collapsed, we can only assume that the remark about wearing a demon mask and brandishing a rod had to do with a scene in the play about the miracle manifested by the guardian deity of Mount Hiei, Sannō Gongen. The remark in Nakahara Moromori's diary that day about the stands being completely destroyed *after* the play supports this argument.[23]

In *Sarugaku dangi*, Zeami characterizes another play, *Sano no Funabashi* (The boat bridge of Sano), as basically a dengaku piece that he had revised. An early noh play that was also performed in dengaku, he said, it had a long history (ZZ 291). Dengaku is thought to have put on demon plays at subscription events, including ones on the theme of attachment or obsession such as *Funabashi* (Boat bridge), as the work is now known.[24] The play depicts a man and woman from the village of Sano in Kōzuke Province (now Gumma Prefecture) who appear before a mountain ascetic and ask him to make a donation to build a new bridge. It turns out that they are the ghosts of lovers who drowned when the woman's parents removed the bridge planks to prevent them from meeting. The second part of the play depicts the man's sufferings in hell.

The dengaku repertoire primarily consisted of acts such as *chūmonguchi* (the musical opening piece), the use of stilts, knife juggling, and joint dances (*tachiai*) that centered on physical skills. The lack of a narrative thread made it difficult to project a religious message, a circumstance that presumably necessitated staging demon noh—that is, sarugaku plays—as religious dramas at dengaku fundraising events. Zeami's remark about *Sano no Funabashi* being an early noh play that was later taken up by dengaku is suggestive, in light of the belief that demon plays originated in sarugaku and were later added to the dengaku repertoire. The essential nature of dengaku as a maskless mode of performance makes it difficult to believe that demon plays were a dengaku invention.

THE DEVELOPMENT OF SUBSCRIPTION SARUGAKU EVENTS

A total of eight subscription sarugaku performances are mentioned in contemporary records prior to 1400, that is, before Zeami is believed to have perfected his unique type of noh:

Date	Location	Performer	Source
1317	Hōryūji, Nara	Kesa Tayū	*Kagenki*
1339	Hatagawa-dera, Kii	unknown	temple records
1364	Yakuōji, Kyoto	Yamato sarugaku troupe	*Moromori ki*
1371	Fukushōji (Settsu)	Kan'ami	temple records
ca. 1372	Daigoji	Kan'ami	*Ryūgen Sōjō nikki*
1380	Ayanokōji riverbed, Kyoto	Inuō	*Kōyōki*
1383	Takakura Jizōdō hall, Kyoto	unknown	*Yoshida-ke hinami ki*
1399	Ichijō Takenohana, Kyoto	Zeami	*Kōyōki*

Although at first glance the list may seem short, historical records are silent on the subject of events, such as the subscription performances by the Yamato actors Konparu Gonnokami and Kongō Gonnokami in Kyoto that are touched upon in *Sarugaku dangi* (ZZ 298). What elite circles felt about subscription sarugaku (and dengaku) presumably was an important factor, since that stratum of society kept the written records. For instance, Nijō Yoshimoto's steward Higashibōjō Hidenaga admits in his diary *Kōyōki* in 1380 that he had watched in utmost secrecy a subscription sarugaku performance by the famous Ōmi sarugaku actor Inuō. After watching a fundraising dengaku performance at the Daigoji Lecture Hall on the thirteenth day of the Fourth Month of Jōwa 2 (1346), Kenshun, the head of the Sanbōin subtemple at Daigoji, noted in his diary that he went there in great secrecy but felt compelled to refrain from doing so again in the future.

In 1420, an account of traditional religious and secular customs and manners called *Ama no mokuzu* includes the following comment regarding attendance at subscription dengaku and sarugaku performances: "In the past, nobody of consequence went to these events. Recently, however, the Nijō regent attended for the first time. The Kajii abbot also attended from the ranks of *monzeki* (monks from elite imperial, aristocratic, or warrior families). Since then, aristocrats and monks from monzeki temples often go to performances."

The attendance by the regent Yoshimoto and the abbot Cloistered Prince Son'in at the dengaku event in 1349 provided a precedent for appearing in the stands. Although the practice subsequently became commonplace, in 1380, even Hidenaga, who had an open-minded aristocrat in Nijō Yoshimoto for an employer, wrote about attending a performance at the Ayanokōji riverbed in Kyoto in utmost secrecy. Inasmuch as events combining entertainment and fundraising activities, by nature, were venues open to commoners that the elite shied away from, it is fair to assume that subscription sarugaku (and dengaku) were held rather frequently around the country, even if they do not appear in historical records.

ASPECTS OF RELIGIOUS PLAYS

Of course fundraising noh events were not limited to the dramatization of paintings that depict punishments suffered in hell. Many religious (*shōdō*) plays also featured a person who, after going to hell, recounts the past and confesses his or her sins—a type of play reminiscent of the tales featuring dreams that were discussed at the beginning of this chapter. We can, of course, readily imagine that the religious plays about hell mentioned above also contained scenes of this sort.

Kayoi Komachi (Courting Komachi), an early work also known as *Shii no Shōshō*, is a representative example. The play depicts the celebrated Heian poet Ono no Komachi's courtship by the Lesser Captain of the Fourth Rank (*Shii no Shōshō*), a member of the Imperial Guards from Fukakusa. According to *Sarugaku dangi*, "the play was created by a preacher (*shōdō*) from Mount Hiei. Konparu Gonnokami performed it at Tōnomine. It was later rewritten" (ZZ 291). These comments clearly indicate that the original version was composed by someone whose function was to conduct sermons to enlighten the masses, an activity that overlapped in many respects with that of kanjin holy men.

The following remarks by Koyama Hiroshi offer a thought-provoking view of the evolution of the play:

> The ghost of the Lesser Captain of the Fourth Rank from Fukakusa appears and reenacts before a monk how he visited Ono no Komachi for a hundred consecutive nights long ago. When the monk says, "Expiate your sins by making a confession," the Captain turns to Komachi and says: "Tell how you waited a hundred nights at the carriage stand. I will imitate how I came to visit for one hundred nights."
>
> The explicit remark about recounting the past as a confession of one's sins can be viewed as a vestige of the teachings conveyed in preachers' sermons. Although it must originally have had a didactic meaning, the focal point in this play, too, has shifted to enjoyment of the interesting scene in which the one-hundred-night courtship is recounted. This approach evolved until the speech by the monk likewise came to express the idea that he, too, was a spectator watching a show. In the early seventeenth-century Kurumaya-bon text, as well as in performances today, the monk says, "Imitate how you commuted one hundred nights to the stand where the carriage was set down."[25]

Koyama argues that the process by which noh was established needs to be examined from various angles. One possibility, he says, would be to consider how it shed its ties with religious plays, as *Kayoi Komachi* suggests.

In *Kayoi Komachi*, the art of *monomane*, or dramatic imitation, a specialty of sarugaku, has been transformed into the mimetic representation of a confession regarding the captain's courtship of Komachi, a central motif in the play. Sarugaku simultaneously attracted spectators and enlightened them through the art of dramatic imitation. That was presumably the aim of the original playwright, a preacher from Mount Hiei. Yet the same could be said of works about hell that centered on the punishments inflicted there. It is safe to assume that most of the plays of this type—such as *Kayoi Komachi*, which features the confession of a dead person who has gone to hell; and the play about Tōru the Minister, which depicts sufferings in hell—were works written by preachers or kanjin holy men for subscription noh performances.

The original version of *Kayoi Komachi* composed by a preacher apparently premiered at a performance by Komparu Gonnokami in a competitive setting in which new works were pitted against each other: namely, the sarugaku program accompanying the Eight Lectures on the Yuima (Skt, Vimalakīrti) sutra at the Tanzan shrine on Tōnomine. The demand for this type of play is thought to have sprung chiefly from subscription noh venues.

It also might be worth noting that a document from 1528 belonging to the school of *kotsuzumi* drummers states that a fundraising monk had a craftsman carve a new mask after an Okina mask was destroyed in a fire on Tōnomine in the Ninth Month of 1506. The remark that the monk—a kanjin holy man—supplied a new mask by having a craftsman under him carve one suggests the existence of special ties between noh masks and kanjin holy men.

Noh plays like *Jinen Koji*, too, gained much greater immediacy in subscription noh settings. In the aforementioned study of tales about hell collected and disseminated by itinerant holy men, Tokuda cites several examples of temple and shrine histories compiled by holy men who depict the achievements of their predecessors, including *Yūzū nenbutsu engi* (An account of the origins of the Yūzū nenbutsu sect) and *Shinnyodō engi* (An account of the origins of Shinnyodō temple).[26] His research has led him to conclude that writing about the activities of earlier kanjin holy men and employing temple and shrine histories in sermons was a means of boosting the authority and achievements of contemporary kanjin holy men in their temple communities. This practice readily segues into the structure of *Jinen Koji*, as a noh play depicting the religious activities of one kanjin holy man, which was staged at a subscription event that another kanjin holy man organized. Its performance at this kind of event must have delighted spectators and kanjin holy men alike.

Plays about mad or distraught persons (*monogurui*) such as *Hyakuman* and the piece about a celestial maiden performed by the famous Ōmi sarugaku actor Inuō can also be regarded as religious dramas that suited subscription events. The former stresses the important role of the miracle manifested by Shakyamuni, the historical Buddha, the principal deity enshrined at Seiryōji temple on the western outskirts of Kyoto, in bringing about a reunion between the dancer Hyakuman and her son.[27] The latter play casts Inuō in the role of a bodhisattva of song and dance who enters holding a sutra and performs a dance extolling the Buddhist law. The metamorphosis and progress manifested in plays involving preachers is illustrated by the setback dealt a monk by Ono no Komachi, a lay person, who out-duels him in a debate on Buddhist doctrines in *Sotoba Komachi* (Komachi on the stupa). When viewed from this perspective, a majority of early noh plays could be seen as falling under the category of shōdō religious plays.

On the other hand, the religious aspect is thought to have been weak in three of the four plays listed in a record of the special festival at Kasuga shrine in Nara in 1349, which is often cited in discussions of early noh. The lone exception was one identified as a piece about Prince Hanzoku, an Indian ruler who converted to Buddhism. The plays were an attraction offered by amateurs—priests and shrine maidens attached to the Wakamiya shrine at Kasuga—and should probably be classified as a program featuring works from the past that were not part of the mainstream.

SUBSCRIPTION NOH SETTINGS

A variety of religious dramas are thought to have been performed and developed in this way at fundraising events. A central place was occupied by plays that took the form of a memorial service seeking the salvation of individuals who had gone to hell, such as *Kayoi Komachi*, *Funabashi*, *Ukai*, and the play about Tōru the Minister. *Ama* (The diver) and *Motomezuka* (The sought-after grave) are two other examples.

The impact of the plays was greater in fundraising venues that were in close proximity to the land of the dead. The incident that occurred during a subscription performance of the *Heike* at the Yata Jizōdō hall in 1418 is a case in point. According to Prince Sadafusa, spectators listening outside the hall to the *Heike* recitation that day witnessed a miracle before their very eyes: "The bodhisattva Jizō shook his staff," he wrote. "The statue moved slightly."[28] The incident offers a glimpse of the intense religious atmosphere at fundraising events.

Subscription noh venues, however, were not merely intense religious fields. Sarugaku before then had been no more than a religious ritual offered on behalf of Shinto and Buddhist deities, and spectators who attended the events merely looked on from the sidelines. Subscription noh settings, however, were different: for the first time, performers found themselves in a situation in which they directly faced the audience. Increased responsibility meant a better fee. The going rate at subscription noh performances from the Age of the Northern and Southern Courts onward into the fifteenth century was fifty *kan*, a vastly different sum than the amount received for sarugaku performed in front of a deity.[29]

Conversely, *Sarugaku dangi* relates the fate that befell the actor Komparu Gonnokami, whom Zeami disparaged as having a countrified style. The subscription event in Kyoto in which he was participating was so poorly received that the shogun did not bother to attend, so the actor was forced to call it quits after only two days instead of continuing for the usual three (ZZ 298). One aspect of fundraising noh venues was their nature as sites where fierce competition ruled, placing a premium on popularity.

The advancement of sarugaku and dengaku into this new arena where religiousness and worldliness fiercely clashed led to the creation of a new type of play in which a monk traveling around the country holds a memorial service on behalf of a dead person—a role suggestive of kanjin holy men. Further refinements were made while being exposed to the fickle critical gaze of spectators.

This kind of play eventually formed the core of the repertoire and became much more stylized under Zeami, who was directly impacted by another major shift in attendance as spectators from elite circles became standard. Although how that happened cannot be discussed in detail here, the end result was that Zeami introduced the format of a dream (*Kayoi Komachi*, for example, is not cast as a dream), creating two-act plays with a more advanced structure in which the past and present converge in a single figure. Formally, however, his perfection of the two-part dramatic dream structure represented a return to the kind of tale introduced at the beginning of this chapter. At the pinnacle of its refinement, noh returned to folklore and this perhaps assured it a long stable existence.

5

BEAUTIFUL TEMPLE BOYS AND THE EMPEROR SYSTEM

Mishima Yukio's novel *Forbidden Colors* (*Kinjiki*; 1951) mentions a text that had secretly been handed down by Buddhist clerics in the middle ages. The novel centers on a beautiful youth named Yūichi, who was under the sway of an elderly writer named Shunsuke, a person who possessed a vast store of knowledge about medieval Japanese literature and unusual tastes. After experiencing his first erotic encounter with a boy, Yūichi paid a call on Shunsuke and listened as the elderly writer talked about the medieval text in his study:

> "Can you think of something in medieval Japan that corresponds to the worship of the Virgin Mary in Europe during the middle ages?" Shunsuke asked. Anticipating a negative answer, he continued, "It's the worship of boys. I have a copy of an interesting secret book from that period, a time when boys occupied the seat of honor at banquets and drank wine from their master's cup before everybody else." He removed a slender bound manuscript from a nearby shelf and showed it to Yūichi, saying that he had asked someone in the Tendai Archives on Mount Hiei to transcribe the manuscript.

Yūichi asked him how to pronounce the Chinese characters on the cover. Shunsuke replied that they were read *Chigo kanjō* and said, "The text is divided into two parts: *Chigo kanjō* (*The Initiation of Catamites*) and a secret text called *Kō chigo shōgyō hiden* (*Secret Transmission of the Teachings on Catamites*). The gloss appended to the latter title attributing it to Eshin is of course a complete fabrication: even the period is wrong. I would like you to read the section explaining in detail the ritual of the caress in the *Secret Transmission of the Teachings on Catamites*. (What exquisite terminology! The organ of the youth who is loved is called the Flower of the Law; that of the man who loves him, the Flame of Darkness.) I'd like for you to understand this thinking behind the initiation of boys."

Shunsuke impatiently turned the pages with his elderly fingers and read aloud the passage, "You are a being in an advanced state of enlightenment, a Buddha from antiquity. You have come into this world to save all sentient beings."

He explained that the remark was addressed to a boy and said, "It was customary to recite these mystic words of praise and exhortation after the naming ceremony, proclaiming 'From now onward, the suffix -*maru* shall be appended to your name.'"[1]

Mishima, however, did not actually see the *Secret Transmission of the Teachings on Catamites* with his own eyes. The remark that the manuscript was divided into two parts—*The Initiation of Catamites* and *the Secret Transmission of the Teachings on Catamites*—may have sprung from a misunderstanding: this scene in the novel seems to have been written solely on the basis of quotations in the Tendai monk Kon Tōkō's story "Chigo" (1946), to judge from Kon's afterword to the 1973 edition, which expresses displeasure at Mishima's unauthorized use of material.[2]

But the unauthorized use of material is not what concerns us here. Given Mishima's enthrallment with the emperor in his later years, it is intriguing to contemplate what might have happened if he had actually seen the *Secret Transmission of the Teachings on Catamites*, for the overall account of the initiation of boys, in it and in variant texts, is not limited to their erotic and sacred nature. It also has to do with the profound hidden meaning of imperial power, which includes both aspects, and with the sexuality and sacredness residing deep inside the emperor system.

THE ADULATION OF BOYS IN MEDIEVAL JAPAN

The term *chigo* (rendered above as "boy") could also be translated as youth depending on the individual's age as well as the cultural and historical context. In Japanese religious and aristocratic circles, it referred to acolytes and pages. In temple society, especially, it acquired homoerotic and aesthetic connotations when acolytes were the object of the monks' sexual desire. Hence, it is not infrequently translated as catamite, temple boy, or beautiful boy.

The comment in *Forbidden Colors* that chigo drank wine from their master's cup before everybody else underscores the place of honor accorded them in the middle ages. The incident in which Zeami as a boy sat in the grandstands with Ashikaga Yoshimitsu (1358–1408), the third shogun, at the Gion festival and drank from his wine cup must have been familiar to Mishima, who wrote a story called "Chūsei" (The middle ages; 1946) about the eighth shogun Yoshimasa, his son and successor Yoshihisa, and the object of their affections, a young *sarugaku* actor named Kikuwaka.[3]

Chigo formed a unique existence that sprang from homosexual practices in temple society. The phenomenon of homosexuality spread to court circles during the twelfth century, when retired emperors maintained control over the government, and by the late thirteenth century it had permeated warrior society as well. Chigo were prized as a flower in all three segments of society. They also participated in the arts; for instance, a *waka* collection called *Shokumonyō wakashū* compiled in 1305 prominently featured love poems exchanged by monks and chigo. Nor does the field of linked verse lack for examples such as the *renga* session at the Ise shrine described by the elderly professional poet Saka Jūbutsu in which a chigo composed a brilliant verse that captivated him. The Muromachi period (1336–1573) even gave rise to a unique literary genre called *chigo monogatari*, which depicts love affairs between monks and temple boys. Early on, the art of flower arranging, too, was sustained in part by chigo and their Zen counterparts, *kasshiki*, who studied it as part of their curriculum.

Figures that had formerly been represented as adults now began to be depicted as boys. The bodhisattva Monju (Mañjuśrī); the legendary Japanese Prince Shōtoku (574–622); and Kūkai (Kōbō Daishi; 774–835), the founder of the Shingon sect of Buddhism in Japan, are a few examples. Images of them as chigo circulated widely in the middle ages, beginning in the twelfth century when retired emperors held the reins of power. Literary heroes, too, were represented as boys. For instance, a commentary on *Ise monogatari* (*Tales of Ise*) compiled prior to 1300 maintains that the famous Heian courtier-poet Ariwara no Narihira (825–880) as a child was a beautiful boy named Mandara (Mandala) who studied under the monk Shinga (the younger brother of Kūkai).[4] Moreover, the hero of *The Tale of Genji* appears as a boy in act 2 of *Suma Genji* (Genji at Suma), a noh play possibly by Zeami that is mentioned in *Sarugaku dangi* (ZZ 279).

FIGURE 5.1 Portrait of Kōbō daishi (Kūkai) as a child/*chigo*, from *Chigo daishi zō*

Courtesy of Kōsetsu Museum of Art

Particularly noteworthy is the statue of Prince Shōtoku as a boy that was produced in 1069 soon after the accession to the throne of Emperor Go-Sanjō (1034–1073; r. 1068–1073), whose reign anticipated the era when retired emperors controlled the government. That year the monks at Hōryūji temple in Nara made an image of the seven-year-old prince and installed it as the main object of worship at the memorial service, a pacification ceremony (*goryō-e*), on the anniversary of the prince's death, replacing one of Guse Kannon (the World Savior Avalokiteśvara), which was viewed as an actual likeness of the prince. From a Shinto perspective, the belief in vengeful offspring deities (*wakamiya*) also began to flourish during that time. The tradition that the Wakamiya festival in Nara was launched by the regent Fujiwara no Tadamichi in 1136—during the rule of Retired Emperor Toba—also comes to mind as a symbol of this development.

The period from 1130 to 1156 when Retired Emperor Toba wielded power coincided with the emergence of openly homosexual figures such as Tadamichi's younger brother Yorinaga, the Minister of the Left.[5] Sexually, it was a transitional age when androgynous phenomena surfaced in personal attire and the performing arts. According to *Ama no mokuzu* (1420), an account of ancient court customs and usages, stiff costumes began to replace soft ones in Retired Emperor Toba's day. Before then, males never plucked their eyebrows, bound their sidelocks, or blackened their teeth. Everything has reached a state of extreme ornamentation in this final degenerate age, the writer laments, saying that such tastes did not exist in China even in the present day. The depiction of nobles in the Taira clan wearing makeup in the *Heike* was part of this trend.

Conversely, *Essays in Idleness* declares that the performance of dances by beautiful women in male attire began during that period: "The court musician Ō no Hisasuke said that the lay-monk Michinori [d. 1159] taught a woman called Iso no Zenji interesting dance movements that he had selected. Because she had on a short white cloak with wide sleeves (*suikan*), carried a dagger at her waist, and wore a man's *eboshi* cap, her performances were referred to as male dances. Her daughter Shizuka passed down the art. That is the origin of *shirabyōshi*.[6] The dance marked the beginning of gender crossing in the performing arts, a phenomenon that flourished in noh.

Various factors may have been involved in the representation of adults as boys and androgyny, but I believe that the most fundamental reason lay in the unusual ontological structure of the imperial institution during the middle ages. Beginning in the twelfth century emperors wielded power as a retired emperor after ceding the throne to a son. The groundwork for this development had been laid two centuries earlier when the regency system was introduced. Under the *ritsuryō* legal system established in the seventh century, the emperor possessed both power and sacredness. The extent of his power, however, declined as the system weakened and fell apart. The establishment of regency rule in the ninth century placed real power in the hands of the emperor's maternal relatives, members of the Fujiwara clan, who maintained a hereditary hold on the office of regent (known as a *sesshō* when the emperor was a child and *kanpaku* when he was an adult). The emperor was kept isolated, and only his authority was guaranteed. Even then, however, the source of power and authority formally continued to reside in the emperor at the apex of the ritsuryō system, meaning that regents were only able to issue important orders in the form of imperial decrees.

Although much of the absolute power and sacred authority of the imperial house were temporarily restored in the twelfth century, in actuality the formal integrity preserved under the ritsuryō system was clearly split between two separate entities: the retired emperor as a despot who took over the Fujiwara clan's power in a more potent form; and the emperor as a figurehead whose authority was unadulterated. The task of governing was generally conducted by means of orders or decrees issued by the retired emperor who became the undisputed guardian of his son after he stepped down from the throne.

Child emperors were not just an inevitable product of this system involving a father (retired emperor) and son (emperor). They also naturally emerged as a symbol of the purity of the emperor's authority and sacredness. Emperors ascended the throne, on average, at the age of sixteen (by Japanese reckoning) and reigned fifteen years and five months during the regency period, which spanned the reigns of fourteen emperors from Yōzei (r. 876–884) to Go-Reizei (r. 1045–1068). Conversely, the twenty-three emperors who reigned from the twelfth century until the first quarter of the fourteenth century ascended the throne, on average, at the age of eight years and ten months and remained there for ten years—a time span that corresponded exactly to the age of a chigo.[7]

Child emperors became increasingly cut off from government compared to their position during the regency period because of the despotic retired emperors; while their isolation in a vacuum concomitantly heightened their sacredness. The structure of the imperial institution in the middle ages, I would argue, gave rise to equivalent phenomena: the representation of sacred figures as boys, and the spread of unisex attire and androgyny in the performing arts. The worship of chigo in temple society and the emergence of child shoguns in military circles, especially when the Hōjō clan exerted political control as shogunal regents during the Kamakura period, correspond to the phenomenon of child emperors.

The following interpretation of Prince Shōtoku as an unrealized emperor has been offered by Yamaori Tetsuo in his book on the religious authority of the emperor. He writes: "Having left the world as an extraordinary crown prince, he was placed in a golden frame as the person most legitimately able to represent the ideal type of emperor. Perpetual expectations surrounded him retrospectively as an ideal heir to the throne. Of course, perpetual expectations are the obverse of perpetual frustration. As long as expectations remain unrealized, frustration does not disappear. Hence the ideal image of an emperor was sought in the glittering golden space behind the tragic image of Prince Shōtoku in the religious consciousness of the people in the middle ages."[8]

As mentioned earlier, a statue of Prince Shōtoku as a seven-year-old boy was installed as the chief image at the memorial service held for him at Hōryūji in 1069, replacing that of Guse Kannon the World Savior wearing a golden halo, which was regarded as an actual likeness of him. To force Yamaori's argument slightly, it was a simplified visual rendering of him as an unrealized emperor. Moreover, in our context, the image of him as a boy, which could also be perceived as a symbol of regeneration, was a visual expression of the emperor's isolation as simply a sacred existence during the regency period. This anticipated the actual transformation of the emperor into a child during the twelfth century when retired emperors ruled. In any event, the hollow center in the emperor system that had existed in Japan since antiquity came to be deeply tinged with issues involving the beauty, eros, and sacredness of boys at the point at which the emperor, a child, was placed at the empty center in the middle ages.

THE LEGEND OF THE
IMMORTAL YOUTH JIDŌ

The Japanese psychologist Kawai Hayao has argued that the key to the structure of the Japanese psyche lies in "the model of a powerless, functionless center that maintains a suitable balance between opposing forces, rather than in a model of social unity forged by the wielders of authority or power."[9] This argument closely resembles the theory of the medieval Japanese state advanced by Kuroda Toshio, which is predicated on the existence of ruling elites, or *kenmon*. Kuroda argues that the ancient ritsuryō legal system was brought to an end by the advent of government by retired emperors. From that point onward, that is, during the middle ages, the Japanese state rested upon complementary relationships among the court nobility (including the emperor), temples, and warriors.

The close resemblance between Kuroda's approach and Kawai's model of a balance of power maintained by a hollow center is readily apparent from the following remarks by Kuroda regarding the state and religion in the middle ages:

> The emperor as sovereign was regarded as an authority with profound religious and ideological significance. In the medieval Japanese state, the sovereign was referred to objectively and substantively as though he were a regent, retired emperor, shogun, or the like. In actuality, however, the opposite was true. The fallacy of the system of ruling elites was underscored by the fact that the sovereign was restricted to a merely nominal existence as emperor. The emperor suited the system, which simply demanded transcendent authority, not transcendent power, of the sovereign. In part, this was because the emperor possessed sacredness as a descendant of the rulers of the ancient autocratic state, but it was

not the only reason. Over time, various norms and precedents accumulated that formed an abstract idea of the emperor and endowed him with a mystique as simply an authority figure.[10]

The establishment of the system of ruling elites in the middle ages naturally also altered the relationship between the emperor and Buddhist institutions that had existed since antiquity. The change is explained thus by Kuroda in a study on the power of medieval temple-shrine complexes:

> In ancient times, Buddhism considered its mission to be the protection of the state. Buddhist institutions were not entities whose task was to expound the truth as bodies independent of the secular world; rather, they were intended to serve the state, hence their subservient relationship to it. The aristocracy, which comprised the bureaucracy, expected shamanic powers from monks and nuns to protect the state. By touting that type of benefit, Saichō [the founder of the Tendai sect] and Kūkai [the founder of the Shingon sect] secured public recognition for their respective institutions. But the situation had now changed. Regardless of how much authority they possessed, the wielders of state power (whether regent or retired emperor) were essentially members of an elite group or faction. Conversely, the temples in essence were a faction that was vital to the protection of the state, placing them on a par with the wielders of governmental power. The temple monks who formed the heart of the temple-shrine power structure accordingly reveled in their own position and stressed their equal footing with secular authorities. The meaning of protecting the state consequently shifted from subservience to a position of equality.[11]

The expression "mutual dependence of Imperial law and Buddhist law" was an ideological formulation of the parity that existed between the two sides. A document submitted to Tōdaiji by one of its land estates in 1053 put it this way: "The equivalence between Imperial law and Buddhist law in the present day can be likened to the two wheels of a carriage and the wings of a bird. If one wheel or wing is missing, a carriage cannot move, a bird cannot fly. Without Buddhist law, how could Imperial law exist? Without imperial law, how could Buddhist law exist?"

The secret ritual was added to imperial accession ceremonies in medieval temple circles, based on this concept of the interdependence of Imperial law and Buddhist law. At the time, the accession ceremony consisted of the Great Harvest Festival (Daijō-e), which had existed since the founding of imperial rule in antiquity, and the succession and accession rituals, which were instituted in the mid-ninth century under the influence of the Chinese imperial accession ceremony. The new ritual was inserted in the Japanese ceremony at the point where a Protector Monk, or a regent carrying out his wishes, taught a hand gesture (mudra) and incantation (mantra) to the new emperor when he mounted the Takamikura throne.

Abe Yasurō has presented evidence showing that this secret ritual may have begun in 1068 when Emperor Go-Sanjō ascended the throne—in other words, during the early phase of rule by retired emperors.[12] He quotes a document on the origin of the mudra and mantra performed during the accession initiation that was given to the fifteenth-century Shinto scholar Yoshida Kanetomo by a high-ranking court noble, Ichijō Fuyuyoshi (or Fuyura, 1464–1515). According to the document, Go-Sanjō's enthronement in 1068 marked the start of the accession protocol (*sokui hō*). As proof, it quotes a statement in Ōe no Masafusa's diary that a Daigoji monk conferred the protocol on the new emperor and had him make a mudra when he ascended the Takamikura throne.

The comment is noteworthy, says Abe, because it accords with the remark by the Tendai Abbot Jien (1155–1225) in *Musōki* (Record of a dream) that Masafusa's diary contains a description of the protocol regarding the Takamikura throne. In fact, a document about the accession of Emperor Go-Sanjō contains a gloss attributed to the eleventh-century Palace Minister Minamoto no Morofusa concerning what transpired while the new emperor was seated on the throne. The gloss, which is by no means unfounded, states: "During that time, his majesty put his hands together and made a mudra like that of Mahāvairocana (Dainichi Nyorai, the Cosmic Buddha)."

There were two types of secret accession rites: the Tendai sect protocol; and its counterpart, the Tōji protocol in the Shingon sect. The initiation of boys in the Tendai sect is predicated on prior knowledge of the Chrysanthemum Boy, or Kiku Jidō (Ju Citong in Chinese), a legend that sprang up in medieval Tendai circles to explain the genesis and efficacy of the Tendai accession protocol.[13] The story of Jidō was also taken up in noh and other medieval performing arts. A favorite of King Mu of Zhou in China, Jidō violated a taboo against traversing the king's pillow, for which he was banished to a distant place called Lixian at the advice of the king's vassals. But the king took pity on him and taught him a magic spell consisting of two verses from the *Fumon* ("Gateway to Everywhere") chapter of the Lotus Sutra that were transmitted during enthronement ceremonies. Jidō inscribed the spell on chrysanthemum leaves in Lixian, whereupon the dew that fell from the leaves turned into a heavenly elixir, which he drank. As a result, he remained a boy even when he reached the age of eight hundred. This story is usually recounted together with one about how King Mu came to receive the verses.

Different versions of the story exist, including its narration in Tendai circles as an orally transmitted secret about the origins of the Tendai accession protocol. The following account from the *Taiheiki* is a representative example that contains nearly all of the basic story elements [the numbering has been added by the translator]:[14]

1. Long ago, eight heavenly horses appeared during the reign of King Mu of Zhou. The king was able to ride anywhere in the world on them. One time, he traveled westward 100,000 *li* over mountains and rivers until he reached the country of Śrāvastī in India. Shakyamuni was preaching the Lotus Sutra on Vulture Peak at the time. King Mu dismounted and approached the assembly. He promptly bowed to Shakyamuni, withdrew, and sat down. The Buddha asked, "What country are you from?" King Mu replied, "I am the King of China." The Buddha then said, "You have come here at a good time. I know a means of governing countries. Would you like to learn it?"

King Mu replied, "I fervently wish to learn how to virtuously govern the people and rule the kingdom in peace." Shakyamuni taught him a *gāthā* consisting of eight verses in Chinese from the four key chapters of the Lotus Sutra. They were the passages conveying the innermost secrets regarding the doctrines and precepts set forth in the Lotus Sutra today. After returning to China, King Mu kept the verses hidden deep inside his heart and did not transmit them to the world.

2. King Mu doted on a boy named Jidō. As a result, the boy was always by his side. Once while passing by the throne, Jidō stepped over the royal pillow by mistake. After conferring, the king's vassals announced, "When we consider precedents, his transgression is not shallow. Nonetheless, it was unintentional, so the death penalty should be commuted and he should be punished by being exiled to a faraway place." The decision could not be overturned so Jidō was banished to a remote mountain called

Lixian 300 *li* from the capital. In the remote mountain shrouded in clouds, birds did not sing and tigers and wolves abounded. Consequently, nobody who entered this mountain, however briefly, ever returned alive. King Mu took pity on Jidō and secretly transmitted to him two verses from the "Gateway to Everywhere" chapter of the Lotus Sutra. "Each morning, bow in all directions and recite this passage," he said.

In the end, Jidō was banished to Lixian and abandoned in a dark valley deep in the mountains. Obeying the ruler's august instructions, he chanted the passage once each morning. Lest he forget it, he inscribed the passage on low chrysanthemum leaves nearby. Dew from the leaves fell little by little into the water that flowed through the valley. All of the water turned into a heavenly elixir that Jidō drank when he was thirsty. It tasted like the sweet dew of heaven and surpassed the finest delicacies in taste. Not only that, heavenly beings came offering flowers, and fierce deities humbly attended him, so that he did not fear wild beasts such tigers and wolves. Instead he became an immortal who was able to fly. Moreover, the three-hundred and more households that drank the water downstream in the valley were promptly cured of illness and enjoyed long life without growing old or dying. Ages passed and for more than eight hundred years Jidō still possessed a boy's figure with no sign of infirmity or old age. During the time of Emperor Wendi of Wei, he changed his name to Pengzu and taught this secret of longevity to the emperor. After learning it, the emperor passed around a cup of wine with chrysanthemum blossoms in it in celebration of long life. This was the origin of today's Chrysanthemum Banquet on the ninth day of the Ninth Month.

3. Since then, when a crown prince inherits the Throne of Heaven, he always receives this passage first. As a result, the "Gateway to Everywhere" chapter can be regarded as the most

precious scripture in circulation today. It was transmitted to our land and taught to generation after generation of virtuous rulers on the day they ascend the throne. When the imperial regalia are conferred upon a child emperor, the regent receives the passage and teaches it to him at the start of his rule. These eight verses transmitted in the three kingdoms provide a method for governing the world and enabling the people to live in peace. The verses are an excellent means of warding off disaster and promoting happiness.

4. This is solely due to the blessings bestowed by King Mu's heavenly horses. The appearance of this fleet horse now is a sign of the prosperity of Buddhist law and Imperial law and everlasting imperial rule.

The above account from the *Taiheiki* is cast as an official's report to the throne in response to an inquiry by Emperor Go-Daigo about whether a magnificent horse presented to the court was auspicious. The first three parts—King Mu's reception of eight verses from Shakyamuni, Jidō's story, and the Tendai accession protocol—are summed up as deriving from the virtue of King Mu's heavenly horses. The court official, Tōin Kinkata, concluded that the arrival of the swift horse was an auspicious omen signifying the flourishing of Buddhist law and Imperial law and the never-ending prosperity of imperial rule.

The focus in the Tendai world, of course, was not on horses. The story of King Mu and Jidō was created and transmitted as a tale that explained the origins and benefits of the Tendai accession protocol, which formed the basis for the prosperity of the Buddhist law and Imperial law and the longevity of imperial rule. Jidō is a symbol of chigo on Mount Hiei, a perspective that requires explanation. A popular saying on Mount Hiei in the middle ages was "first chigo, then Sannō" (*ichi chigo, ni sannō*).

According to a Shinto document called *Gonjinshō* (1414) and other sources, when Saichō, the founder of the Tendai sect, ascended Mount Hiei, a wondrous youth (a manifestation of the Hiei shrine deity Jūzenji) appeared first, followed by a great figure in human form (a manifestation of Sannō Gongen, the guardian deity of Mount Hiei). As worship of chigo intensified, the saying came to signify the belief that the position of chigo was higher than that of the Sannō deity. The view of chigo as sacred representatives of Mount Hiei is illustrated by the statement in *Shokoku ikken hijiri monogatari* (Tales of a holy man traveling around the country; 1387) that the manifestations of Sannō Gongen were all chigo.[15] It was within this conceptual framework that chigo were worshipped and treasured.

Accordingly, the story of King Mu and Jidō can be interpreted in the following way: Sakyamuni's bestowal on the king of the eight verses from the four key chapters of the Lotus Sutra is reflected in the protector-monk's bestowal of the Tendai accession protocol—namely, the eight verses from the sutra—on the new emperor during the succession and accession rituals when he receives the three imperial regalia and ascends the throne. Mount Hiei can be viewed as the Japanese version of Vulture Peak in India and Mount T'ient'ai (Jp = Tendai) in China. In this instance, it represents their luminous aspect.

Jidō's banishment to, and decentralized rule over, Lixian after receiving from King Mu the two verses from chapter 25 of the Lotus Sutra bespeaks a recognition of Mount Hiei's decentralized governance from the perspective of the emperor's position as the secular authority. Desolate Lixian, deep in the mountains, is a metaphor for the dark aspect of Mount Hiei, which protects the Demon Gate in the northeast quadrant of Kyoto. Furthermore, Jidō, who continued to live as a boy for eight hundred years, changed his name to Pengzu and presented to Emperor

Wendi of Wei the two verses that he had received from King Mu in the Chinese capital. This process is presumably a reflection of the repeated Tendai transmission of the accession protocol to emperors in Japan.

In this way, Mount Hiei and the temple community (i.e., Buddhist law) are divided into the dual aspects of light and darkness, both of which possess a transhistorical nature. Placing Shakyamuni's transmission of the accession protocol to King Mu at the beginning of the story suggests the fundamentality of Buddhist law and its superiority over Imperial law. The key passages from the Lotus Sutra serve as a medium linking them to the emperor (Imperial law) on multiple levels. The story as a whole expresses the interdependence of Imperial law and Buddhist law, as well as their mutual prosperity and the existence in perpetuity of the imperial throne.

THE INITIATION OF TEMPLE BOYS

The story of King Mu and Jidō, however, does not simply explain the interdependence and nonduality of Imperial law and Buddhist law. The secret initiation of chigo on Mount Hiei, where it was actually conducted, allows us to view from afar the emperor system in the middle ages, which is clearly mirrored in Mount Hiei.

The following hypothesis has been offered by Abe Yasurō about when and by whom the story was created as an account of the origins of the Tendai accession protocol:

> The protocol, which originated in the days when retired emperors controlled the government, consisted simply of a mudra and mantra. (The regent is said to have secretly transmitted it on the Takamikura throne during the emperor's enthronement

ceremony.) The addition of a secret oral explanation of its significance in narrative form is thought to have occurred during the Kamakura period, when the protocol was secretly handed down. At first, the mudra and mantra were transmitted by esoteric Tendai monks (such as Jien). The shift to a form that entailed a secret oral transmission seems to have involved the participation of medieval Tendai monks specializing in the study of the Lotus Sutra (particularly the scholar-monks of the Eshin school), who emphasized the secret oral transmission of the Law.[16]

As mentioned earlier, Mishima Yukio's alter ego Shunsuke declares in *Forbidden Colors* that the *Secret Transmission of the Teachings on Catamites* was falsely attributed to the monk Eshin (Genshin), who died in 1017 and thus was not even from the same period. If anything, the attribution shows how the chigo initiation ceremony was identified with the branch of Tendai Buddhism founded by Eshin. In other words, it was a secret rite generated by the same imaginative powers that produced the story of King Mu and Jidō.

The initiation of chigo promoted in the dark, secret chambers of medieval Eshin-school monks was designed to consummate encounters deep within the chigo's sacred erotic body. A counterpart could be found in the secret ceremony called *Genshi kimyōdan* (Reception of secret teachings and pledge of faith before the altar) performed by the Danna school, another scholarly lineage on Mount Hiei. In its affirmation of the principle of eroticism, the initiation also corresponded to the praxis and teaching of the doctrine of "becoming a Buddha in one's present body" (*sokushin jōbutsu*) through heterosexual intercourse promoted by the Tachikawa school, a medieval offshoot of the Shingon sect.

Since our endeavor here is to view the secret chigo initiation ritual from the perspective of the imperial institution in the middle ages, I will defer to Kon Tōkō's novella *Chigo* in a discussion of matters such as the etiquette governing what transpired after the initiation ceremony, when euphemisms such as *hosshō no hana* ("Flower of the Law") and *mumyō no hi* ("Flame of Darkness") were used. The two original manuscripts in the Tenkai Collection on Mount Hiei consulted by Kon which explain that part in detail, however, remain off limits, so let us examine the secret initiation ritual using a slightly different, abbreviated manuscript called *Chigo kanjō shiki* (A private record of the initiation of chigo), dating from the early seventeenth century, in the Tendai Archives' Shinnyo Collection.[17]

At the beginning of *A Private Record of the Initiation of Chigo*, the explanation of how chigo are led into the world of Kannon's boundless mercy and compassion is prefaced by the statement: "In this practice hall (*dōjō*) in the Great Land of Japan in the World of Human Beings, revering the vow of Kannon of Great Compassion and invoking the deities in the Lotus Realm (Padma-kula), the Initiation of the Four Mandalas and Three Mysteries shall now be conferred on the boy who possesses an affinity with the Buddha."

This passage is followed by an account of the rigorous weeklong austerities prior to the initiation rite that the chigo undergoes under the direction of the officiating monk, a Ritual Master (Ajari). The text goes on to describe the actual initiation, saying that it was first conducted in Japan by the monk Ennin (known posthumously as Jikaku Daishi, 794–864), and that its general principles follow the Womb and Diamond Initiations (Abhiṣekas).

The process of decorating the practice hall where the initiation was conducted is described thus: "A space should be specially constructed for the occasion, and the practice hall should be decorated in a grand and solemn manner. First, screens are set up in all four directions, and the initiation site is placed facing south. The main object of worship is a Kannon mandala. To the left and right of it are hung images of Sannō Gongen [the Guardian Deity of Mount Hiei] and Dengyō Daishi [Saichō]. A jar filled with votive water is set down. An arrangement of seasonal flowers is created and a bowl of holy water is placed in front of the image. A prayer is performed while waving the *vajra*. Separate secret transmission. Low tables are covered with a cloth after they are set down to the left and right of the Ritual Master. A set of toiletry items—including black ink and a brush, toothpick, mirror, and comb—is placed on the left-hand table. Formal ceremonial attire, a crown, and the like, are placed on the right-hand table."

With this, the preparations for the site were complete and the ceremony conducted by the Ritual Master began. The chigo undergoing initiation then entered the room naked from the waist up.

> The Ritual Master counts the prayer beads as he chants. After the prayer to the main object of worship [Kannon] has been chanted five hundred [out] of one thousand times, the instructor [the chigo's attendant] brings in the chigo, dressed only in wide divided trousers (*ōkuchi*). The Ritual Master is seated on a low prayer stool facing west. The mudra is the Nowhere-That-Is-Not-Reached mudra. The mudra and mantra performed while the chigo is being led in are the Original Vow (*Mula-samaya*) mudra and mantra [secret transmission]. The chigo spreads out a prayer mat and bows three times. After doing so, he sits down. He sits on the mat after bowing three times. First, the instructor has him apply incense to his body. The Five Vows come next. After that, the Pledge on Entering the Way of the Buddha (*Buddha-pravesa-samaya*) mudra and mantra are performed seven times, followed by the Birth in the Realm of the Law (*Dharmadhātū-pāda*) mudra

and mantra three times, the Turning of the Wheel of the Law (*Dharma-cakra pravartana*) mudra and mantra three times, and the Nowhere-That-Is-Not-Reached mudra and mantra three times. Next the Ritual Master hands the toothpick to the chigo. After that he has him drink votive water. Then he takes the brush, dips it in tooth blackening, and applies it to the chigo's teeth three times. After that, the chigo applies it under the direction of the instructor. Next the instructor has the chigo wipe his mouth and then shaves his eyebrows, applies his makeup, and has him dress in formal attire. He also places the crown on the chigo's head.

After the makeup has been applied and the costume and crown are put on, the boy being initiated formally acquires the figure of a chigo. The Ritual Master steps down from the raised platform, and the chigo takes his place. At this point, rituals are performed that simulate a new emperor's ascent of the Takamikura throne and the performance of the accession protocol when the imperial regalia are bestowed and the accession rite is conducted. "The Ritual Master descends from the platform and has the chigo ascend it. The Ritual Master consecrates the water in the jar, confers the mudra and mantra, and performs the purificatory rite. (The secret transmission is recorded on separate paper.) Next, the Ritual Master intones an oral transmission three times. According to a certain text, it is two verses."

It is probably correct to assume that the verses were the two from "The Gateway to Everywhere" chapter of the Lotus Sutra, known as the Kannon sutra, that Jidō received from King Mu. After that, the Ritual Master's lecture begins. That is, after the chigo ascends the platform, receives the mudra and mantra, is purified (has water sprinkled on his head), and receives the two verses, the Ritual Master announces that he is the bodhisattva Kannon:

"From this day onward, the suffix -*maru* shall be affixed to your name. The initiation represents the initiation into Kannon's Great Mercy. By possessing mercy and compassion, you will save all sentient beings. If you lack mercy and compassion, you will incur the punishment of the Buddhas of the Ten Directions and Three Worlds, especially Kannon, as well as the Sannō deity. You are a being in an advanced state of enlightenment, a Buddha from antiquity. You have come into this world to save all sentient beings. Your heart, luminous and pure as the moon, inherently possesses the Sanskrit letter 'A.' When you received this unction now, the letter 'A' (the unborn buddha-nature) was activated. You are the bodhisattva Kannon. As Kannon, you embody mercy and compassion. I devoutly pray for you to save all sentient beings using mercy and compassion. Of the six *pāramitās* [perfections] by which a bodhisattva attains Nirvana, this prayer represents the practice of generosity. In the Fourfold Great Vow, it is the vow to extinguish blind passions, however great. If you put into practice the vow to save all beings in this way and attain Buddhist enlightenment within yourself, realizing the truth embodied by the buddhas and bodhisattvas, you will create positive karma for attaining release from the laws of transmigration in the life to come. This concludes my instructions."

After that, the chigo descends from the platform and sits on the mat again. The Ritual Master ascends the platform once more and performs the final prayers. Then he chants the closing prayer transferring merit to other beings:

"The great mercy and compassion of the Buddhas of the Past,
    Present, and Future
All converge in the body of Kannon.
The Eight Cold and Eight Burning Hells
One person out of Great Compassion suffers on others' behalf."

The passage is chanted three times, whereupon the ceremony as a whole comes to an end.

Immediately after spelling out in detail the protocol followed in the chigo initiation, *A Private Record of the Initiation of Chigo* makes an intriguing comment before turning to the story of King Mu and Jidō: "This initiation is a ritual conducted during the emperor's accession ceremony. After that, the term 'king' or 'maru' is employed. Kannon is the chief image of worship on this occasion. The teaching handed down during the accession is the transmission of 'The Gateway to Everywhere' chapter. In short, it is two words: mercy and compassion."

These remarks bespeak a recognition by medieval Eshin-school monks themselves that the chigo initiation was conducted as a ceremony equal to, rather than in imitation of, the imperial regalia and accession rites. The monks clearly regarded the chigo, a Kannon possessing infinite mercy and compassion, in the same light as the emperor, who was expected to govern with mercy and compassion. The identification of the unrealized emperor Prince Shōtoku as the avatar of Guse Kannon in the middle ages clearly sprang from the same imaginative roots, as did his transformation into a chigo. The legend about the black horse of Kai in medieval biographies of the Prince is the Japanese version of the eight horses of King Mu. Moreover, a document known as *Sokui hōmon no koto* (Teaching on the imperial accession) by a scholar-monk of the Eshin school, Sonkai (1253–1332), identifies the Chinese immortal Pengzu as Guse Kannon and states that he was known as Nan-yüeh in China and Prince Shōtoku in Japan.[18] This remark reflects a perception that Jidō, Pengzu, and Prince Shōtoku were one and the same. Prince Shōtoku embodied both King Mu and Jidō: in other words, he was an incarnation of Kannon as an emperor and chigo.

We need to persist a bit longer here, however, regarding the relationship between the chigo's actual circumstances and the image of Jidō. A guide to customs and manners called *Uki* (Notes on the right, 1202) by Cloistered Prince Shukaku, the abbot of Ninnaji temple in Kyoto, states that the "age for taking the tonsure should be set at seventeen, or perhaps nineteen. Consequently, a countenance with beautiful eyebrows, rouge, and white makeup lasts a mere four or five years."[19] The passage indicates that the time spent as a chigo, which included painting the eyebrows and wearing lip rouge and white face makeup as well as blackening one's teeth, usually lasted only a few years. But cases existed such as that of Taira no Tsunemasa; according to the *Heike*, he became a chigo under Cloistered Prince Shukaku's predecessor at Ninnaji at age eight and underwent the coming-of-age ceremony (*genpuku*) when he was thirteen.

The earliest Tenkai Archives manuscript on the initiation of chigo, which is dated 1450, describes the start of a chigo's day thus: "In the morning, he should arise early, use a toothpick, and wash his hands and face. . . . After combing his hair four or five times and temporarily tying it in back, he should apply makeup. After that he should comb his hair and tie it properly, and then go over the scripture that he read the previous day. He should carefully ask his mentor about passages he has forgotten. After that he should practice calligraphy."[20]

The account also states: "He should always carry a mirror and toothpick on his person. He must never let people see him wipe his face; nor should he allow his toenails and fingernails to become long and unkempt. He should not use a lot of force to open and close outer doors, and must never shut slide doors in a rough manner. He must not leave outer doors ajar when he shuts them. It would be unsightly."

These passages indicate that chigo underwent rigorous training in terms of personal grooming and etiquette. In Cloistered Prince Shukaku's words, they were polished and nurtured in temple circles as "beings for whom charm and grace (*yūen*) are everything." The strict regulations governing a chigo's looks and behavior represented nothing less than a powerful desire to purify him and turn him into a null symbol. Certainly, for a boy himself, the lustrous moment of beauty as a chigo did not last long in terms of his overall lifetime—just a mere four or five years. Even so, another chigo emerged to provide continuity when a chigo's age limit was reached, thereby preserving the overall radiant youthfulness of the system. This structure of the "eternal youth" in the chigo system was embodied by Jidō, who remained a boy for eight hundred years. The word Jidō is a collective noun for chigo. If King Mu's alter ego—a being that received two of eight verses from the Lotus Sutra—was Jidō, then it was also an affirmation of the secret behind the state of being "forever young" possessed by the emperor and the emperor system. Mishima's description of the character Matsugae Kiyoaki in *Honba* (Runaway horses) as a "non-volitional agent like a beautiful radiant particle that remains forever unchanged" does not refer just to Kiyoaki's beautiful countenance and way of life observed in the past by the narrator Honda Shigekuni.[21] It also suggests the beauty and nature of the emperor symbolized by chigo.

At the same time, however, the image of Jidō as a boy who lives for eight hundred years also seems to have been inspired by the coexistence of old men and boys in Taoist imagery. Of course this metamorphizing body originated in the bodhisattva Kannon, who assumes thirty-three forms to aid sentient beings. It is also intriguingly intertwined with the issue of an emperor system slowly permeated by imperceptible changes in the marginalized emperor.

We must not forget here that the chigo whom the monks sexually violated was a Kannon. Conversely, the idea that such acts were prohibited when a chigo was not a Kannon is expressed in *A Private Record of the Initiation of Chigo*:

> We sentient beings are all without sin as long as we entrust ourselves to Kannon's great mercy and reject darkness and blind passions. Hence it is known as a natural precept. However, we must not willfully commit transgressions. If we are tempted by mistaken and deluded ideas and our blind passions become enflamed, we will commit transgressions. If we do, we should violate chigo who have been initiated in this way. Violating chigo who have not been initiated will form a seed causing rebirth in the Three Evil Paths. . . . If one does commit transgressions, one should place complete faith in Kannon and look upon the chigo as a being in an advanced state of enlightenment, and oneself as a bodhisattva residing at the first stage. It means eliminating darkness and blind passions at that level by means of wisdom at the final stage prior to the attainment of perfect enlightenment (buddhahood).[22]

The Tendai concept of nonduality, which holds that worldly passions themselves constitute enlightenment (*bonnō soku bodai*), could be construed here as nothing more than a rationalization on the part of Tendai monks about how to cope with sexual desire. The equation of chigo with Kannon in the middle ages, however, is readily apparent from the large number of tales that depict them as an incarnation of the bodhisattva, beginning with the early fourteenth-century *Chigo kannon engi* (Story of Kannon's manifestation as a youth), the title of which speaks for itself.

Moreover, the thinking that informs the initiation of chigo, which Mishima's alter ego Shunsuke wished Yūichi to understand, concerns the belief that a chigo was a being at an advanced stage of enlightenment, a Buddha from antiquity who has come into this world to save all sentient beings. In other words, the chigo whom it was permissible to violate possessed absolute sacredness as someone who saved sentient beings. What medieval monks concomitantly worshipped and violated were chigo who were incarnations of Kannon as well as the alter ego of the emperor. It is possible that Mishima's agenda—a vow of devotion to the emperor as an absolute being—was already intuitively grasped in the initiation described in *Forbidden Colors*.

FROM THE MIDDLE AGES TO MISHIMA YUKIO

After watching Luchino Visconti's 1969 film *The Damned* (*La caduta degli dei* [officially subtitled *Götterdämmerung*]), Mishima wrote, "The camera showed the half-naked youth in female attire at an hour of wild pleasure and inebriation in the early morning darkness amid the distant roar of automobiles along the shore of the lake. The scene was filled with dark inexpressible lyricism like absorbent cotton soaked with alcohol. Whether good or bad (irrespective of what kind of youth he was), it was a foreshadowing of his brutal murder" [see editor's note].[23]

If we tone down the rhetorical level in the expressions "Wagnerian taste," "Germanic grotesqueness," and "gloomy terrifying lyricism" permeating the scene in Visconti's movie, it comes to resemble passages in medieval Japanese tales about chigo in which a monk falls in love with a youth. Take the following example from the scene in *Aki no yo no nagamonogatari* (A long tale for an autumn night; 1377) in which Keikai, a Master of Precepts on Mount Hiei, falls in love with a youth named Umewaka:[24]

As he passed Miidera temple, a misty spring rain began to fall lightly on his face. Deciding to wait a while until the sky cleared, he headed in the direction of the main hall. In the garden of the monks' quarters at the Shōgoin was an ancient tree with tinted blossoms that were unusually beautiful. The upper branches spreading beyond the fence resembled a blanket of clouds. Enticed by the idea expressed in a Chinese verse about "glimpsing a dwelling from afar and promptly entering the gate lured by the flowers," he approached the gate.

A sixteen-year-old chigo emerged from behind a screen and stood in the garden, seemingly unaware that he was being watched. He wore a wide-sleeved gauze cloak (*suikan*) with a water-and-fish pattern over a multilayered rose-colored underrobe. He had slender hips and his soft trousers were loose around his ankles. Breaking off a small branch weighed down with white blossoms like snow, he composed a poem:

Furu ame ni	Even if they are moistened
nuru to mo oramu	by falling rain, I shall pluck
yamazakura	the mountain cherry blossoms,
kumo no kaeshi no	for a cloud-dispersing
kaze mo koso fuke	breeze is blowing.

His figure moistened by raindrops from the blossoms, too, resembled a flower.

The figure of the young chigo in female attire dampened by the blossoms in the gentle spring rain exuded an aura that is identified as *shiore* (a moist or wilted state), a term denoting decadent beauty in medieval Japan. The flower that appeared in the misty spring rain truly merits the term *yūgen*, an aesthetic term variously translated as mystery and depth, elegance and grace, graceful beauty, and so forth. The aspect of yūgen possessed by the chigo consisted of an extremely gentle graceful flower-like beauty that welled up from the quiet spiritual depths that lay within, a description that resembles the characterization of the murdered woman in Mishima's novella *Extracts from the Philosophical Diary of a Murderer in the Middle Ages*: "her small white porcelain-like chin rose from the depths of the darkness like a moonflower." The common belief expressed in Jien's history of Japan (*Gukanshō*; ca. 1220) that emperors naturally possessed graceful elegance and depth (*yūgen*) as well as gentleness bespeaks the underlying attributes shared by emperors and chigo.[25]

The initial encounter between the Master of Precepts Keikai and Umewaka at Miidera, however, was a premonition of the latter's brutal murder, not unlike the foreshadowing Mishima described in Visconti's film *The Damned*, Umewaka's abduction by a mountain ascetic (i.e., a *tengu*) prompted the Miidera monks to burn down the mansion of his father, the Hanazono Minister of the Left, and erect an ordination platform, the source of a long-standing dispute between the temple and Mount Hiei. Fighting broke out, as a result of which the temple's magnificent buildings were all burned to the ground. When he saw with his own eyes what had happened, Umewaka threw himself into the Seta River and drowned. Extreme violence sprang up around the sacred but powerless chigo, and he took his own life. In the tale, however, his suicide is expressed in terms of the true spiritual awakening of Keikai, who, as the holy man Sensei, later made a name for himself as the founder of Ungoji temple in the Eastern Hills. Umewaka's story offers a concrete example of the chigo's role as Kannon ("One person, out of Great Compassion, suffers on others' behalf") expressed in *A Private Record of the Initiation of Chigo*.

The medieval tale *Suzuri-wari* (Broken inkstone) is introduced by Mishima in *Forbidden Colors* as a "story that had nurtured [Shunsuke's] poetic sensibilities through its depiction of the extraordinary philosophical resignation of the young master, who was beheaded by his father after taking upon himself a sin committed by the family retainer Chūta." This tale, too, depicts a chigo who took the suffering of others upon himself. The elderly writer Shunsuke must have been moved by the intense feeling of masochism underlying the tale.[26]

In *Yama no oto* (The sound of the mountain), Kawabata Yasunari describes the elderly protagonist Shingo's strange erotic response to the Jidō noh mask, which he contrasts with a kasshiki mask representing a young Zen acolyte:

> Kasshiki has the face and eyebrows of a man, whereas Jidō's countenance is rather ambiguous. There is quite a bit of space between the eyes and the eyebrows, and the gentle crescent shape of the eyebrows too resembled those of a girl.
>
> When [Shingo] moved his eyes close to the mask from directly overhead, the surface, which had a maidenly smoothness, softened in his elderly eyes. In the process, it took on the warmth of human skin, and the mask smiled vibrantly. It took his breath away. When his face was three or four inches from the mask, a live woman was smiling. It was a pure lovely smile. The eyes and mouth were truly alive. Dark pupils appeared in the hollow openings of the eyes, and the red lips looked moist and lovely. Shingo held his breath. When his nose was almost touching the mask, the dark pupils rose to the surface and the lower lip was full. He was on the verge of kissing the mask. Letting out a deep breath, he pulled his face away. At a distance, it seemed like a lie. For a time, his breathing was ragged.

Mishima once compared Kawabata to a fellow writer Inagaki Taruho, saying that they resembled each other in different respects regarding their pursuit of eroticism in medieval literature. Both writers, Mishima said, grasped the ineffable pathos in medieval literature and the pure eroticism that runs through it. This remark also captures the basic nature of his own sensibilities expressed at age twenty in his elegiacal short story "The Middle Ages."

6

ZEAMI AND THE GRACEFUL AURA OF A BOY'S FIGURE

Zeami was a man of the theater who attached great importance to the looks and demeanor of a boy. For instance, in his 1421 treatise *Nikyoku santai ningyō zu* (Sketches of figures representing the two arts and three role types; ZZ 124), he declares that the figure of a boy forms the basis of *yūgen*. Unlike his earliest treatise *Fūshikaden* (Transmission of acting styles and the flower), completed around 1418, which says that the charm of a boy's acting does not constitute the true flower but merely a temporary one, this treatise makes the graceful figure of a boy the foundation of the system of noh training. A similar sentiment is expressed in his 1420 treatise *Shikadō* (The path to achieving the flower; ZZ 112).

The phrase "figure of a boy" is a translation of *koshi* (*chigo no sugata*). In other contexts, chigo could also be translated as youth, depending on the individual's age. In Zeami's own case, discussions of chigo have invariably centered on matters regarding his boyhood beauty and homosexual relationship with the third shogun Ashikaga Yoshimitsu rather than directly addressing his image of chigo, despite the importance that he attached to chigo, their appearance, and the effect that they created. A reexamination of Zeami's view of chigo in light of their actual circumstances in his day, however, reveals the roots of his noh aesthetics by raising questions regarding his image of a chigo's figure and his own position as a beautiful boy as well as the nature of chigo. Such an undertaking concomitantly opens up another avenue for interpreting his life and theories on noh.

The noh scholar Kōsai Tsutomu has drawn attention to similarities in the figure of the boy in *Nikyoku santai ningyō zu* and that of a chigo in a sixteenth-century Buddhist text called *Kenro seiyo*. In both cases, the figures have artificial eyebrows shaped like a large elongated Chinese character "eight" (*hachi* 八) and long flowing locks fastened at the nape of the neck with a cord in a manner resembling a girl's hairstyle. These similarities led Kōsai to conclude that the sketch of the boy in Zeami's treatise conforms to the representation of temple boys in medieval love stories about chigo.[1]

But the image of a temple boy surely does not end just with Zeami's vision of chigo: an impression of Zeami himself as a temple boy emerges from the famous letter by Nijō Yoshimoto describing the boyish beauty of Fujiwaka, the name that the former regent had bestowed on Zeami a couple of years earlier:

> If Fujiwaka has time, please bring him again. It was a wonderful day. I was completely swept off my feet. Nothing further need be said about his own art; even his skill at such things as court football and linked verse is exceptional. Above all, his looks and bearing exude an enchanting aura as well as firmness and crispness. Little did I imagine that such a wonderful boy existed.

> In *The Tale of Genji*, the outlines of young Murasaki's eyebrows are described as being hazy, meaning that they have soft, enchanting contours. The remark likening her to a "mountain cherry tree overflowing with blossoms that is visible through the spring dawn mist" denotes a flowerlike figure that has an aura around it. Court poetry and linked verse are judged to be good when they create an interesting effect and display yūgen. The way in which this boy moves his hands, stamps his feet, and waves his sleeves

FIGURE 6.1 A *chigo* (young boy) dancing, from *Nikyoku santai ningyō zu* Omote Akira and Katō Shūichi, eds., *Zeami, Zenchiku*, Nihon shisō taikei (Iwanami shoten, 1974), 123.

when he dances seems more supple and graceful than a young willow in the Second Month swaying in the breeze. It surpasses the flowers on the seven autumn grasses moistened by evening dew.[2]

Yoshimoto goes on to cite a legend about the Tang dynasty emperor Xuanzong and his concubine Yang Guifei, as well as the poet Li Bo:

> Long ago Emperor Xuanzong of the Tang dynasty built a structure of aloe wood whose fragrance was said to extend for two or three *li*. He called it the Aloe-wood Pavilion. Yang Guifei enjoyed

viewing the peony blossoms there. She waved her sleeves as she performed the dance of the Heavenly Maiden set to the strains of Rainbow Skirt and Feather Cloak composed for the flute by the emperor following a visit to the Moon Palace. The interesting verses by the poet Li Bo that were sung, too, reflect my feelings now. The scene beneath the cherry blossoms at sunset during the Flower Festival when Hikaru Genji danced to the strains of the "Warbling of the Nightingale in Springtime" must have been just like this.

The special favor shown by the shogun is completely understandable. Good timing is rare, even in the case of an extraordinarily talented individual such as this. If swift horses had not encountered the trainer Be Le, their potential would not have been realized. It took three reigns for the statesman Bian He's jade to be recognized as a precious stone. The true nature of something comes to naught if it remains hidden. To have been granted such an opportunity is extraordinary. Please be sure to bring Fujiwaka with you again soon.

I cannot help feeling that a flower still blooms in the heart of someone relegated to obscurity like a buried log.

Please burn this letter at once.

The recipient of the letter is identified only as the Sonshō'in, the name of a subtemple and by extension the high-ranking Buddhist official who headed it. Yoshimoto's aim in writing the letter was to ask the official to bring his young companion for another visit: if Fujiwaka (i.e., Zeami) has time, please bring him again.

The letter is dated the seventeenth day of the Fourth Month without specifying the year. Happily, a fragmentary record known as *Fuchiki*, dated the twenty-fifth day of the Fourth Month of 1378, gives Zeami's age as sixteen and states that the name Fujiwaka had been bestowed on him by the former regent when he was thirteen, meaning that his first visit to Yoshimoto with the Buddhist official took place in 1375.³ Yoshimoto's letter entreating the official to bring Fujiwaka for another visit was composed not long after that.

Efforts to identify the recipient of the letter have been hampered by the existence of multiple Sonshō'in subtemples in the Kyoto and Nara areas. A compelling argument has been made by Omote Akira, however, that a monk named Kyōben, the twenty-fifth head of the Sonshō'in subtemple at Tōdaiji in Nara, was the person who brought Yoshimoto and Zeami together.⁴ Omote presents two Tōdaiji documents as evidence. The first, a list of the heads of the Sonshō'in subtemple, states that Kyōben was appointed intendant (*bettō*) of Tōdaiji in 1379, and that he resumed the post on the fifteenth day of the Fourth Month of 1396, followed by another stint beginning on the fourth day of the Fifth Month of 1402. The second document, which lists Tōdaiji intendants, identifies him as a deputy lesser sangha administrator (*gon shōsōzu*) and states that he was formally appointed the 131st intendant of Tōdaiji on the fourteenth day of the Tenth Month of 1379. In small print, it identifies him as the Sonshō'in and as a member of the Kegon sect of Buddhism and says that he had received verbal notification of the appointment on the ninth day of that month.

The argument that the official was Kyōben, the head of the Tōdaiji subtemple, is reinforced by the diary of Yoshimoto's steward, Higashibōjō Hidenaga, which describes in detail a pair of flower parties (*hana kai*) at Yoshimoto's mansion in 1180 (Kōryaku 2).⁵ As the earliest references to this type of event, the entries in the diary, *Kōyōki*, are already well known to historians of the art of flower arrangement.

In the entry for the ninth day of the Sixth Month, Hidenaga writes: "Top secret flower party today at the mansion. I was in charge of the preparations. The twenty-four participants were divided into left and right sides. The winners received fans." He goes on to list the courtiers, high-ranking warriors, and monks who made up the group, by rank. Yoshimoto headed one side; his son Morotsugu, the other. Hidenaga also lists the winners (there was one draw) and the materials, such as bronze, lapis lazuli, and lacquer, from which the vases and stands were made.

A week later on the seventeenth, Hidenaga writes: "Clear day. Went to mansion to attend flower party. People again brought a variety of vases. It was enjoyable. The left and right sides were chosen by lot. Winners, who received fans, were decided by the whole group. Today's meeting was requested by the losers the other day." Once again, he lists the participants and the winners. Inasmuch as the flower party that day was held because the losers on the ninth had requested a rematch, the basic composition of the group remained unchanged. Aside from an apparent error in transcription that lists Seikōbō instead of Reikōbō, the only exceptions were the *sōzu* (sangha administrator) Kyōben and the courtier Muneharu, whose names appear only on the ninth; and the high-ranking monk Sōshin, the courtier Norinobu, and the Sonshō'in, who are mentioned only on the seventeenth. Since the above-mentioned Tōdaiji documents indicate that the head of the Sonshō'in who served as the intendant of Tōdaiji in 1380 was named Kyōben, the individual by that name at the flower party on the ninth was clearly the same person as the Sonshō'in who was present on the seventeenth. In other words, the diary entries reveal that Nijō Yoshimoto and Kyōben (aka the Sonshō'in) attended the same parties.

The fourteenth day of the Sixth Month—namely, three days prior to the second party—coincided with the end of the Gion festival in Kyoto when the portable shrine bearing the shrine deity wended its way back to the Gion shrine from its temporary site. Hidenaga's diary indicates that the shogun watched the spectacle from lavishly appointed stands furnished by a leading daimyo. Nijō Yoshimoto was also in attendance. The shogun and the former regent had both been present a week earlier on the seventh, when the portable shrine bearing the deity was transported to the temporary site. After the festival they went to the imperial palace, where they enjoyed themselves until dawn: "A party was held beneath the southern steps all night under the moon," writes Hidenaga. "Yoshimoto and the shogun left at dawn." It was probably then that the shogun learned of the secret flower party on the ninth. Since at the time he was already operating the Hana no Gosho (Flower Palace), the shogunal residence in the Muromachi district, it seems unlikely that this event would have escaped his notice.

A third flower party was scheduled for the nineteenth, this time at the shogun's residence. Roughly the same members who had been present on the ninth and seventeenth seem to have gathered for the occasion. This event represents the first known flower party hosted by the shogun, who, after leaving office in 1394, would hold grander flower competitions (*hana-awase*) celebrating the Tanabata festival on the seventh day of the Seventh Month, most often at his Kitayama villa in the northern hills of Kyoto.

The diary entries indicate that the Sonshō'in (Kyōben) was a member of Yoshimoto's cultural circle. He also seems to have displayed artistic sensibilities regarding flower arranging, inasmuch as he is listed as a winner at both flower parties at Yoshimoto's mansion in 1380. Not only is the source valuable in identifying the Sonshō'in; it also sheds light on Yoshimoto and Zeami.

ARISTOCRATIC PASTIMES

After expressing a desire to see Fujiwaka again, Yoshimoto praises the young actor's talents, saying that he excelled even in areas such as *kemari* (court football) and linked verse, not to mention his own art of *sarugaku*. He also praises the boy's looks and demeanor and notes the special favor shown him by Ashikaga Yoshimitsu, who had discovered his father Kan'ami and him at performance of sarugaku at Imagumano in Kyoto in 1374, the year before his first visit to the former regent's mansion. Zeami is also known to have attended the Gion festival with the shogun in 1378, a circumstance that incurred the displeasure of the courtier Sanjō Kintada, who fulminates:

> The Yamato sarugaku boy (the son of the actor named Kanze) was summoned to watch the Gion festival from the shogun's box. Recently, the shogun has doted on this boy. He keeps him by his side and offers him his wine cup. An activity such as sarugaku is the occupation of beggars, yet he treasures the boy and keeps him by his side. It is a sign that the world has gone mad. Elite people bestow valuable possessions on him. Those who give him presents gain the shogun's favor, so the daimyo vie with each other to give him things. Enormous amounts are being expended apparently. It is completely outrageous.[6]

An anecdote in *Sarugaku dangi* regarding a performance of *Jinen Koji* by Zeami's father at an event that the young actor attended with Yoshimitsu further attests to his interaction with the shogun. Kan'ami, who was in his forties at the time but looked as if he was only twelve or thirteen, sang the section containing the lay preacher's sermon so skillfully that Yoshimitsu joked to Zeami, "No matter what stratagems you employ, there's no way you can outdo him in this regard" (ZZ 265).

It has been suggested that Zeami began studying court football and linked verse under the shogun's influence.[7] But it is not clear when the shogun first took an interest in aristocratic pursuits such as court football. And, even if Zeami did begin to study them at his prompting, it is a bit of a stretch to assume that the boy, however much of a genius he may have been, progressed far enough after less than a year to impress the former regent, who had a thorough knowledge of both fields. It has even been argued that the former regent asked a person such as the Sonshō'in to serve as an intermediary in the realm of love because his position at the apex of the court nobility precluded writing directly to Zeami, whose lowly station was equivalent to that of a beggar on a riverbank. Yet if Zeami was always by his father Kan'ami's side during that period, Yoshimoto should have been able to send for him directly without resorting to a letter.

Writing a letter to the Buddhist official asking him not just once, but twice, to bring Fujiwaka again can be attributed to Zeami's position at the time under the official's supervision. Indeed, the letter contains evidence suggesting that Zeami was in fact a celebrated chigo under the official's wing. Moreover, Zeami served as his chigo.

To begin with, the skills of court football and linked verse cited by Yoshimoto were accomplishments typical of a temple boy's education. In *Tango monogurui* (Madman of Tango), an early play rewritten by Zeami, for instance, a father who placed his young son in a temple to be educated, remarks, "It goes without saying that a chigo's accomplishments include *waka* and *renga*; court football and the small bow (*koyumi*) are fine too."[8] As this comment suggests, court football and linked verse were representative skills acquired by temple boys. Court football, especially, was an aristocratic pastime that a boy raised as a sarugaku performer would not ordinarily have had any opportunity to learn.

Chapter 5 shows how the worship of boys on Mount Hiei involved strict training in grooming and etiquette to enable them to fulfill both their sexual and sacred roles. The method in which they were nurtured and polished placed a premium on the elements of charm and grace (*yūen*). Cloistered Prince Shukaku's comment that the period between seventeen and nineteen was a suitable age for taking the tonsure means that the period when a boy beautified his face with makeup and blackened his teeth lasted only a few years.

Another consideration is the role of flower arranging (*rikka*) in the education of chigo. The illustrated scroll *Boki ekotoba*, for instance, depicts the monk Kakunyo placing cherry blossoms in a vase and composing poems with his grandson, a chigo named Sōkō.[9] In addition, the earliest treatise on flower arranging, *Sendenshō* (Selections from an immortal's teachings), contains headings on subjects such as "flowers when inviting boys" and "flowers for attracting the attention of boys and others." A fourteenth-century work on flower-arranging etiquette called *Rikka kuden daiji* purportedly by Sasaki Dōyo stresses the importance of yūgen with regard to flowers used to decorate the rooms of boys and girls. Even if chigo did not create flower arrangements themselves, one can readily imagine that flowers were indispensable in decorating their rooms. The link between chigo and flower arranging is further suggested by an entry in Hidenaga's diary for the seventh day of the Seventh Month of 1401 stating that the Tanabata flower competition that year was held at the residence of the boy Keigyo-maru, a favorite of Ashikaga Yoshimitsu.

Young temple attendants known as *kasshiki*, the Zen counterpart of chigo, likewise had close ties with flower arranging. In an entry in *Kanmon nikki* in 1425, Prince Sadafusa comments that his young daughter, a kasshiki in a nunnery, was going to make her first flower arrangement the following day. He says that he had the plants and flowers that she wanted sent around from various places. In addition, the lady in the eastern quarter (one of his father's wives) donated money for refreshments and provided rushes and the like to commemorate her first flower arrangement. This entry suggests that there was an educational purpose behind the mastery of flower arranging by kasshiki beginning at an early age.[10]

THE AESTHETICS OF BEAUTIFUL BOYS

The former regent's description of Zeami as a boy draws on language in *The Tale of Genji* and critical terms in his renga treatises. It also echoes the depiction of chigo in medieval tales, reinforcing the impression that Zeami was in fact a chigo. With regard to Zeami's face and figure, Yoshimoto says, "His looks and movements exude a gentle aura as well as crisp firmness." *Hokehoke* (translated here as "gentle aura") is a renga critical term that Yoshimoto often employed in the sense of a hazy aura. The following quotations from *Kyūshū mondō* (Kyūshū dialogues; 1376) are a case in point. Yoshimoto characterizes a truly outstanding renga style as one that "has an aura and is steeped in yūgen, a vivid style that exudes the aura of fragrant blossoms." A little earlier he says that a truly outstanding style consists of "verses without artifice or conventional word associations that somehow convey an aura."[11]

Moreover, in *Jūmon saihishō* (Top secret treatise on ten questions; 1383), a treatise composed at the age of sixty-four, eight years after writing to the Buddhist official about young Zeami, Yoshimoto declares, "What exudes an aura and is deeply felt is generally best." In other words, in his treatises the term *hokehoke* signifies something that triggers a hazy, indistinct feeling. In his letter he pairs it with *kenarige* (translated here as "crisp firmness"), a term denoting firmness and vigor. In short, Zeami was a beautiful, impressive (*ririshii*) youth with clearly defined features and crisp movements, and, at the same time, a boy in full flower (*hana no chigo*) who exuded an enchanting aura.

The kind of beauty possessed by Zeami as a boy is likened by Yoshimoto to that of young Murasaki in *The Tale of Genji*.[12] "The contours of young Murasaki's eyebrows are described as being hazy, meaning that they have a soft enchanting (*hokete*) shape," he says, alluding to the following description of her as a young girl in chapter 4 ("Young Murasaki"): "Her face was charming; the contours of her eyebrows were hazy, and her forehead from which the hair had been childishly pushed back was very pretty, as was the way her hair grew around her face." The business about her eyebrows refers to the fact that their shape was softened by newly sprouted hairs, producing an artless enchanting (*hokete*) effect. The description must have evoked in Yoshimoto's mind an image of a chigo's painted eyebrows that are softened around the edges.

The remark likening Murasaki to a blossom-laden cherry tree visible through the dawn mist alludes to the scene many years later in chapter 28 ("Typhoon") when Genji's son Yūgiri caught a glimpse of her during a storm: "The screens had been folded up and placed to one side because of the raging wind, leaving a clear view of the person sitting in the room along the outer corridor. It was impossible to mistake her for anybody else: her dignified beauty exuded a warm glow. It was like looking at a lovely blossom-laden cherry tree through the spring dawn mist." The metaphor suggests a flowerlike figure that has an aura around it. Like a gaily flowering cherry tree that clearly emerges through the mist, graceful beauty wells up from the quiet background, or, conversely, exudes an aura that fills the surrounding space.

After commenting that court poetry and linked verse are judged to be good when they create an interesting effect (*kakari*) and display yūgen, Yoshimoto offers the following critique of Fujiwaka's dancing: "The way in which this boy moves his hands, stamps his feet, and waves his sleeves when he dances seems more supple and graceful than a young willow in the Second Month swaying in the breeze. It surpasses the flowers on the seven autumn grasses moist with evening dew."

The conventional rhetoric comparing Fujiwaka to cherry blossoms, willows, and autumn grasses and the reference to his "moist" (*shioretaru*) aura cast into relief the image of a temple boy, as the following quotations from medieval literary texts demonstrate. For instance, the thirteenth-century guide *Taregami ōrai* that I mentioned earlier (see chapter 3, note 7) describes a boy as having "slender hips as pliant as a young willow tree swaying in the breeze, and a lovely face that possessed the freshness and beauty of crimson cherry blossoms covered with dew."

A love story called *Toribeyama monogatari* (The tale of Mount Toribe) describes the luminous countenance of a chigo faintly visible through the loose tresses around his face, adding that he looked like a dew-covered flower at dawn, a willow bending in the evening breeze. Similar imagery can be found in the scene in *The Story of Kannon's Manifestation as a Youth* in which an elderly monk first comes upon a chigo on the way home from a pilgrimage to Hasedera temple:

> At daybreak, he reluctantly departed from the mountain and headed homeward. As he passed the foot of Mount Obuse, he noticed a boy of thirteen or fourteen whose moonlike face and attire were divine. The lad wore white silk over a lavender *kosode* underrobe and elegant loose trousers (*hakama*) the color of fallen leaves. He was playing a plaintive melody on a Chinese flute. He

had a bamboo ornament in his long hair, which was tied in back with a cord. He had the look of being moist with dew on the morning of the eighteenth day of the Eighth Month, and seemed more supple and graceful than a willow disheveled by the breeze in springtime.[13]

The monk Genmu's first glimpse of the chigo Hamamatsu at the Hall of the Four Kings on Mt. Hiei in *Genmu monogatari* (The tale of Genmu; 15th c.) is described thus:

> A chigo of sixteen or seventeen was in the company of two monks who looked to be his traveling companions. He appeared to have come from a distant province for his feet seemed to be sore. He had been about to depart after having taken vows, but the snow was falling heavily so he approached the Hall of the Four Kings to wait for it to stop. Genmu noticed that he seemed lost in thought and had a somewhat dispirited (*uchi-shioretaru*) air about him, perhaps because of fatigue from the journey. At an hour when all was quiet around him, he had the look of cherry blossoms at night wilting in the spring rain, and his thick tresses were disheveled like willow fronds at dawn. The way he looked was impossible to describe in words; no painter's brush could do it justice.[14]

Although chigo at major temples were mainly the offspring of courtiers and warriors, a case exists of a lowly dengaku performer's son who entered a temple as a chigo. The actor, Fukuwakamaru, was born seventy years after Zeami. His early life as a dengaku performer and chigo at the Jūshin'in temple in Kyoto is known from an account that was composed and presented to him by his mentor, Jitsui (d. 1454), the head of the temple. The account focuses on his role as a star, including the dengaku performances at the temple on the seventeenth and eighteenth of the Third Month of that year (1446), to which a number of aristocrats had been invited.[15]

Fukuwaka-maru's skill and looks are extraordinary, writes his mentor. It was obvious when he entered the temple at an early age that he planned to leave soon and return to his former life, but he was deeply aware of a bond with Buddha and with his teacher, and defied expectations by living there for several years. That year he was seventeen, so he had probably acquired the figure of a chigo around the age of twelve or thirteen, as was usually the case.

The performance on the eighteenth was even more successful than the previous day's, we are told. Fukuwaka-maru sat near the guest of honor, a monk from the Shōgoin in Kyoto who was a son of the sixth shogun. He performed in a variant style wearing a costume and reciting the dialogue while seated. His treatment clearly differed from that of the other dengaku players stationed further away a step below in the open area under the extended eaves (*hirobisashi*). As a lowly dengaku performer, he was presumably able to sit near the aristocrats in his capacity as a chigo. The scene brings to mind Zeami's attendance at the Gion festival with the shogun, an event that incurred the criticism of the conservative courtier Kintada.

Fukuwaka-maru accompanied his mentor Jitsui to the Fushimi no Miya palace a few days later at the invitation of the latter's cousin Prince Sadatsune, an ardent fan who had been the guest of honor at the performance on the seventeenth. The aristocratic gathering on the twenty-first featured court football and a waka party, activities in which Fukuwaka-maru would naturally have participated. Everybody marveled at his singing and dancing, which he performed without the usual instrumental accompaniment. "When he began singing, the entire audience was deeply moved," says Jitsui. "When he waved his sleeves, everyone was dazzled." The actor received a *kosode* robe from Prince Sadatsune that belonged to the empress, the prince's mother, who had also given birth to Emperor Go-Hanazono. The gift was accompanied by a request for a dance. "He took the robe and said, 'I am a poor humble woman living in the Mano area of Nishi Ōmi.' His quick wit and gentle aura (*shioretaru keshiki*) moved everybody to tears before he even danced. He also performed *shirabyōshi* dances while the courtiers, who had a fondness for the performing arts, marked the beat."

The image of this young performer taking part in an aristocratic gathering where he was the star owing to his outstanding talent and beauty almost exactly matches that of the young Zeami, who attended a party at Nijō Yoshimoto's mansion in the company of the Sonshō'in and melted Yoshimoto's heart. In all probability, when Zeami watched the Gion festival with Ashikaga Yoshimitsu as a boy and even drank from his wine cup, he was in the shogun's entourage in his capacity as a chigo. The anecdote in *Sarugaku dangi* about the shogun and Zeami watching Kan'ami perform, too, conjures up the image of a performance jointly attended by an aristocrat and a chigo.

It should be noted that Fukuwaka-maru's acting was restricted to singing and dancing, as was true throughout the dengaku account. His first performance in front of Prince Sadatsune in 1444 had consisted of six dances and a number of songs. On the seventeenth and eighteenth of the Third Month of 1446, he appeared only in dengaku plays, and did not participate in original dengaku arts such as the opening musical pieces (*chūmonguchi*) performed at the gates of aristocratic mansions and temples, or joint dances and knife juggling. The skills employed in dengaku acrobatics did not suit a gracefully and charmingly (yūgen) polished chigo who was expected to have gentle refined manners.

Even in dengaku plays, his role would clearly have been limited to aspects that showcased his beautiful face and aura. If that is indeed the case, then Zeami's system of noh training represented by the arts of song and dance and the three modes of acting—aged, woman's, and martial role types—surely needs to be reexamined as well from the vantage point of these aesthetic and physical rules governing chigo.

In *Shikadō*, Zeami declares, "At the start of his training, a boy should thoroughly master singing and dancing under the direction of his teacher. He should not study the Three Modes for a while during the period from around the age of ten when he still has a boy's figure. He should perform roles on stage without altering his appearance as a child. In other words, he should not wear a mask and should perform all roles in name only, wearing attire suitable for a child" (*ZZ* 112).

Zeami's comment about the initial period around the age of ten when an actor still has a child's appearance suggests that his acquisition of court football and renga as a temple chigo started around that time. Regular presence at the temple, however, would have impeded his sarugaku training. Moreover, he must have traveled around performing with his father Kan'ami—for instance, at Imagumano in 1374 when he was twelve. Consequently, it is likely that he was accorded special treatment as a chigo who often returned home.[16]

Zeami's remarks about a child's training—that he should carefully learn the Two Arts of singing and dancing, and refrain from studying the Three Role Types for a while during the period from around the age of ten—should not be viewed simply as a theory about training that continues to apply today: namely, that his artistic skills would not improve after he became an adult but would remain limited in scope if he merely studied detailed representational techniques (*monomane*) during this early period. Rather, this passage from *Shikadō* explains the importance of putting on stage *as is* a chigo who in daily life possessed an artificially constructed figure that anticipated kabuki actors later on who specialized in woman's roles. The pursuit of representational skills and techniques would inevitably invite a situation that exceeded the aesthetic and physical limits placed on a chigo for whom grace and charm were everything. The arts of singing and dancing were demanded, in fact, as a way to take full advantage on stage of the chigo's figure and movements.

In *Nikyoku santai ningyō zu* Zeami states, "If the Two Arts are performed when the chigo's figure is transferred to the Three Role Types, the visual effect of yūgen will naturally be expressed in them" (*ZZ* 124). Since the beautification of boys itself took a direction that approximated Heian court ladies, or the image of women that resided in the medieval yearning for the Heian court, the figure of a chigo readily formed a link with the Woman's Mode, which was modeled on the "inexpressibly beautiful appearance of aristocratic ladies," as Zeami notes in *Sandō* (Three techniques; 1423), his treatise on writing noh plays (*ZZ* 137).

Chigo, however, are still chigo. A description of boys in terms of yūgen can already be found in the record of a specially scheduled festival at the Kasuga shrine in 1283, which states that the dancing boys' faces with delicately drawn eyebrows possessed yūgen. More than a century later, Zeami declares in *Nikyoku santai ningyō zu* that the figure of a chigo forms the foundation of yūgen, while *Shikadō* ends with a poetic image of yūgen: "A white swan with a flower in its beak: this perhaps is the epitome of an elegant, graceful figure on stage (*yūgen no fūshi*; *ZZ* 119)." The elegant, graceful figure of a white swan holding a flower in its beak is nothing less than a metaphor for the dancing figure of a chigo transformed into sweet limpid eroticism.

The refinement and grace of a chigo's figure expressed the appeal on stage of chigo actors who further inverted the fiction of daily life and sexual identity lived as a chigo. Zeami's awareness of his own duality, his own multiple layers, must have been honed even more by having lived this kind of dual fiction. It was a driving force behind the vitality that informs his treatises. Above all, the two-part dream plays that he invented are a unique type of drama created by means of a protagonist (*shite*) and the multiple temporal layers that constitute his life. Zeami's masterpiece *Izutsu* (The well-cradle) is a case in point. The main character, a woman longing for her childhood sweetheart Ariwara no Narihira, is played by a male actor. In the course of the play, the actor dressed in woman's attire dons Narihira's cloak and court cap and performs a dance. In other words, the gender of the shite rapidly changes like shifting images in opposite-facing mirrors.[17]

THE AESTHETICS OF YOSHIMOTO AND ZEAMI

Zeami was eighteen when the above-mentioned flower parties were held at Yoshimoto's mansion in 1380, two years after he attended the Gion festival with the shogun. At the time, he was probably at the age when his voice was changing, a point that he would later identify in *Fūshikaden* (ZZ 16) as beginning around seventeen or eighteen. (Recall that Cloistered Prince Shukaku gives the years between seventeen and nineteen as the age limit for a chigo.)

In addition to throwing light on the identity of the Buddhist official who took Fujiwaka (Zeami) to visit Yoshimoto, the diary of the former regent's steward is a valuable source regarding Yoshimoto and Zeami. One can readily imagine Zeami even in 1380 soaking up the ambiance of the salon formed by Yoshimoto, the shogun, and the Sonshō'in, as well as others such as the renga poet Bontōan (a former warrior), and the waka poet Reizei Tamemasa, at events such as flower parties and the Gion festival. This kind of social network is not the only reason to believe that Zeami attended flower parties. Another is the role played by the art of flower arrangement in the education of chigo that was discussed earlier.

In *Kyushu mondō*, Yoshimoto characterizes a truly outstanding renga style as one that has an aura and is steeped in yūgen, a vivid style whose brilliance is like a fragrant flower. As this remark shows, the concept of the Flower (*hana*) inherited from the Nijō school of poetry was transformed into a more dynamic concept in Yoshimoto's renga treatises. Zeami, for his part, continued throughout his life to pursue the Flower on stage while thoroughly examining it on a theoretical level. Both men's concept of the Flower can be seen as a reflection of first-hand experience with flower parties and flower arranging. Zeami's aesthetic concept is obviously an abstraction of actual flowers, but I believe that he was able to realize its full potential as a theater concept precisely because the foundations for grasping a real flower as an aesthetic object had been nurtured at flower parties.

Omote Akira has pointed out that the word *motogi* (literally, "main tree") used by Zeami to refer to the chief character in a play was adapted from works such as *Sendenshō*, where it signified the principal material used in a flower arrangement. Moreover, the first section of the "Separate Secret Transmission" (Besshi kuden) in the holographic copy of *Fūshikaden* ends with a comment about countless vases being used to decorate large meeting places—so many, in fact, that it was a sea of flowers.[18] This statement bespeaks Zeami's firsthand knowledge of the use of flower arranging in decorating rooms. Also, in *Sarugaku dangi* he likens a performance by the dengaku actor Kiami in the play *Sumiyaki* (Charcoal burner) to looking at a bronze object. What he had in mind was surely a flower vase—the kind of Chinese object on display at the flower parties in the Sixth Month of 1380.

YŪGEN

The concept of yūgen was inextricably linked to the beauty of chigo, especially for Yoshimoto and Zeami. As noted earlier, Yoshimoto describes Zeami's boyish beauty using a renga critical term: Fujiwaka's looks and bearing, he says, possess a gentle aura (*hokehoke*) as well as liveliness and strength. Although he does not apply the term yūgen directly to a chigo's looks unlike the account of the festival at the Kasuga shrine in 1283, his use of yūgen to denote extreme youthfulness and charming beauty is considered a distinctive element in his aesthetics.[19]

For instance, in *Jūmon saihishō* a chigo-like sense is conveyed by his remark that language possessing yūgen sounds fresh and smooth, and by his advice to employ smooth, delicate (*hosoku*) language to create an overall configuration characterized by yūgen. At the beginning of *Renga jūyō* (Ten renga styles; 1379), he maintains, "The effect (*kakari*) and overall configuration are crucial in renga. No matter how fresh or unusual a verse is, if the overall configuration and flow of words are bad, it will not seem the least bit interesting. It is like a girl wearing coarse hemp attire. Gentleness and yūgen should be given precedence."

Judging from Yoshimoto's stress on making the figure of a girl in a coarse robe convey charm and grace, his yūgen sprang from a sensual bias toward the beauty possessed by girls and chigo (or may have become more pronounced in his later years).

This was Yoshimoto's idea of yūgen. In other words, his letter describes the young Zeami in terms of yūgen, albeit in an oblique manner. To the former regent, who declared in his letter that waka and renga are judged to be of high quality when they create an interesting effect and display yūgen, the figure of Fujiwaka appearing before his eyes embodied his poetic ideal. For Zeami, too, yūgen leaned toward what is exemplified by the beauty of a chigo; it is not simply a feminine type of grace and beauty. In declaring that a chigo's figure represents the foundation of yūgen, and by equating yūgen with a white swan holding a flower in its beak, Zeami articulated an important thread in his understanding of the concept that represented an extension of Yoshimoto's view.

MOISTNESS (*SHIORE*)[20]

The third section of *Fūshikaden* consists of a series of questions and answers, including a discussion of *shiore*, which Zeami identifies as a frequently heard critical term (ZZ 35). Zeami acknowledges that it is impossible to express what it means in writing, adding that the artistic effect is not manifested outwardly. "Nevertheless," he says, "acting that produces that kind of appeal does in fact exist.... It can be said to represent a higher level than the Flower. However, without the Flower it would be meaningless; it would be damp and cheerless. The wilted or moist effect (*shiore*) of a beautiful flower is interesting. What is interesting about flowerless plants and trees that have wilted? The attainment of the Flower is difficult, but shiore is a truly difficult level to attain since it ranks higher."

He offers two poems as examples of the aesthetic effect created by shiore. The first one, by Fujiwara no Kiyosuke, is from the *Shinkokinshū* ("Autumn," I: 340):

Usugiri no	Morning dampness
magaki no hana no	of flowers on a woven fence
asajimeri	visible in light mist:
aki wa yūbe to	who said that evening
tare ka iiken	was best in autumn?

The second poem, by Ono no Komachi, is included in the first imperial waka anthology, *Kokinshū* ("Love," V: 797):

Iro miede	What changes
utsurou mono wa	without any visible signs
yo no naka no	is the flower
hito no kokoro no	that blooms
hana ni zo arikeru	in the human heart.

The morning moisture of flowers blossoming on a bamboo fence in the light mist represents what is for Zeami a slightly off-target example that barely captures the meaning of shiore.

Although Zeami is silent on the subject, Yoshimoto and the question of chigo are intertwined regarding shiore as well as yūgen. Konishi Jin'ichi offers the following analysis of the use of shiore in Yoshimoto's renga treatises, beginning with the passage in *Renri hishō* (Secret notes on the principles of linking; ca. 1349) in which the former regent writes: "The verses of a person who uses language effectively convey heartfelt sensibilities [*shimijimi to shioretaru*]. They seem easy to link and are interesting.

One should make a note of, and deeply reflect upon, language redolent of yūgen that skilled poets regularly employ."[21]

A few years later in *Gekimoshō* (1358), Yoshimoto uses shiore to describe the link between the following verses: *hana ya mukashi no / nagori naruran* (The flowers evoke / memories of the past) and *kasume to wa / omowanu tsuki mo / namida nite* (Veiled in mist / unexpectedly, the moon too / seems clouded by tears). "The words are characterized by shiore. Moreover, various sentiments are conveyed by them. The phrase *omowanu tsuki* (unexpectedly, the moon) is the most wonderful of all."

Then, in *Kyūshū mondō*, he writes, "Superior verses incorporate few items from the natural world. Their sentiments are deep, and their words are delicate [*hosoku*] and moist or soft [*shiore*]. As a result, the assembled poets' excitement mounts, making it easy to link all the verses."

Konishi goes on to quote a passage from a renga manual by Yoshimoto's student Bontōan that associates Yoshimoto's own mentor Gusai with shiore. "Although Gusai did not reject any style, he employed considerable thought and seemed to focus on shioretaru aspects," writes Bontōan. "He created verses that suggested a solitary poet sitting near a verandah as the misty spring moon shone faintly through cracks in the blinds of a rundown dwelling with an earthen fence and a tilting cypress-thatched roof overrun with ferns and where no visitors come."

> From the perspective of classical sensibilities, Bontōan's remark about a rundown dwelling without any visitors creates a tasteful setting befitting the portrayal of charming romantic love. The misty spring moon evocative of Narihira long ago is a perfect image of courtly grace and charm (yūen) faintly glimpsed through a veil. In that sense, it is noteworthy that the example from

Gekimōshō above echoes Narihira's famous poem (*Kokinshū*, "Love," 15: 747):

Tsuki ya aranu	Is that not the moon,
haru wa mukashi no	and the spring not the spring
haru naranu	of long ago?
waga mi hitotsu wa	Yet only I remain
moto no mi ni shite	as I was before.

Hana ya mukashi (flowers ... the past), *kasume to wa* (veiled in mist), and *tsuki mo namida* (the moon too ... tears) are all expressions that gently suggest the charming yet melancholy love evoked by Narihira. They are words that are characterized by shiore. What Bontōan calls the shioretaru aspect, too, is none other than this sort of gentle charm and grace.

I have no issue with this definition of shiore but would like to take a closer look here at a few examples from medieval chigo love stories describing the aura that shiore evokes and the way it captivates men. For instance, the story about the monk Genmu describes his first glimpse of the chigo Hanamatsu on Mount Hiei thus: "A very moist (*uchi-shioretaru*) aura enveloped the figure who seemed lost in thought. At that quiet hour, he had the look of cherry blossoms at night wilting in the spring rain, and his thick tresses were disheveled like willow fronds at dawn." In a similar fashion, *The Story of Kannon's Manifestation as a Youth* characterizes the chigo as looking as though he was "moist (*shioretaru*) with dew ... and he seemed more supple and graceful than a willow disheveled by the breeze in springtime."

The next example comes from the scene in "A Long Tale for an Autumn Night" in which the Master of Precepts, Keikai, invites the chigo he has fallen in love with to his quarters for the first time:

> When he heard [the chigo's attendant speak], Keikai became light-headed and his heart pounded. He did not know where or who he was. His emotions were wrung by the repeated tolling of the temple bell as he waited impatiently while the moon moved around to the south. Hearing somebody opening the gate, he looked out of the door in the study and saw the youth in the distance holding a translucent lantern containing glowing fireflies. In the dim light, the young master wearing a gauze *kinsha* cloak with wide sleeves (*suikan*) had a graceful *uchi-shioretaru* figure. He stood there beneath the flares as if aware that he was being observed. He looked so utterly like a young willow sapling with slender streaming branches that Keikai was immediately smitten and seemed in a complete daze.[22]

A couple of uses of the term to describe women can be found in *Tamura no sōshi* (The tale of Tamura). The first example comes from a passage about the shogun Toshisuke's encounter with a serpent that had transformed itself into a beautiful woman:

> In the deepening autumn, he set out through the fields of Saga. The colors on the fields and hills had deepened, the grasses were lonely, so too the crying of insects, whose melancholy voices fit the occasion. Such was the setting in which an extremely beautiful woman appeared out of nowhere. Gazing up at the moon of the sixteenth night, she composed a poignant verse:
>
> | kusamura ni | When I hear |
> | naku mushi no ne o | the sound of insects crying |
> | kiku kara ni | in the grasses, |

| itodo omoi no | my feelings |
| masari koso sure | deepen even further. |

No painter's brush could do justice to her uchi-shioretaru appearance. Willow branches swaying in the spring breeze and crimson lotus blossoms in the rain must have seemed like that too. She had no attendants but stood there alone looking completely lovelorn.

Shiore occurs again later in a scene in which the shogun Toshihito (Toshiyuki's son) secretly approached the eastern main gate and saw a girl, aged fifteen or sixteen, standing outside the gate weeping "in an uchi-shiorete manner."[23]

These two examples, like the earlier ones, have to do with an initial encounter that marked the start of love. (In "A Long Tale for an Autumn Night" it was a secret assignation.) The shioretaru aspect of the girls and chigo was so seductive that it bewitched men. Since chigo were polished to perfection at temples in the manner of Heian court ladies, it is not surprising to find the term being applied to both sexes, but bear in mind that the preponderance of examples in the middle ages dealt with chigo.

Shiore is also employed regarding the dengaku performer Fukuwaka-maru, who, after being presented with a robe, identified himself as a poor humble woman living in the Mano area of Nishi Ōmi. His quick wit and gentle aspect, we are told, moved everybody to tears before he even danced. Likewise, Zeami's artistry is praised by Nijō Yoshimoto, who writes that the "way he moves his hands, stamps his feet, and waves his sleeves when he dances seems more supple and graceful than a young willow in the Second Month swaying in the breeze. It surpasses the flowers on the seven autumn grasses moistened (*shioretaru*) by evening dew."

Shiore is employed in both cases as a critical term regarding the artistry of a boy. The former regent's letter, in particular, pays homage to Zeami as a chigo. Zeami's discussion of shiore at the age of thirty-eight in *Fūshikaden* undoubtedly sprang from a desire to explain a word that was widely employed as a critical term. I believe, however, that he ignored the term's association with chigo when he wrote that section of the treatise out of a conscious desire to avoid addressing the images and nature of chigo.

7

THE POETICS OF SPACE IN NOH

In his later years, Zeami occasionally employed an obscure word *enken* ("distant view"). Altogether, fifteen examples can be found in his treatises, from *Shikadō* in 1420 to *Sarugaku dangi* in 1430. Yet the term has received little attention, perhaps in part because of the difficulty of assigning a single overarching definition to it, unlike *riken* ("detached view"), another word coined by Zeami. Whereas the latter denotes the heightened experience of a noh actor regarding theatrical time and space (for instance, while dancing), enken can be regarded as a unique term that he invented regarding the poetics of space.

The following example comes from his remarks in *Sarugaku dangi* about *Obasute* (The discarded old woman), a play about an infirm old woman who had been abandoned on Mount Obasute in Sarashina (present-day Nagano prefecture):

> In *Obasute*, the verse "how shameful being seen in the moonlight" is like finding gold lying on a road. The distant view (enken) forms the foundation of *sarugaku*. It should be performed in a full, unhurried manner. It would be unsightly for the old woman to bend over hiding her face with her fan from the person opposite her, without looking at all at the moon when the words are sung.

> At the words "being seen in the moonlight," the actor should make an ambiguous gesture, holding his fan up high so that the focus is on the moon as he looks slightly at the other person. Doing so will create an interesting effect. (ZZ 269)[1]

The verse "how shameful being seen in the moonlight" is from the first chant (an *ageuta*) sung by the chorus in act 2. Since it conveys the old woman's feeling of shame at appearing before a person in the moonlight (a man from the capital played by the *waki*, or secondary actor), a gesture or action conveying that emotion to the other person should suffice: that was the traditional way of performing representational actions (*monomane*). Zeami, however, disagreed, maintaining that the actor playing the old woman should perform a gesture signifying shame as he looked out from the stage at an invisible object, the moon, an action that concomitantly created the effect of moonlight streaming down onto the stage. Unlike plays such as those by his father Kan'ami that depict concrete conflicts between human beings, Zeami placed the focus on one person—the *shite*—while pursuing dramas on a deep human level but keeping classical sensibilities, represented by or harmonizing with nature. For him, the act of looking into the distance—in other words, enken—was inevitably called upon to conjure up vividly on stage an object or scene from the external world of nature. For that reason, he went so far as to declare that the distant view formed the basis of sarugaku and should be performed in a full unhurried manner.

Zeami's comment about the distant view is repeated on the two other occasions in which it is used in *Sarugaku dangi*. In the first example, he remarks: "The play about the Genji forces descending on Yashima was written in such a way that the distant view formed the foundation, but since the person looking into the distance is headed into battle, the feeling that is conveyed should be different from that of an excursion in the hills" (ZZ 289). By this he means that the line about the Genji descending on Yashima was written so that the act of looking into the distance was central, but it conveyed the impression that someone heading into battle was on a sightseeing excursion in the hills, producing an unintended effect. The work is no longer extant and the playwright is unknown, but it may have been an unsuccessful piece by Zeami in which enken was used as a foundation.

The second example is noteworthy because it occurs in conjunction with the rhetorical strategy of pointing out famous places (*meisho oshie*). The passage in question concerns a play called *Furu* that begins with an encounter between a mountain ascetic from Kyushu (the waki) and a woman (the shite) at Furu River in Nara.[2]

> If the usual order had been followed in *Furu*, the story about the sword of Furu would have followed the spoken exchange (*mondō*) between the mountain ascetic and the woman about washing cloth in the river. The ageuta beginning "The first snow falls [*furu*] / [on] Furu's high bridge" (*hatsu miyuki, furu no takahashi*) is sung instead because the distant view provides a foundation. The desirability of using famous places connected with the main subject matter derives from this strategy of the distant view. If the subject lends itself to actions on stage, one can follow the usual order and begin by telling about the origins of the place. (ZZ 288)

Furu was once attributed to Kan'ami, based on a comment in Zeami's treatise *Go on* (Five types of singing): "*Furu*: 'The first snow falls /[on] Furu's high bridge, gazing around (*Hatsumi yuki / furu no takahashi / miwataseba*).' Written by my late father"

(ZZ 209). But now it is regarded as a new work by Zeami that incorporated the above verses from an independent song by Kan'ami quoted in the treatise.

In Zeami's holograph copy of the play, dated 1428, the exchange between the waki and the woman about washing cloth in Furu River leads into a simple exchange of dialogue pointing out famous nearby places, followed by the chorus's first chant, an ageuta, containing the verses found in *Go on*. The section recounting the story of the sword of Furu comes after that. In other words, by inserting a segment about famous places that features the distant view—namely, the dialogue describing the famous places and the ageuta sung by the chorus—before telling the story of the sword (which forms the heart of the first part of the play), Zeami has sought to firmly establish the story's setting while at the same time creating a space imbued with a classical aura. Hence the end of the quotation from *Sarugaku dangi*—"If the subject matter is able to generate effective action, one can follow the usual order and begin by recounting the story about the place"—can be taken to mean that, if the story that serves as the centerpiece in the first part of a play is able on its own to create space redolent of classical sensibilities, it can be inserted straight away without prefacing it with a section that points out the famous places connected with the setting.

The technique of pointing out famous places, which centers on gazing in the distance, was developed and widely employed by Zeami to foster a sense of space with a classical aura in the first part of a play. The strategy is in fact found chiefly in his plays. In addition to *Furu*, they include *Tōru* as well as *Yorimasa*, *Matsura*, and the *rongi* section of *Ukon*. Two works by other dramatists—*Kanehira* and *Shigehira*—contain similar segments, although it would be more accurate to say that these examples, which may have been modeled on Zeami's, point out Shinto and

Buddhist architecture. *Shigehira*, in particular, seems to have emulated Zeami's example.

The grandest in scale and most poetic of all the explanations of famous places created by Zeami is located in *Tōru*. The spatial configuration that he sought in noh is expressed in almost a perfect form by the aesthetic space portrayed in the play. When a traveling monk (the waki) visits the site of the Kawara riverside villa in the Sixth Ward of Kyoto where Minamoto Tōru lived long ago, a mysterious old man (the ghost of Tōru), played by the shite, appears carrying buckets for drawing salt water. After telling Tōru's story, he points out the famous places and poetic place-names around Kyoto that are visible from the villa.[3]

MONDŌ

WAKI: Say, old man, the mountains visible around here are all famous places, it seems. Please tell me about them.
SHITE: Ask me about them, and I will tell you.
WAKI: First of all, is the place over there Otowayama (Sound-Feather / Rumor Mountain)?
SHITE: Indeed, that is Otowayama.
WAKI: A poet once wrote of "Otowayama:[4]
'tis said to be on this side of Meeting-Slope-Barrier (Ōsaka no seki)," so Meeting-Slope-Mountain (Ōsakayama) must be nearby too.
SHITE: Indeed, the poem talks of this side of the barrier,
but the mountain lies on the far side,
so it is hidden by Otowa Peak (Otowa no mine)
and cannot be seen from here.
WAKI: Well, then, please tell me about each famous place in the range of mountains stretching from Otowa Peak.

SHITE: The subject is limitless, but that is poetic Uta no
   Nakayama and Seiganji, and Imagumano lies over there,
WAKI: followed by a grove of trees around a cluster of houses.
SHITE: Look upon them as a guide.
   Since it is autumn and the cold rains have yet to
   fall, the leaves are still green on Mount Inari (Inariyama).
WAKI: Beyond the wind-blown clouds suggesting nightfall,
   the treetops, too, are green, displaying autumn's hue.
SHITE: It is autumn now in Wisteria Wood (Fuji no mori),
   where wisteria were viewed in spring, as its name suggests.
WAKI: The fields and hills reflect the deep blue sky.
   What of the village that lies beyond them?
SHITE: Over there, "when evening descends,
WAKI: the autumn wind blowing across the fields
SHITE: pierces the soul,
WAKI: and a quail plaintively calls out
SHITE: in the deep grasses." That is Fukakusayama
   (Deep-grass mountain).[5]

UTA

CHORUS: Mount Kowata, Takeda in Fushimi,
   Yodo and Toba, too, are visible.

RONGI

CHORUS: Off in the distance,
   the sky wears a mantle of white clouds,
   the sky wears a mantle of white clouds.
   Darkness has begun to descend upon the distant hills

whose heavily wooded peaks are visible.
What sort of place is that?
SHITE: *That* is famous Ōhara Field[6]
and Mount Oshio, too: today
must be your first chance to see them.
Please continue asking questions.
CHORUS: As I listen to your words, the autumn
wind blows; in the west, from which the autumn
wind is said to blow, a range of peaks is visible.
SHITE: Autumn has already
passed its midpoint. Amid the wind in the pines,
Pine Ridge (Matsunoo) and Storm Mountain
(Arashiyama) are visible.
CHORUS: As the fierce wind (*arashi*) blows in the
deepening autumn night,
the moon rises in the clear sky. In the moonlight
SHITE: the full tide has already turned.
CHORUS: At an hour when there is no time to lose,
gazing at the bright cloudless moon,
SHITE: so engrossed
CHORUS: I have forgotten
my place. There is nothing to be gained
from a long tale on an autumn night.
I shall begin drawing sea water, he says.
Holding the buckets (*tago*) of Tago Bay (Tago no Ura),
the hem of his salt-gathering robe tucked up in
the eastern style,
he draws water. The moonlight too lodges in his
moistened sleeves.
Returning to the shore at night when the waves
roll in, he appeared
as an old man. Hidden by clouds of spray,

his figure disappeared without a trace;
he disappeared without a trace.

As he tells the story of Tōru the Minister, the old man begins to point out Kyoto's famous places and poetic place-names seen from the Kawara riverside villa. The description of the sights in the long sequence follows an arc from the eastern hills around to the south, and then to the western hills. During the mondō, the old man stands at the shite's fixed position (*jōza*) as he points out the famous places. At first, he looks out past the front of the stage and then shifts his gaze about forty-five degrees to the right to the *naka-shōmen*, before looking at stage right (*waki-shōmen*). The monk, standing at the waki's position (*waki-za*), does likewise. During the chorus's song (*uta*), the shite takes the waki's sleeve and leads him to stage front, where they look around. During the ensuing *rongi*, the last song prior to the shite's exit, both actors return to their original positions and look around once more toward stage front, followed by the *naka-shōmen* and stage right. This is how the sequence is performed by the Kanze school today, but Zeami's staging probably did not differ much with regard to the strategy of inscribing a visual arc as they gaze around.

In the course of slightly changing direction as he looks intently at and explains each famous place, the old man clarifies the linear relationship between the famous places and himself on stage (i.e., at the Kawara riverside villa). In so doing, he affirms the centrality of the old man (shite) as the point where those visual threads converge. Moreover, the internalization of talking and singing about waka and stories that have accumulated regarding each famous place simultaneously transforms him into a refined, elegant embodiment of collective memories. In this way, the old man forms a focal point on stage that radiates outward. He becomes a mediator in the spatial configuration unique to noh, the stage's central axis that emerges through the outward expansion of space.

In *Sarugaku dangi*, enken refers to a concrete action—looking into the distance—that creates the outwardly diffused physical space of the shite in conjunction with the language. The example from the section on itinerant entertainers in priestly attire (*hōka*) in *Sandō*, Zeami's treatise on writing plays, can be viewed in a similar manner:

> After the opening section [when the waki makes his entrance] is completed, the musical instruments should play energetically while waiting [for the shite to appear]. [The shite], dressed as an itinerant entertainer, should deliver the recitative (*sashi-goe*) in a smoothly flowing manner on the bridgeway. He should recite seven or eight lines that contain interesting language and are familiar to the ear—whether they be old songs and poems or other famous verses—intermixed with plain speech, and then begin the entrance chant (*issei*). In this type of role, it is especially important to create an entrance that makes effective use of the act of looking into the distance [enken] on the bridge while vocally building up interest. Write plays bearing this in mind, find appropriate words, and seek material that generates interesting actions. (ZZ 139)

This passage is almost identical to the structure of the shite's entrance section in *monogurui* ("mad-person") plays, which deal with performers or distraught persons whose heightened emotional state is conducive to the performance of a dance. A strategy that rhetorically makes maximal use of the act of looking into the distance on the bridgeway can be found during the shite's entrance in Zeami's famous plays of this type—*Lady Han* (Hanjo) and *The Flower Basket* (Hanagatami), as well as in the quasi-monogurui play *The Reed Cutter* (*Ashikari*)—none of which may have existed in 1423 when Zeami wrote *Sandō*. (The lines below that are recited while the shite looks into the distance in today's performances have been placed in italics.)

In *Lady Han*, a woman named Hanago (the shite) who is employed at an inn in Mino Province becomes so lovesick for a traveler who spent a night there that she is dismissed by the innkeeper. The following song is performed during her entrance in act 2 as she wanders in search of the traveler:[7]

SASHI

SHITE: "*On Kasuga Meadow, the young shoots*
    poking through the snow are barely
    visible, like my brief glimpse of [him]."
It was foolish to become attached to such a person.
Like multilayered robes the days pile up, the months go by,
but beyond the coldness transmitted by the autumn wind,
there is no one to bring word of him.
    "*Past the banner of clouds at dusk I gaze,*
    lost in thought,"
    my restless spirit wanders,
leaving my life in ruins.
May the gods and buddhas take pity
and grant my wish. . . .

The second play, *The Flower Basket*, depicts a woman named Teruhi no Mae (the shite), whose lover Prince Ōatobe left her to return to the capital to ascend the throne.[8] After a messenger bearing a flower basket and letter comes to inform her of the Prince's departure, she makes her way to the capital with her servant (the *tsure*) hoping to meet him. The following sequence is performed during their entrance at the beginning of act 2:

SASHI

SHITE: *Yonder traveler, please tell us*
  the way to the capital.
  What if I am a distraught person,
  I ask precisely because distraught people
  have longings too.
  Why do you unfeelingly fail to tell us?

KAKEAI

TSURE: Even if he does not tell us,
  there is a guide to the capital:
  Look over yonder at the wild geese
  winging through the air.
SHITE: What of the wild geese winging through the air?
  Indeed, I recall very well
  in autumn, wild geese always make their way
  southward through the sky.
TSURE: It is no empty talk; the place where his lordship resides,
  the capital, it's said, lies in that direction.
SHITE: *Let us rely on them as companions whose cries*
  will serve as a guide.
TSURE: *The trusty wild geese in the rice fields will lead us*
  along the Koshi Road.
SHITE: *Then, too, there is Su Wu's famous*
  traveling wild goose. . . .

The third play, *The Reed Cutter*, depicts a man named Saemon (the shite) who survives by peddling reeds in Naniwa after falling on hard times and abandoning his wife.[9]

SASHI

SHITE: *The spreading hills may be covered in mist,*
but across from Naniwa Bay lies wave-filled Awaji Lagoon.
The setting affords a delightful view of other bays
and Naniwa's boats floating on the water:
What a pleasant refreshing scene at dawn!

Lady Han draws on two poems from the first imperial waka anthology, the *Kokinshū*, beginning with one by Mibu no Tadamine ("Love," I: 478) that is quoted in its entirety:

Kasuga no no	On Kasuga Meadow
yukima o wakete	the young shoots poking
oi-ide kuru	through the snow
kusa no hatsuka ni	are barely visible,
mieshi kimi ka mo.	like my brief glimpse of [him/you].

The following anonymous poem ("Love," I: 484) is alluded to a few lines later:

Yūgure wa	At dusk
kumo no hatate ni	past the banner of clouds
mono zo omou	I gaze, lost in thought,
amatsu sora naru	yearning for a person
hito o kou tote	in the heavens far away.

The Flower Basket enlists a famous legend mentioned in the *Heike* and elsewhere about a Chinese emissary named Su Wu (Sobu), who had been captured by northern nomads and held against his will for many years. One day, he attached a message to the leg of a wild goose. When the goose flew south, it was shot down by the emperor, who thus learned that he was still alive.

The Reed Cutter alludes to a poem in the eighth imperial waka anthology, the *Shinkokinshū* (Shun'e, "Spring," I: 6):

Haru to ieba	Speaking of spring,
kasuminikeri na	mist has descended.
kinō made	Until yesterday
namima ni mieshi	it was visible between the waves:
awajishima yama	mountainous Awaji Island.

In all three plays, the italicized passages employ language linked to the familiar world of classical sensibilities that describes the act of looking into the distance while at the same time evoking space that suits the distant, absent gaze characteristic of distraught persons. These passages adhere to Zeami's advice in *Sandō* to "seek appropriate language while bearing in mind interesting seeds for actions and gestures" (ZZ 139).

There is a clear-cut precedent for the strategy of looking into the distance on the bridgeway: the acting of Kiami, the renowned *dengaku* player from the Shinza troupe, in *Sumiyaki* (The charcoal burner), a lost play. In *Sarugaku dangi*, Zeami reminisces:

> Kiami stood in the middle of the bridgeway wearing a hemp wig, the top of which was folded toward the front of his crown. He wore a monochromatic old man's mask now used by Zōami, and

a *nerinuki* silk robe under a three-quarter length plain-weave robe with broad sleeves that were rolled up and fastened at the shoulders. He carried firewood on his back and held a cane. Clearing his throat, he recited,

> "Is yonder mountain rustic's load a light one?
> Do you hasten on the homeward path?
> Do you hurry along because the fierce wind is cold?
> Do you hurry because 'tis said that a person living in the same hills also
> should cut a sprig to wear in their hair?
> Through the tree tops on mountain after mountain. . . ."

At the end, he began singing the *issei* entrance chant. His skill was masterful. It was like looking at an object made of bronze. (ZZ 262)

The dengaku performer's acting and singing on the bridgeway seem to have made a powerful impression on Zeami, who in later years incorporated the entire sequence in the shite's entrance speech in act 1 of *Akoya no matsu* (The pine tree at Akoya), the kind of play that he maintains in *Sarugaku dangi* could never be equaled by future playwrights (ZZ 286).[10]

What's more, the shite's entrance speech in the first part of Zeami's holograph copy of *Unrin'in* (Unrin'in temple) mimics the stream of questions in Kiami's speech:[11]

> Did someone break off a branch scattering the blossoms?
> If not, was it the breeze from a bush warbler's wings?
> The soughing of a pine tree? A person?
> Was that so, or not? A breeze in the lower branches . . . ?

Four examples can be found of the use of enken simply in the sense of a distant prospect without any connection with performance. In *Yūgaku shudō fūken* (Views on modes of training in the arts of entertainment; undated), for instance, it occurs in a discussion of Fujiwara no Teika's famous poem in the *Shinkokinshū* ("Winter," VI: 671):

Koma tomete	There is no shelter
sode uchiharau	where I can halt my horse
kage mo nashi	and brush off my sleeves:
sano no watari no	The Sano crossing
yuki no yūgure	in the snowy dusk.

Zeami writes, "This poem conveys no special admiration for the snowy landscape. It simply seems to describe a journey with no place to rest or find shelter in a setting that offers no distant view (enken) suggesting the traveler's location" (ZZ 166).

The second example comes from the description of the Style of the Correct Flower (*shōkafū*), the fourth highest level of performance in *Kyūi* (Nine levels), a brief treatise on the stages of an actor's training culminating in the highest artistic level known as the Style of the Wondrous Flower (*myōkafū*). Zeami describes the Style of the Correct Flower thus: "The mist is bright, the sun is setting, and the mountains all around are crimson. The Style of the Correct Flower is embodied by a distant view (enken) of the mountains all around vividly illuminated by the radiant sun in the blue sky. This artistic level is superior to the Style of Breadth and Detail (*kōshōfū*); it represents the first step toward the realm in which the Flower is attained" (ZZ 174).

In *Shūgyoku tokuka* (Finding gems and attaining the flower; 1428), Zeami writes the following regarding the Three Role

Types: "The basic principle for performing dramatic actions in the Aged Mode is expressed in [*Nikyoku santai ningyō zu*] as 'a still mind and distant eyes.' In other words, Keep your mind still as your eyes look in the distance. It is a type of performance that suggests an old man with clouded vision who cannot see clearly into the distance [enken]" (ZZ 192–93).

The fourth example comes from *Go ongyoku jōjō* (Items concerning the five types of singing), a treatise in which the various effects produced by noh singing are likened to different kinds of trees. Under the heading "Japanese cedar" (*sugi*), Zeami lists the "style of supreme virtuosity (*rangyoku*):" "The cedar has an extremely imposing appearance. As sacred trees surrounding august shrines, cedars stand out from other trees when viewed from a distance (enken)" (ZZ 200–201).

The last half-dozen uses of enken are problematic. The two most notable examples occur in *Nikyoku santai ningyō zu*. Regarding the woman's dance, Zeami declares:

> The woman's dance is an especially ideal type. It is the expression (enken) on stage of a wondrous figure (*myōtai*) suffused with graceful beauty (*yūgen*). The Woman's Mode ranks highest among the visual effect of a boy's singing and dancing and the Three Role Types. The actor must not forget to "make the mind the foundation and abandon forcefulness," and inwardly maintain that state throughout his singing and dancing. The woman's dance represents the pinnacle of our art. Acting that gives spectators the indescribable impression that the singing and dancing have been fused into one resides in this graceful style. (ZZ 126)

The passage is accompanied by the slogan "The source of graceful beauty (yūgen) and refinement."

In the section on the dance of the celestial maiden, Zeami writes: "The music should form the foundation. The actor should mentally infuse his entire body with energy as he dances and is swept up in the dance. He should express differences in tempo, and like a bird playing among the blossoms in the spring breeze, create the vision on stage (enken) of a wondrous aura and subtle depths, in which the skin [overall effect], flesh [training and experience], and bones [innate ability] are expressed as one. It is danced in an expansive manner. It must be carefully studied and practiced" (ZZ 130). The explanation is accompanied by a sketch of the dancing figure of a celestial maiden and the caption, "Inwardly attuned to the music."

These two uses of enken have been characterized as being virtually synonymous with *kenpū* ("visual effect"), an interpretation that lacks the sense of distance in the first syllable (en-) of enken.[12] When the word follows phrases such as "wondrous figure suffused with yūgen" (*yūgen myōtai*) and a "wondrous aura and subtle depth" (*myōfū yūkyoku*), it surely does not refer to a mere visual effect, but rather the space created by the shite that radiates outward, as seen above in the act of pointing out famous places in *Tōru*.

After watching an experimental performance by the French actor and director Jean-Louis Barrault and the great noh actor Kanze Hisao in Tokyo in 1977, Nakamura Yūjirō, a philosophy specialist, made the following observation regarding the space physically generated by the shite:

> In Barrault's case, a subtle disparity was generated the more he tried to approach the spirit of noh, for his acting tangibly restricted space, something foreign to the noh stage. Conversely, Hisao's performance demonstrated that noh movements and gestures spring from a place that causes something tangible to radiate

outward into space with intense directionality. It also demonstrated that theater space is created in terms of relationships rather than being formed externally.[13]

During a symposium on spatial aspects of the noh stage three years later, Yuasa Jōji, a composer and music specialist, linked the shite's physical creation of space to Zeami's treatise *Kyūi*. The actor's awareness, he observed, spreads in all directions, becoming one with space. In other words, undifferentiated space is created in which actor and space become one. The treatise characterizes low-level performances as ones in which the power of the shite's presence is conveyed straightforwardly. The more the actor merges with the space around him, the more highly regarded the performance is. The pinnacle of the nine levels of performance, known as the Style of the Wondrous Flower, said Yuasa, is a state in which the actor merges completely with the surrounding space.

Upon further reflection, the woman's dance and the dance of the celestial maiden in *Nikyoku santai ningyō zu* correspond to two of the five modes of dancing outlined by Zeami in *Kakyō* (Mirror of the flower; 1424): *butaifū chi* and *bu chi*. Zeami describes the former as a "style in which dance is central, movements and gestures (*shu*) subordinate. It represents a flow, a temporal process, rather than outward visual effects (*mushi*)." Regarding the latter, he writes, "Although 'movements and gestures' have to do with dancing, in the 'method of dancing' (*bu chi*) dependence is not placed on the hands and feet. Instead the dancing figure as a whole forms the foundation. It is an approach in which dancing is expressed without conspicuous movements or techniques on stage. It is like a bird gliding through the air without moving its wings. This mode of dancing is what is known as *bu chi*" (ZZ: 87–88).

Attention needs to be paid here to the expressions "without outward visual effects" (*mushi*) and "dancing figure without conspicuous movements" (*mushu mufū naru yosooi*). Although *shu* (literally, "hand") in *mushu* is understood to mean dance movements and patterns, in both instances the dancing figure of the shite seems to embody a type of performance that, in Nakamura's words, "causes something palpable to radiate into space," or, as Yuasa says, a performance in which "the actor becomes one with the space around him." The woman's dance and the dance of the celestial maiden truly constitute a wondrous figure (*myōtai*), a wondrous aura (*myōfū*), respectively. I would argue that Zeami viewed enken in terms of a situation in which the dancing figure of the actor appearing in this wondrous chronotopic state dissolves into the surrounding space and disperses into the distance.

The following use of enken in *Shūgyoku tokuka* can be interpreted in a similar fashion: "The singing captivates spectators' eyes and minds causing people to focus solely on the shite," writes Zeami. "As a result of the distant view generated by the shift in focus from the singing to the aura surrounding the shite's movements, the entire audience is moved and accolades are bestowed. When that happens, it can be considered an ideal performance that delights one and all" (ZZ 185). The use of enken here in *sono renjō yori fūshi ni utsuru enken* (literally, a distant vision in which there is a shift from the singing to the movements) can be regarded in terms of the expansion of the space created by the actor's figure, when the eyes and minds of spectators, which had been drawn to the actor's singing, shift their focus to his movements. Moreover, from my perspective, the idea of his figure merging with the surrounding space is perceptible as well in the following example from *Kakyō*: "A consummate actor excites more and more interest when a vision (*enken*) of his singing and dancing emerges without conscious intent from a mastery of many plays and the training of his body and mind" (ZZ 103).

The third example of enken, however, has to be interpreted as meaning *kenpū*, namely, the effect produced on the audience by an actor's performance: "In mastering a specific role type, an actor should perform it in such a way that his acting and the visual effect (*enken*) that is produced display a degree of ease commensurate with his innate talent or potential. This is important in our art." (ZZ 190).

The final example comes from *Shikadō*: "An effect (enken) is created in such a way that an unorthodox performance is transformed into a good one. In other words, it is an indirect effect that transforms the negative into the positive by means of a consummate actor's skill" (ZZ 114). Since the first syllable in enken here denotes the distance between the two extremes, in this instance, too, it seems equivalent to *kenpū* (i.e., acting that is manifested outwardly).

The foregoing discussion demonstrates the variety of ways in which enken is employed in Zeami's treatises. At its core, however, his treatment of the term seems to refer to the outwardly radiating figure of the actor in space, the merging of body and space, whether it concerns the technique of looking into the distance or dances performed while playing women's roles. The space informed by it, however, would never have come into existence unless the shite himself served as a powerful magnetic field. This poetics of space was sought by Zeami simultaneously with his discovery of the motionless body, which forms the subject of the following chapter.

8

ZEAMI'S VISION OF THE ACTOR'S BODY AS A MEDIUM

A vivid sense of Zeami in his fifties can be found in a fifteenth-century commentary on the Chinese classic *Records of the Grand Historian* by Tōgen Zuisen, a Zen monk at Tōfukuji temple in Kyoto. In a passage about a visit to a well-known temple in neighboring Ōmi Province in 1477, Zuisen tells he how he found himself in the company of an elderly monk when he went to take a bath at a nearby temple. After discussing the performances by the noh actor Kanze Jūrō starting that day at another temple in the area, their conversation turned to the subject of Jūrō's grandfather Zeami. "The elderly monk said that Zeami was short in stature," writes Zuisen. "When he stood up off the floor, he moved with agile footsteps. It was a natural outgrowth of long training. He was always laughing and talking in the presence of their teacher Funi and introduced Zen-inspired talk that made everybody laugh."[1]

This anecdote describes Zeami standing up and moving with nimble footsteps, the apparent product of years of training in the art of *sarugaku*. In addition, he was always talking and smiling in the presence of their teacher Funi, namely, Giyō Hōshū (1361–1424), a prominent Zen scholar-monk who spent his final years in retirement at the Rikkyoku-an, a Tōfukuji subtemple. It was probably there that the elderly monk saw Zeami, and even after the passage of a half century, the figure of Zeami with his agile movements and engaging talk still remained a vivid memory.

The meaning in the original of the word translated above as "footsteps" is ambiguous and could refer either to standing up off the floor or walking. Whatever the case, the elderly monk, with his acute observation of how Zeami moved his feet, had sharp eyes, for Zeami did in fact seem to have agile feet. But this gift was not necessarily an asset in artistic terms; rather, it was the source of a lifelong complex. In *Sarugaku dangi*, his younger son Motoyoshi writes, "Zeami confided that, unbeknownst to anyone, there was an aspect to his art that was inferior to Kan'ami's. When I asked what it was, he replied, 'It's the quickness of my feet'" (ZZ 314). In trying to clarify his enigmatic remark, the usually straightforward Zeami uses the agility of his feet to measure the level of his artistry against that of his father; along with the comment "unbeknownst to anyone," his negative assessment reveals that the deep-seated complex was hard for others to imagine.

Another hint can be found in the anecdote in *Sarugaku dangi*, mentioned earlier, involving Kan'ami's performance as the young lay monk Jinen Koji. On stage Kan'ami looked as if he was only twelve or thirteen, and when he adeptly began singing the section containing the sermon, the shogun Ashikaga Yoshimitsu turned to Zeami and joked, "No matter what stratagems you employ, there's no way you can outdo him in this regard." The shogun's jest, which plays on a sumo technique consisting of suddenly grabbing an opponent's inner thigh and throwing him to the ground, is premised on the nimbleness and cleverness of Zeami's art. Moreover, an image of Zeami as a child with nimble feet and a talent for court football is evoked by Nijō Yoshimoto's letter.

In his later years, Zeami put his innate gift to use in a type of performance called the "style of quick intricate movement" (*saidōfū*) that generates excitement using energetic movements and foot stamping (ZZ 128). His concern for acting techniques that involved footwork, including foot stamping, is manifested by the detailed explanation appended to *Nikyoku santai ningyō zu* that is headed "The distribution of foot stamps in a sequence of vigorous actions while performing quick intricate movements in our troupe" (ZZ 131).

What is important, however, is that Zeami, at least late in life, considered the innate agility of his feet to be a burden. After the age of forty, Zeami adopted the changed attitude toward the actor's body that underpinned the new art of the noh; any acting that utilized his agility was incompatible with these ideas. Or perhaps I should say that he devoted himself later in life to a sense of movement and tempo beyond the raw physical level that was produced by restraining his body, which moved too quickly.

This approach looked like, but was inherently different from, the type of acting described by Zeami at age thirty-eight in 1400, when the first section of *Fūshikaden* was completed. At that point, he expressed the following view of actors who had reached age forty-four or forty-five: "From this time onward, an actor should avoid overly detailed realistic actions (monomane). . . . He should refrain from vigorous plays that entail quick intricate movements of the body." After age fifty, Zeami continues, the actor's "only strategy in general is nonaction" (ZZ 18–19). Although both approaches have to do with aging, there is a world of difference between acting that merely involves not moving and acting that finds positive value in it. In the section of *Kakyō* called "Moving the mind ten-tenths, the body seven-tenths," Zeami writes:

> An actor should follow his teacher's instructions when learning the correct way to extend his hands (*te o sasu*) and move his feet. Once he has thoroughly mastered the movements, he should not

extend his arms or draw them back (*hiku*) quite as much as he does in his mind. Instead he should physically execute the movements with somewhat more restraint than he does mentally. This should not necessarily be limited just to dancing and physical actions (*hataraki*). In his overall bearing and demeanor, if the actor performs in such a way that his body is more restrained than his mind, his body will form the foundation of his acting and his mind will create overtones, producing an interesting effect. (ZZ 84–85)

It is noteworthy that this section, which follows general remarks about singing at the beginning of *Kakyō*, offers guidelines regarding the noh actor's body overall. The motionless body is defined here in the sense of restrained acting (moving the body seven-tenths) in a tension-filled figure that dynamically performs nonaction and concentrates inwardly, that is to say, "moves the mind ten-tenths."

THE THREE ROLE TYPES AS AN ACTING SYSTEM BASED ON MASKS

The question as to how the concept of the motionless body took shape in Zeami's mind is closely linked to his awareness of, and discoveries that he made concerning, the technique of performing with a mask. The same is true regarding his formulation of the arts of song and dance (*nikyoku*) and the aged, woman's, and martial odes (*santai*) as the basis of noh training, our focus here. In *Fūshikaden*, the section on dramatic imitation (monomane)—the hallmark of the Yamato sarugaku style of acting—is divided into nine character-types: women, old men, roles performed without a mask, mad persons (*monogurui*), priests (*hōshi*), warriors (*shura*), Shinto deities, demons, and Chinese roles. At this juncture, the thirty-eight-year-old Zeami's emphasis was on the subjects of representational acting that an actor should perform.

Two decades later in *Shikadō*, however, the system of acting was reformulated under the heading of Two Arts and Three Role Types:

> Various items on training in our art. Although noh encompasses a wide range of styles and techniques, a beginner's training should not go beyond the Two Arts and Three Role Types. "Two Arts" refers to singing and dancing; "Three Role Types" the three basic modes of performance.
>
> At the start of his training, a boy should thoroughly master singing and dancing under the direction of his teacher. He should not study the Three Role Types for a while during the period from around the age of ten when he still has a boy's figure. He should perform roles on stage without altering his appearance as a child. In other words, he should not wear a mask and should perform all roles in name only dressed in attire befitting a boy. The same is true of *bugaku* court dances: when boys perform masked pieces such as Ryō-ō and Nasori, they do so in name only. They are dressed as boys and do not wear a mask. This training lays the foundation for preserving graceful beauty (*yūgen*) in the actor's performance techniques in later years.
>
> After coming of age and acquiring an adult's figure, an actor may perform many roles in which he dons a mask and changes his appearance by wearing an appropriate costume. Even then, however, the initial steps in attaining true artistry should be limited to the Three Role Types, in other words, an old man, woman, and warrior. After thoroughly studying roles pertaining to an old man, woman, and person of vigor [warrior], he must employ the arts of singing and dancing that he has studied since

childhood in a wide range of roles that are subsumed under the Three Role Types. There is no other way to learn our art. (ZZ 112)

From the age of ten onward, says Zeami, a boy should seek to master the fundamentals of noh—song and dance—while performing without a mask and eschewing concrete representation. As an adult, one should master mimetic techniques wearing a mask, but one must first and foremost thoroughly master the three basic role types.

In *Shikadō*, the various kinds of roles discussed in his earliest treatise have been reduced to three basic types: the aged, woman's, and martial modes. But Zeami did not just randomly choose three types from abstract physical forms and acting techniques. He must have received a hint from somewhere that inspired him to make categories that led to the creation of the Three Role Types. In all likelihood, masks provided that hint.

The Three Role Types can be viewed as physical forms and acting techniques that correspond to the noh masks with a human expression representing aged men, women, and adult males that remain when the Okina and demon (*oni*) masks, which retain a close link to sarugaku's shamanistic roots, are excluded. The section on masks in *Sarugaku dangi* provides information about what they were like in Zeami's day (ZZ 301–302). After discussing Okina and demon masks (the latter include *tobide*, *beshimi*, and Tenjin), the subject turns to the following types of masks:

> [In Ōmi] these days, the mask maker Echi from the Zazen-in is an outstanding maker of woman's masks.
> In Echizen, the mask maker Ishiō-hyōe was followed by Tatsuemon, Yasha, Bunzō, Ko-ushi, and Tokuwaka. Until the time of Ishiō-hyōe and Tatsuemon, anybody could wear their masks;

the effectiveness of the masks by Yasha and those after him depended on the actor. The mask worn by Kongō Gonnokami was a genuine Bunzō mask. In our troupe, the old man mask was made by Tatsuemon. The smiling old man mask (*warai jō*) praised as suiting *Koi no omoni* (The heavy burden of love) was made by Yasha. The one used in the second part of *Oimatsu* (The aged pine) and other plays was carved by Ko'ushi.

Masks carved by Echi were given to Ōmi sarugaku. The ones Zeami received as the renowned Yamato sarugaku performer using Iwadō as an intermediary were the woman's mask that now belongs to Hōshō Dayū and the slender-faced old-man mask. The latter has been repainted and used for the title role in *Genzanmi* (*Yorimasa*). Recently, masks of men produced by Chigusa are highly regarded. Tatsuemon is a maker of young man's masks. . . .

Our troupe's mask of a slightly older woman was made by Echi. Zeami wore it in woman's plays. Other famous masks no doubt exist.

Masks with a human expression are clearly categorized here by Zeami under the rubrics of the old man (*jō*), woman, and man. At the same time, old man's masks, which emerged early on, include specific names such as the smiling old man mask, whereas masks of women and men do not. Despite the reference to Echi, a noted recent maker of woman's masks from the Zazen'in (an Enryakuji subtemple on Mount Hiei), and the comment about young man's masks by Tatsuemon from the past, the remark that recently Chigusa's masks of men were highly regarded suggests that masks representing young men and women, particularly the latter, began to be produced in earnest in Zeami's day. Although masks had been worn by actors since the earliest days of sarugaku, it is thought that they usually had a surface function in performances to indicate the role played by the actor. Even when

Zeami wrote the section on monomane in *Fūshikaden*, his main concern did not lie in the performance of mimetic actions while wearing the mask, but rather in the characters depicted using mimetic actions.

In his forties and fifties, however, Zeami underwent a radical shift toward acting that centered on wearing a mask, as though in response to rapid advances in the production of masks representing human beings, particularly women, during that period. The change was not limited to the theory of Three Role Types, which subsumed the various subjects of dramatic representation under three fundamental acting modes based on the type of mask. This major change extended much further down to a deep level in the human body and even altered the nature of the noh text.

THE MASK AND THE ACTOR'S BODY

The transformation in Zeami's thinking occurred during a process of trial and error on various fronts. In fact, he could be said to have shouldered a lifelong contradiction between dramatic imitation and abstract acting for which wearing a mask provided a catalyst.

Although Zeami is thought to have possessed subtle noh masks like the *ko-omote* woman's mask traditionally ascribed to Echi, his views on performing woman's roles while wearing this kind of mask are not exactly clear to us today. Obviously, the caption "make your mind the foundation and cast aside forcefulness" in the section on the Woman's Mode in *Nikyoku santai ningyō zu* can be regarded as a major advance in the level of abstraction, especially compared to the treatment of woman's roles in *Fūshikaden* (ZZ 21), which focuses on outward imitation, emphasizing costumes and the age of the actor in accord with

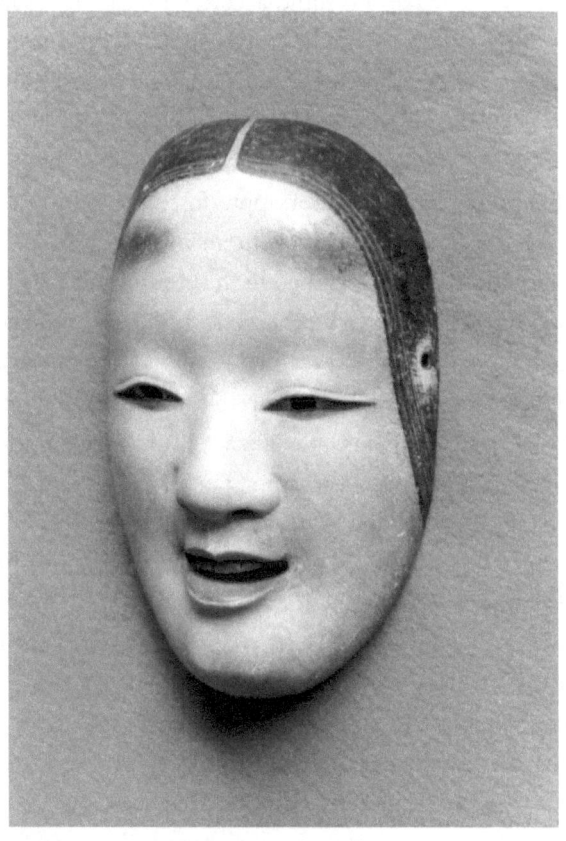

FIGURE 8.1 Woman's *ko-omote* noh mask, attributed to Echi
Courtesy of Tessenkai

Zeami's declaration that woman's roles suit the kind of dramatic imitation performed by young shite actors.

Various remarks by Zeami, however, suggest that *kokoro* (*shin*; heart, mind, idea) manifests a concern for representation that entails the mindset or idea of being completely transformed into a woman, rather than a concern for the actor's mental concentration. For instance, the caption "Make your mind the foundation and abandon forcefulness" is glossed in *Shūgyoku tokuka* as: "If the actor makes his mind accord with the figure he represents, force will forthwith be cast aside" (*ZZ* 193). In addition, the section of *Kakyō* headed "First transform yourself into the person, then skillfully imitate the person's actions" offers this advice: "When playing the role of a woman . . . an actor should keep his body pliant, and not apply force mentally" (*ZZ* 86). The evolution from an external to an internal theory of dramatic imitation can be discerned in these examples, albeit without escaping completely on a theoretical level from the yoke of representational action. Nevertheless, the key point in acting has shifted from external imitation to the actor's mind, and the actor's inner state has become a matter for discussion for the first time regarding the Woman's Mode, the second of three basic role types set forth in *Nikyoku santai ningyō zu*. These circumstances necessitate taking a look at the development of the subtle woman's mask and its impact on acting.

There is a huge difference between acting while wearing a large demon's mask with a clear-cut expression, such as a tobide or beshimi mask, and doing so when wearing a relatively small woman's mask with a restrained expression. Kanze Hisao was an actor who keenly understood the difference:

> Regarding noh masks, those that represent demons are somewhat different as they fall under the category of masks that have a fixed expression. . . . The expression on masks that belong to the woman's category is extremely profound and subtle. When using that kind of mask, the actor has to wear it with his jaw protruding a little. The performer's jaw and head both fit inside a *gigaku* mask. In the case of gagaku masks, the performer's head is not completely covered by the mask, but his jaw is. As a result, the person who performs wearing that kind of mask is either transformed into something or negates his self, whereas in noh if a mask that

depicts a woman's face is worn without the jaw protruding, the mask dies to a considerable extent. Hence the jaw is slightly visible. As a result, the actor performing the role and the mask clash, they repel and conflict with each other, at which point something dramatic is born.[2]

Unlike large masks, which completely hide the actor's face, wearing a woman's mask so that the actor's jaw is slightly visible causes the element of dramatic imitation—completely assuming the role of someone using the mask—to recede into the background. Conversely, the mask is drawn toward the actor's face. While mask and actor conflict with each other, the latter remains central.

The nature of the woman's mask whose expression is extremely profound and subtle, a mask that seems to hide and condense primal emotions, requires inner concentration on the part of the actor to enable it to change and express a variety of emotions in a play. The phrase "make your mind the foundation" in the slogan "make your mind the foundation and abandon forcefulness" in *Nikyoku santai ningyō zu* may not refer to this inner concentration, but Zeami's remarks in the section headed "One mind connecting all actions" in *Kakyō* clearly address the issue of the actor's inner concentration:

> Spectators make comments such as "places with no action are interesting." This derives from the care secretly taken by the actor deep within himself. The arts of song and dance along with gestures, movements, and dramatic imitation are all actions performed by the body. "Places with no action" refers to the moments between them. The reason why these intervals of nonaction are considered interesting derives from the inner working of the actor's mind as he constantly strives to connect the intervals

between actions. It lies in the vigilance he maintains throughout not to let up after he stops dancing or finishes a song, or between all intervals in words and actions. The outward intimations of an actor's inner state are interesting.

However, the actor's inner mental state must not be manifested outwardly. If it is visible, it is already a conscious act and ceases to be non-action. One should link what comes before and after moments of non-action on an unconscious level so that one's mind is hidden even from oneself. This, in short, is the expressive power produced by connecting all actions by means of "one mind (*isshin*)." (ZZ 100)

The effect produced in this way corresponds to the use of *kokoro* (*shin*) in the above advice from *Kakyō* about "moving the mind ten-tenths, the body seven-tenths," which refers to the actor's inner concentration. *Kokoro* here denotes the concentration maintained by the actor throughout the intervals after he stops dancing, after he finishes a song, or between all actions entailing language and dramatic imitation. The actor adheres to this psychological principle to unify mimetic acting as well. This mental state is not required of masks with fixed expressions, such as demon masks, but, rather, is imperative when wearing a type of mask that must hold the audience's attention on stage for a long time—namely, human masks with a restrained expression, such as those representing an old man, woman, or adult male.

Placing masks with a human expression, especially the woman's mask, at the core of acting shifts the focus to the actor and heightens the degree to which it is concentrated inwardly. The actor is reduced to an even more passive state owing to the destabilization of his field of vision by the woman's mask, which has two small eye holes. He foregrounds his physical nature by concentrating inwardly as a way of pushing back against the mask.[3] One is, of course, speaking generally, inasmuch as no direct ties between the woman's mask and the performance of woman's roles were made by Zeami. Nevertheless, guidelines on acting as a whole, such as "moving the mind ten-tenths, the body seven-tenths" and "one mind connecting all actions," must be thought of as theories that sprang from an awareness of a deep bond between mask and body.

Dramatic imitation was inevitably forced to retreat as a result of the revolution in acting brought about by representing human beings with masks so subtle as to even seem expressionless. In *Kakyō*, Zeami's advice to concentrate inwardly while simultaneously performing restrained movements ("moving the mind ten-tenths, the body seven-tenths") comes at the start of the treatise after advice on singing, while the discussion of monomane drops back to the fifth section, which is titled "First, completely transform yourself into the person; then skillfully imitate the person's actions." This change frankly demonstrates the foregrounding of the actor's physical self in place of the emphasis on role playing in *Fūshikaden*, a development that occurred in Zeami's forties and fifties, that is, around the time that *Kakyō* was written.

"Moving the mind ten-tenths, the body seven-tenths" may also suggest an orientation toward abstract movements. But, even leaving aside that issue for now, the consistent principle regarding the noh actor's body—inward concentration and the simultaneous suppression of movements—represents an appropriate response to the dynamism lurking in the woman's mask itself, which appears expressionless while hiding and condensing primal emotions within it. The actor's body is reconstituted by the mask. Zeami was the first person to be acutely aware of this and formulate theories about the body and an actor's training to transmit to future generations. Theater in which the actor's physical state has absolute priority—the noh that we watch today—had begun.

MASKS AND THE COMPOSITION OF DREAM PLAYS

The invention of subtle masks and the reconfiguration of the noh actor's body did not, of course, flow unilaterally from mask to body. The connection between the two clearly deepened while interacting with each another. Something else was involved: namely, the production of noh texts. Innovations regarding masks and the actor's body also had a major influence on the composition of noh plays. Kanze Hisao has pointed out the close connection between the woman's mask and the perfection of the mugen noh form by Zeami:

> The birth of the woman's mask, I believe, is intimately linked to Zeami's perfection of the dream structure of noh plays, the greatest event from the point of view of the history of noh. The plays imbued with yūgen sought by Kan'ami, followed by the *mugen* noh plays perfected by Zeami, marked a huge advance in noh. The birth of plays with a dream structure came about amid the difficulties experienced as a performer following the transformation of sarugaku from a ritual performing art into a splendid theater form at the center of society under the patronage of the warrior aristocracy, and the impact of changes in shogunal leadership.
>
> Zeami invested mugen noh with a strong narrative element. Mugen noh plays emphasize singing and dancing, but that is not all they do. They are unified by the narration of a foundation story (*honzetsu*). True mugen noh plays that are still part of the

repertoire, such as his masterpiece *Izutsu* and *Teika*, a play by his son-in-law Zenchiku, possess a structure in which a story that provides the framework for the play is recounted, usually in the form of a *kuse* (a long, sung narrative). In general, the shite sits motionlessly at the center of the stage during the kuse while the chorus musically recounts a story on behalf of, or regarding, the shite. During the narrative, the stage—nay, the entire theater space—is swept away onto a phantasmal plane that transcends the real world, a realm shaped by the story told in the kuse.

As for the element of dance, the *jo no mai* is a quiet elegant piece in which the actor in the second act, having already been transported to a place beyond the everyday world by the kuse, surrenders himself to the realm of the senses.

The shite in both the seated kuse and the jo no mai dance maintains a quiet composed presence at the center of the stage for an extended period of time. Moreover, he is present there, hiding deep inside himself something that comes welling up from within. The mask has to be able to grant that much time.[4]

The seated kuse in *The Well-Cradle* was clearly a novel experiment by Zeami when he was past the age of sixty. Unlike performances today, which assign the narration of the story to the chorus, it is highly likely that the shite in Zeami's day sang it together with the secondary actor (the *waki*) and the chorus. Even so, the seated kuse formed a dramatic time and space in which the shite had to be present there hiding deep inside something that came welling up from within. It was the ultimate expression of a motionless body.

Moreover, the kuse sequence in *The Well-Cradle* possesses an unusual temporal structure in which the narrative moves backward in time, unlike the twenty-third episode of *The Tales of Ise* (the foundation material).[5] It begins with a *kuri*, a short song by the chorus introducing Ariwara no Narihira, followed by a recitative (*sashi*) that describes his marriage to the daughter of Aritsune and the pain caused her by his visits to a woman in the village of Takayasu. The sequence culminates in their story as childhood sweethearts recounted in the kuse, the aural highpoint of the play which is sung almost entirely by the chorus except for one or two lines sung by the shite. The deepening inward concentration of the masked motionless figure kneeling at the center of the stage perfectly suits the movement of the story back into the past. It is emblematic of the invocation of the past by the emotionally receptive body of the noh actor wearing a mask. The receptive (passive) body of the actor is also closely connected to the world of the passions. Dream noh plays depicting human emotions long ago were woven in this fashion when an inwardly concentrating figure wearing a mask became a playwright.

The importance attached to the telling of a story (*katari*) is cited by Kanze Hisao as a distinctive aspect of Zeami's mugen noh. That kind of world in fact is similar to the oral recitation of the *Heike* by blind storytellers who recited the narrative while playing a *biwa* lute. There is not much distance between the biwa hōshi's powerful recital of the world of the passions using his blindness as a springboard, and a sarugaku actor who thrusts his physical self into the foreground as a result of being forced to exist on stage half in a world of darkness on account of wearing a mask.

Zeami's treatise on writing plays offers the following advice to those writing plays about warriors: "If the foundation source concerns a famous Genji or Heike commander, be very careful to write it exactly the way it is told in the *Heike*" (ZZ 139). All of Zeami's *shura mono* masterpieces—plays about the ghosts of warriors—do, in fact, draw on the *Heike* for material. The underlying similarity at the core of the tale and the warrior plays, however, does not reside so much in spirit pacification as in the depths of the human body where orally narrated tales and noh plays are generated and enacted—a receptive body capable of performing spirit pacification.

THE CHIGO'S BODY

A model for maskless figures was reawakened inside Zeami in the process of formulating the concept of a motionless body that wears a mask and focuses inwardly: namely, the figure of a chigo, a state experienced by Zeami himself as a child.

Zeami's view of childhood in his first treatise differs markedly from his later outlook in *Shikadō* and *Nikyoku santai ningyō zu*. When he laid out an actor's lifelong training in the opening section of *Fūshikaden*, childhood was viewed simply as a special time when a temporary flower blooms:

> **From the age of twelve or thirteen.** Since a boy begins around then to carry a tune and understand performance, he should gradually be taught various plays. Because of his boyish form, whatever he does will possess yūgen, and his voice, too, will be pleasing. These two advantages will hide his weaknesses and accentuate his strong points.
>
> Generally speaking, boys should not be permitted to perform plays requiring complicated acting techniques. Such an approach would not suit the time or place, and would prevent his skill from improving in the future. Once he becomes really accomplished, however, whatever he does will be good. With a boy's figure and voice as well as artistic skill, what can go wrong?
>
> Nevertheless, this flower is not the true flower, but merely a temporary one. As a result, all aspects of his training during this

period can easily be mastered. Accordingly, his level at this point will not determine his lifelong artistry.

Training during this period should take advantage of the pleasing aspects [his physical form and voice]. At the same time, great importance must be attached to the basics: he must learn how to perform gestures and actions precisely, clearly articulate the words when he sings, and firmly master the dance movements. (ZZ 15)

But in *Shikadō* and *Nikyoku santai ningyō zu*, Zeami states that a boy should devote himself solely to mastering singing and dancing, and he should not wear a mask. *Nikyoku santai ningyō zu* goes on to say that a boy's figure forms the foundation of yūgen. In other words, the figure of a boy is now viewed as the source from which a graceful type of beauty arises. Zeami stresses that mastering singing and dancing during childhood will enable an actor to become an outstanding artist who will always perform easily and at a high level. As a result, yūgen will be retained in the aged, woman's and martial modes and will animate what the actor does (ZZ 124).

The section on an actor's training in *Fūshikaden* also expresses the importance of firmly mastering the fundamentals of noh—actions, and singing and dancing—as a boy. During this period, says Zeami, a boy's training should aim to showcase his physical appearance and voice. At the same time, his basic acting skills should be nurtured to enable him to perform vigorous movements (*hataraki*) with precision and assurance, pronounce words clearly when he sings, and execute dance moves properly. In *Shikadō*, however, the business about vigorous movements, which are close to representational acting, has been eliminated, and the contents have been subsumed under the arts of singing and dancing.

The discussion of a boy's training in *Fūshikaden* includes remarks leaning toward a denial of dramatic imitation: as a rule, a boy should not employ very complicated dramatic movements and gestures when performing plays because it would not suit the time and place and might prevent his acting ability from improving later on. Zeami goes on to say that whatever he does will be fine once his art becomes truly outstanding. But since Zeami's advised teaching boys various roles at the beginning, clearly he was not rejecting their performance of representational acting when he wrote that section.

In *Shikadō*, however, Zeami shifts to a complete rejection of dramatic imitation by boys: beginning around the age of ten when he still wears a child's attire and has long hair, he should not study the Three Role Types for a while. He should perform plays attired as a child. In other words, he should not wear a mask and should perform all roles in name only. *Nikyoku santai ningyō zu*, too, advises against allowing an actor to perform the three role types for a while during the period when he has the figure of a child (ZZ 124).

A subtle difference in outlook can also be seen in Zeami's view of the figure of a boy in *Fūshikaden* and the two later treatises. In *Fūshikaden*, he writes that beginning around age twelve or thirteen, when a boy begins to sing on key, acquire an understanding of noh, and learn various kinds of plays, everything he does will be imbued with yūgen because of his childlike figure. This phrasing conveys an understanding that age is central, the boy's figure secondary, as befits the subject covered in the section on the stages in an actor's lifelong training. In *Shikadō* and *Nikyoku santai ningyō zu*, however, Zeami speaks, respectively, of the period from around age ten, when an actor has a child's form, and when the actor has a boy's figure. This wording, which conveys the idea of using a boy's physical appearance as a marker for defining age, makes it clear that the emphasis was on the boy's figure itself. Of course, the difference in wording is also due to the shift in Zeami's views on an actor's training from an espousal of chronological stages over a lifetime to modes of expression, namely, the Two Arts and Three Role Types. That having been said, the very creation of a separate section on the boy's figure as a role type proves that Zeami in his later years was more acutely conscious of (and attached greater value to) it.

The complete rejection of mimetic acting on the part of boys in *Shikadō* and *Nikyoku santai ningyō zu* was driven by Zeami's prioritizing of the figure of a boy. As noted above, the copy of his manuscript of *Nikyoku santai ningyō zu* transcribed by his son-in-law Zenchiku provides a glimpse of his image of a boy's figure. The sketch in the section on the child's dance depicting a boy with artificial eyebrows and long hair bound at the back of his neck with a cord, a hairstyle resembling the way that girls wore their hair, clearly demonstrates that the figure of the boy performing a dance replicates the depiction of temple boys in medieval tales and picture scrolls about chigo. Chapter 6 in this book mentions the possibility that Zeami actually lived as a chigo at a Tōdaiji subtemple called the Sonshōin. Aside from this hypothesis, at the very least Zeami clearly equated the child's form and boy's figure with that of a temple chigo.

Regardless of whether a boy sarugaku performer who had become a temple chigo appeared that way on stage, or boy sarugaku performers were attired in that fashion on stage, the presentation of the figure of a temple chigo was not limited superficially to his face and figure but can be considered an exact replica of temple chigo as a social entity. That is because the figure of a temple chigo itself must have been a drawing card on the noh stage.

During the middle ages, chigo were a common presence at major temples, where they became the love and sex objects of the monks who served as their mentors. The saying "first chigo, then Sannō" shows that they ranked above Sannō Gongen, the guardian deity of Mount Hiei, as an object of worship. To satisfy both amorous and sexual expectations, chigo were educated and polished at temples as "beings devoted entirely to charm and grace." Their rigorous training encompassed everything down to their dress and manners while they were chigo (usually from the age of twelve or thirteen to seventeen or eighteen), including their makeup and hairstyle, in the manner of Heian court ladies.

Chigo are depicted in medieval tales as beautiful radiant figures. For instance, *The Tale of Mount Toribe* describes the young protagonist as having a luminous face that was faintly visible behind his tresses, and compares him to a dew-covered flower at dawn, a young willow swaying in the evening breeze. Similarly, the chigo in *The Story of Kannon's Manifestation as a Youth* looked moist with dew and was more supple and graceful than a willow disheveled by the spring breeze. These descriptions of chigo closely resemble the paean to Zeami as a boy in Nijō Yoshimoto's letter.

The pursuit of representational actions on stage by a child actor as an iteration of temple boys who possessed this kind of socially constructed body would have created a situation that overstepped the aesthetic and physical constraints imposed on chigo, whose lives were devoted to charm and grace. Zeami's complete rejection of mimesis by chigo served to avoid this situation as well. Conversely, skills suiting a child actor—namely, the arts of song and dance—that maximized the appearance and demeanor of a chigo on stage were sought.

Hence Zeami's orientation in later years toward noh that centered on song and dance was accompanied by an active reinterpretation of a chigo's body as a foundation for the arts of song and dance, as he makes clear in *Nikyoku santai ningyō zu*.

He also states that when a chigo goes on to perform song and dance in aged, woman's, and martial roles, the visual effect of yūgen will naturally be manifested in them (ZZ 124). The idealization of beautiful boys approached Heian court ladies, or the image of women that resided in the medieval yearning for the Heian court. As a result, it was easy to link the figure of a chigo to the woman's mode, which, of the three basic role types, was emphasized the most by Zeami, who regarded the ineffably beautiful figure of a noblewoman as a standard and declared that the woman's mode represented the fundamental style of yūgen (ZZ 126). Thus the chigo's body was revived as well in Zeami's orientation in favor of Heian court culture.

Furthermore, even though the maskless figure of a chigo seems to be highlighted in contrast to Zeami's stress on the Three Role Types, which use masks, a chigo's face is amply masklike as a result of wearing makeup. The chigo's androgenous body, achieved by means of his hairstyle and makeup, retains within it a memory of spiritually possessed bodies, as expressed by the term *kami-sage*, which can mean both "hair that hangs down" and "descent of a deity."[6] It also paralleled the Three Role Types, which undergo a kind of possession through the act of donning a mask. In addition, it is linked to the kind of world depicted in *The Well-Cradle*, in which the shite's gender changes like shifting images in a set of opposing mirrors.

As *Shikadō* puts it, a boy should not alter his appearance as a chigo when performing on stage. In other words, he should not wear a mask and should perform all roles in name only. Thus a boy's acting resembles the orientation of the actor's body sought by Zeami that centered on the use of a mask, which forced mimetic elements to retreat. The boy's body could even be said to prefigure the abstract basic posture, or *kamae*, of noh actors who perform all roles using one artificially structured stance.

On a physical level, a boy's body obviously lacks the most important catalyst for performing with a mask: inner concentration. Although in this sense, there is a decided difference between the body and the bodies sought by Zeami that wore a mask, aesthetic constraints prevented a boy from moving very much. On the surface, this point too forms a link with the motionless body characterized by restrained acting based on inward concentration.

For various reasons of this kind, the figure of a chigo was resurrected inside Zeami in his fifties when he was able to look back objectively on his own childhood. Yet he was mindful of individual actors' careers, and he knew full well that boyhood beauty was merely a temporary flower and had no connection with an actor's later years. As he clearly states after the age of sixty in *Yūgaku shudōfū ken* (Views on modes of training in the arts of entertainment): "The graceful aura of a boy's figure will not continue to exist after he becomes an adult" (ZZ 163).

The boy's body was revived inside Zeami as an ideal physical type in which the fundamental element of beauty was concentrated. What is important in the theory of an actor's actual training is the intensive study of the arts of song and dance during boyhood, which laid the foundation for the future. That approach meant that even if an actor lost the graceful aura of a boy's form, the singing and dancing learned during those years would remain, and yūgen would continue to flower in the Three Role Types and other aspects of his art.

9

THE ACTOR'S BASIC POSTURE AND THE ROOF-COVERED NOH STAGE

First-time visitors to noh theaters today are surprised to discover that the stage is covered by its own roof in spite of being enclosed inside a larger roof-covered structure. This unusual configuration is a vestige of noh's long tradition as an art performed out-of-doors.[1] A remark by Zeami in *Sarugaku dangi* about pillars supporting a canopy over the stage indicates that covered stages were already employed at outdoor subscription performances in his day (ZZ 292).

In fact, the use of roofs in the Japanese performing arts began with noh. *Bugaku* court dances, which predate noh by several centuries, were held on an open outdoor stage. The raised platform at Itsukushima shrine on the Inland Sea, which even now contains vestiges of twelfth-century bugaku stages, and the stone platform at Shitennōji temple in Osaka, which retains traces of the structure that existed in the Kamakura period, are two examples. The use of roofs at venues other than subscription noh venues was rare. For instance, performances illuminated by torchlight in front of the Great Southern Gate at Kōfukuji temple in Nara and performances in front of the temporary shrine erected for the Wakamiya festival nearby at Kasuga shrine have been held on a roofless platform for more than six hundred years.

A precedent for roof-covered stages can be found in the temporary huts in which the holy man Ippen and his Jishū followers danced in a circle while chanting Amida Buddha's name. Ippen's illustrated biography states that he began performing the dance at Odagiri (scroll 4). But roughly a dozen priests and nuns, as well as warriors, are merely shown lifting their legs in the air as they dance in front of a warrior's residence while Ippen stands on the verandah striking a bowl. Although the scene in scroll 5 depicts the departure of Ippen and his followers from the residence in Saku rather than the dance itself, the illustration includes a memorable detail of several broken floor boards on the verandah that were left behind in their wake, along with the following explanation: "Several hundred people dancing inside the residence stamped their feet so hard that the floor boards collapsed. Instead of repairing them it was decided to leave them the way they were as a memento of Ippen."[2] The scroll indicates that the broken floorboards resulted from the ecstatic dancing of several hundred people in the house, while the large number of participants would seem to indicate that the dancers were not limited to Ippen and his followers.

The first example of a dance hut with an elevated roof-covered platform occurs in the scene at Katase in Kamakura (scroll 6), which depicts Ippen and his followers chanting the *nenbutsu* and stamping their feet on the floor boards to the striking of a gong as they ecstatically circle the stage in a clockwise manner. They are the only dancers on the stage; ordinary folk are presented simply as onlookers standing below the hut gazing up at the performance. The nenbutsu dance—circling round and round with vigorous stamping feet—superimposed wildly gyrating figures onto an already firmly established practice: the ritual Buddhist ceremony, or *gyōdō*, in which monks circumambulate a temple building or image clockwise while chanting a sutra. The establishment of the nenbutsu dance would have coincided roughly with the period when roof-covered dance huts emerged.

The pattern at Katase was subsequently adopted around the country. Some venues, like the one at Katase, featured an elevated platform, whereas planks were simply spread on the ground at Sekidera. Together with the nenbutsu chanting and the striking of a gong, the pounding of the floor boards by dozens of monks and nuns created a tremendous din. The basic nenbutsu dance with its frenzied movements and novel acoustics, accordingly, attracted enormous curiosity and interest among the populace in the middle ages.[3]

The roof clearly served to amplify the reverberating of stamping feet in the dance huts. The depiction of a roof and no floor at Kumi in scroll 8 and Ninomiya in scroll 11 suggests that the roof possessed more inherent meaning for Ippen and his followers. (It is unclear whether there was a floor at Kumi because the hut is shown flooded with sea water.) One conceivable purpose of the roof was to offer protection from rain and snow. Surely Jishū members shrank from sleeping in the open air while traveling around the country and needed a roof to ward off the elements. Outdoor noh performances such as torchlit events tend to be cancelled today when there is just a slight amount of rain because the costumes and drums are easily damaged by water, but rudely attired Jishū members would certainly have been unfazed by rain or wind as they danced to the metallic beat of a gong. Another possible purpose for the roof was to signify the special space in which the dance was performed, in which case a sacred *shimenawa* rope demarcating the space would presumably have sufficed.

In all likelihood, the roof itself was a prerequisite for creating an enclosed space and defining the center of the group trance.

It was an indispensable covering that enabled all of the Jishū members to enter a trance, a state of ecstasy, as they repeatedly circled the stage at a gradually accelerating pace. Ippen and his followers took no notice of upwardly directed energy. The energy generated by their trance that built up at the center of the roof-covered space was energy that simultaneously spread outwardly in the horizontal space between the roof and the floor (or ground), casting a spell over the spectators and ultimately, it was hoped, reaching the Western Paradise far away.

This perspective regarding the Jishū dance hut closely resembles the attitude toward space manifested by the noh stage. The plays centering on song and dance that developed in Zeami's day are a kind of poetic drama featuring dances (*mai*) that center on circling the stage. In this type of play, spectators are drawn into an ecstatic state by the power of the dance quietly being performed in a circular direction.

Okina, the oldest piece in the noh repertoire, also has close ties with circular movements. Traces of this kind of movement are discernible today only in an actor's circling of the stage in a triangular pattern while stamping his feet in what is known as a heaven-earth-man pattern. *Okina*, however, is referred to as *shushi-bashiri* in the venerable torchlight performances at Kōfukuji. A forerunner of noh, shushi-bashiri were rituals conducted at First Month and Second Month ceremonies by temple attendants (*shushi*) who moved with quick steps as they circled the altar where the temple's chief object of worship was installed. This ceremony was very similar to Ippen's nenbutsu dance in terms of the use of ritual circumambulation. Great emphasis too was placed on ambulation and foot stamping as noh techniques in Zeami's day before the introduction of the distinctive sliding steps known as *suri-ashi* invented by later noh actors.[4]

The dance huts were usually erected in liminal places. A major purpose of the nenbutsu dance performed there was to subdue dead spirits. The reverberation from the intense foot stamping of Ippen and his followers, too, was intended to pacify the souls of the dead writhing beneath the ground who had not attained Buddhahood. The platforms for pacifying liminal spaces intrinsically served a shamanistic function as well in shushi-bashiri and *Okina*, which form the roots of noh. The nenbutsu dance and noh sprang originally from the shamanistic pacification of earth spirits, while the roofs over the dance hut and the noh stage bespeak a consciousness of the earth below.

THE DEVELOPMENT OF THE NOH STAGE

Although subscription venues are thought of as the original source of the noh stage, the configuration of the permanent roof-covered stage in fact evolved from stages erected at warrior estates. For instance, the abbot of Daigoji temple notes in his diary in 1431 that rain began to fall during a performance attended by the sixth shogun at the Myōhōin temple in the Eastern Hills but it soon stopped so the stage was wiped dry and a play was performed, only for the rain to begin again, forcing the performance to be moved indoors.[5] Similarly, a 1509 manual on warrior etiquette belonging to the Ōuchi daimyo family mentions a performance attended by the eighth shogun, Yoshimasa, at the deputy shogun's mansion in Kyoto in the 1440s, during which a heavy evening downpour began to fall while the second play was being performed. As a result, two or three plays were transferred indoors, a change of plans that soured the mood of everyone from the shogun on down.

But an entry in the abbot's diary concerning a performance by the four Yamato *sarugaku* troupes attended by the sixth shogun at the Ichijōin subtemple in Nara in 1429 states that flares were lit on all sides of the stage in spite of the rain, and a temporary roof was quickly provided to cover the stage. In other words, the stage did not have a roof at the outset, but the performance continued after a temporary roof was hastily installed when it began to rain.[6] In the following spring, the abbot notes that there was a dressing room, bridgeway, and roof as usual for a performance attended by the sixth shogun at the Kongōrin'in, the chief priory at Daigoji. His wording suggests that the stage in those days regularly had a roof.

On the other hand, the *Ōuchi* document states that the bridgeway was not protected by a roof at the beginning of a performance attended by the sixth shogun at the deputy shogun's residence at some point between 1429 and 1441. But the deputy shogun, anticipating rain, had prepared a roof in advance. When heavy rain began to fall, he had it hurriedly assembled and installed, and the performance continued. In this case, of course, it is implicitly understood that the stage itself had a roof.

These examples indicate that prior to the mid-fifteenth century, some stages had a roof whereas others, at performances at shrines and temples and on the grounds of warrior residences, did not. Although roofs may have represented a norm, in fact more often than not stages seem to have been uncovered.

The permanent configuration of the roof-covered noh stage was realized in the latter half of the sixteenth century. The oldest surviving example, the Kita (North) noh stage at Nishi-Honganji temple in Kyoto, is said to have originally been constructed prior to 1581 and then moved several times thereafter before finding a permanent home at the temple around 1620.

THE ESTABLISHMENT OF
A PERMANENT NOH STAGE

The unusual theater space formed by the noh stage came about when the demands of noh actors, who sought a horizontally articulated space unique to noh, coincided with those of their warrior patrons, who enjoyed performing and watching noh and wished to possess their own stages. The installation of noh stages at the shogun's headquarters began to occur after the decade-long civil war that broke out in 1467. Shoguns and leading daimyo did not perform noh themselves, whereas the last quarter of the sixteenth century witnessed the emergence of amateur performers, such as Shimotsuma Shōshin, a Honganji temple official whose skill as a noh actor put professional actors to shame; the daimyo Hosokawa Yūsai, an expert *taiko* drummer; and the hegemon Toyotomi Hideyoshi (1537–1598), who enjoyed performing himself as did Hosokawa Yūsai's son. It was during that period that the construction of permanent noh stages began in earnest at temples and shrines and on the grounds of warrior estates.

The function of a bridgeway as an extension of the stage proper and for entrances and exits is evident from Zeami's strategy of the distant gaze, as discussed in chapter 7. When the stage was surrounded by circular stands, as in the case of subscription performances, the bridgeway was usually attached to the rear of the stage in keeping with the pronounced consciousness of left-right symmetry. This type of configuration is evident from *Sarugaku dangi* and the sketch that survives of the famous subscription performance at Tadasugawara in 1464.

The oldest surviving illustration of a subscription performance can be found on a pair of six-panel folding screens depicting scenes in and around the capital that are thought to represent views of Kyoto around 1530. The painting depicts a performance by the Kanze troupe on a small roof-covered noh stage that is open on all four sides. The bridgeway is attached to the left side of the stage (stage right), a configuration that is viewed as a reflection of the reverse influence that permanent noh stages at private residences had on the noh stages erected at subscription performances.[7]

The current practice of attaching the bridgeway at an angle on the left side of the stage has been explained in terms of the restrictions imposed by the construction of noh stages at warrior residences:

> During the Muromachi period, the corridor connecting the main building to the central gate always protruded from the eastern side of the building. Spectators watching performances from that vantage point were regarded as facing the front of the stage (*shōmen*), while the central-gate corridor was considered the place for viewing the left side of the stage (*waki-shōmen*). Hence the placement of the dressing room in a southeasterly direction made sense from the perspective of performing plays. However, the extension of the central-gate corridor from the main building and its temporary function as the waki-shōmen precluded placing the dressing room parallel to the stage. At the same time, the stage inherently needed to be located as close to the spectators as possible; conversely, the dressing room had to be as far away as possible. The bridgeway linking the stage and dressing room had to be long enough to enable it to serve as an extension of the stage. The unusual layout and functions of these architectural elements made the southeast a logical place for the dressing room when the main building was the focus of the performance. Given these circumstances, the bridgeway obviously had to be attached at an angle to the eastern side of the stage.[8]

The practice of covering the entire back of the stage with wooden panels known as mirror boards (*kagami ita*) is inconceivable from the vantage point of stages erected for subscription noh performances, which were open on all sides. An innovation devised for permanent stages whose principal audience faced stage front, the rear wall was designed mainly for acoustical effect. Nor was there any longer a need to consider the view from the far side of the stage, unlike at subscription performances where the audience surrounded the stage on all sides.

This development was viewed with extreme displeasure by Kanze Sōsetsu (1509–1583), the seventh head of the Kanze troupe, whose opinion is expressed thus in a collection of secret noh traditions compiled by Hosokawa Yūsai:

> Strong, thick pillars are detrimental on a noh stage. The performers, particularly the shite, are swallowed up by the pillars. The upper half of the rear of the stage should be open. If it is obstructed by wooden panels, a negative effect would be created when an actor indicates that direction using his body. An effort should be made to enable the dancer to clearly stand out. Blocking the opening is bad because it prevents that from happening.[9]

The remark about panels covering the lower part of the rear of the stage reveals that the practice of covering the entire wall still lay in the future. A large decorative screen, for example, blocks the back of the open noh stage in the famous eight-panel screen depicting a performance of *Okina* hosted by Toyotomi Hideyoshi during an imperial visit to his opulent Jurakudai castle in 1588. The screen dates from the last two decades of the sixteenth century when mirror boards were beginning to develop.[10]

Even now, the boards at the back of the noh stage at Itsukushima shrine on the Inland Sea, a late Muromachi-period feature, are detachable as are the panels covering the rear of the covered bridgeway. The stage, surrounded by the sea, provides the setting for the daylong noh performances during the three-day Peach Blossom Festival held in April every year. The performances are dedicated to sacred Mount Misen, the chief deity (*shintai*) of the shrine, rising some 1,800 feet behind the stage. Precisely because the mirror boards act as acoustical panels, the hollow sound of the *kotsuzumi* shoulder drum can still be faintly heard from the precincts of the small shrine at the summit, a center for the practice of religious austerities.[11]

The custom of painting an aged pine tree on the rear wall of noh stages dates from the following period. Various theories have been advanced as to its meaning, beginning with the notion that it represents the pine tree onto which the deity descends at the annual Wakamiya festival at Kasuga shrine. Another theory suggests that it is a vestige of congratulatory performances called *matsubayashi* (literally, "pine music") that flourished in warrior circles in the middle ages. There is no dispute, however, about the sacred nature of the tree.

The term "mirror boards" probably emerged when the sacred pine tree began to be painted on the rear wall. To noh actors, mirror boards are sacred panels on which a tree is painted just as the mirror room (*kagami no ma*) immediately behind the curtain is a sacred space. Strangely enough, even today the shite's introductory song (*shidai*) in the first part of a play is sung at an angle facing the pine tree rather than the audience or the *waki*. The tree could also be regarded as the eyes of the deity watching the noh actor from behind. In other words, noh actors can be regarded as preserving on the stage a memory of the days when they were viewed from all four sides as they performed on a completely open stage.

For the sixteenth-century actor Sōsetsu, the drawbacks to blocking the rear of the stage with wooden panels began with the negative effect produced by the boards, which was an impediment when one wished to indicate a particular direction. But that was not all; the space behind the dancer should be visible. He thought that blocking the back of the stage had a negative effect because it prevented this from happening. He considered the noh stage a space in which the energy generated by the dance flowed horizontally outward in all directions and thought that boards at the rear of the stage blocked that energy.

Although the development of the mirror boards heightened the focus on the front of the stage, it did not in fact fundamentally alter acting techniques as much as one might think at first. Kanze Hisao performed with a clear awareness of the unusual nature of the noh stage open on all sides, as can be seen in his remarks on the noh actor's physical role:

> In noh, especially phantasmal plays, the actor should be present on that open-sided stage in a way that transcends his physical self.... He must project a presence that is capable of shaping a universe just by standing there. How does the actor maintain that presence? In noh, the act of standing on the stage consists of standing in an equilibrium that is achieved by being pulled endlessly in all directions. Conversely, it means endlessly radiating energy outward. It means infinitely looking out at and controlling space. That is what the *kamae* does.[12]

The actor's kamae, or basic posture, is created by lowering the hips and concentrating tension in the area of the hip joints. The horizontal mode of walking produced by sliding one's feet results from the way in which the actor sets his hips in the basic posture. The sliding footsteps are possible only because of this posture. Or, rather, one could say that the actor is unable to do anything but slide his feet when his hips are lowered.

Intriguingly enough, the development of the actor's basic posture and mode of walking (*hakobi*) in the sixteenth century closely coincided with the formation of today's noh stage. The roof-covered dance hut emerged when the holy man Ippen and his followers, acutely conscious of horizontal space owing to a yearning for the Western Paradise, sought a confined space that facilitated entering a trance. In the same way, roof-covered noh stages developed in earnest when plays centering on song and dance based on circular dances came to form the heart of the repertoire, and awareness of horizontal space intensified as a result of the emergence of the actor's unique stance and method of walking.

Two passages in Zeami's treatises suggest a consciousness of the actor's inner mental concentration as a new way of regarding the actor's body. For instance, in *Yūgaku shūdōfū ken*, he states that the generation of the flowers and seeds in the myriad techniques of musical performance derives from the workings of the mind which fill the body with expressive power (ZZ 167). In *Kakyō*, he declares that the intense concentration generated deep within the actor by the inner workings of his mind, which constantly links all things, excites interest through its outward expression (ZZ 100). But Zeami went no further than consolidating the actor's varied roles under the headings of the aged, woman's, and martial modes.

The artificial stance that fostered inward concentration by focusing tension in the area of the hip joints was an outgrowth of innovations introduced by later actors. Signs can already be evinced in a series of sketches of seminaked figures in a late sixteenth-century work called *Hachijō kadenshō* (Treatise on the transmission of the flower in eight books) that are modeled after Zeami's *Nikyoku santai ningyō zu*. The first three sketches depict the figure of a man (figure 9.1, frontal view of naked man in pose). The middle one offers a frontal view of him standing in a manner that closely resembles the modern kamae. It is accompanied by the following advice about how to hold the upper part of the body:

1. The hips should be firmly set to keep them from shaking when stamping the feet and to enable the actor to maintain the correct posture. Also, the actor should not bend his arms or neck.
2. The knees should be slightly bent, as in archery. The configuration of the body cannot be maintained without regard for the knees and hips.
3. The elbows should be held about six cms away from the body. In plays about demons, however, they should be about nine cms away.
4. Holding the torso this way will not only improve the actor's overall posture but will also help his foot stamping. The hips will naturally remain steady, the feet firm.[13]

The figure in the first sketch does not display this stance, while the third sketch depicts a side view of the stance depicted in the middle sketch. In other words, these three sketches are used to explain the correct way to hold the torso in male roles, a sign of the importance attached to the actor's posture in this type of role.

Yet we should not assume that this included all types of roles. For instance, the tenth sketch, which depicts a woman with a bamboo leaf (*sasa*) in her left hand, indicates the correct way to hold the upper body in *Hyakuman*, as well as in other mad-woman roles. The aim of mad-woman pieces was not to maintain the correct posture, hold one's hips steady, keep one knees firm, or be neatly attired. At that juncture at least, a mimetic way of holding the body was still employed in these roles. One may surmise that the kamae became the usual stance even for madwomen and other female roles by the first half of the nineteenth century when the length of noh performances became roughly the same as today. The comment by the seventeenth-century kyōgen actor Ōkura Toraakira—that the focal point was said to reside in the hips and that the actor's stance appeared to

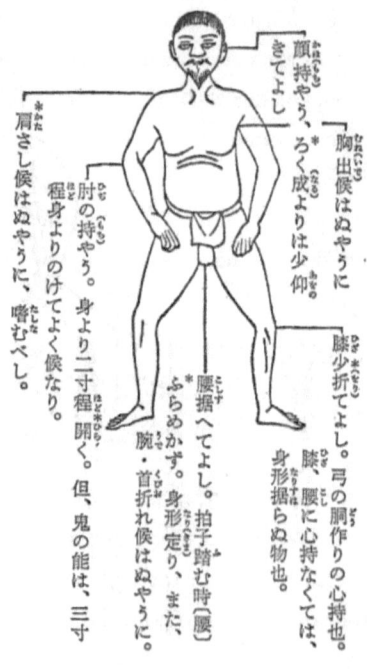

FIGURE 9.1 Frontal view of naked man in pose, from *Hachijō-bon kadensho* Hayashi Tatsusaburō, ed., *Kodai chūsei geijutsuron*, Nihon shisō taikei, vol. 23 (Iwanami shoten, 1973), 597.

be weak if his hips were not bent—can be perceived as part of the process by which the kamae came into general use.[14]

It has been theorized that the sliding steps used by noh actors originated in the footwork of shushi-bashiri temple performers or the slow measured steps used in court ceremonies. Treating the actor's posture and mode of walking as a unit, however, opens up another possibility. A miscellany of the noh actor Komparu Zempō's remarks on various subjects compiled by a disciple around 1513 contains a comment about the applicability of martial techniques and court football to noh. Zempō is also quoted as saying that "holding the hips steady when sparring while wearing *nagabakama* and a sedge hat was a method of training that, if employed in real circumstances, would enable a person to avoid being killed.[15]

A martial arts guide presented to his great-grandson Ujikatsu in 1601 includes sketches of sword fighting techniques performed while wearing nagabakama, long *hakama* trousers that extend behind the wearer like a train.[16] The practice of wearing trousers that hamper footwork has been characterized as training in how to move with a constrained body, but it could be interpreted in a more positive way as providing a thorough training in keeping the hips steady and moving the feet with sliding steps.

A long line of Komparu actors from Zempō's time onward seem to have been accomplished martial artists. Ujikatsu, who was initiated into the inner secrets of martial techniques by a master in the Yagyū Shinkage school of swordsmanship, was one example. But the close association with warriors was not limited to the Komparu family. We should not overlook that this was true of leading noh actors in general during the Muromachi period.

The martial arts and noh were similar in the mental concentration for which Zen provided a model. Interaction between martial artists and noh actors also led to the incorporation by actors of physical aspects of the martial arts, in the process of which the kamae seems to have emerged as a way of holding the upper body in male roles. Indeed, the term kamae itself was unmistakably borrowed from terms such as *seigan no kamae*, which denotes a stance in which the sword is pointed at an opponent's eyes.

The invention of the actor's basic position and manner of walking heightened awareness of horizontal space on the noh stage, a phenomenon foreign to ballet in the West with its frequent use of jumps, or to traditional Japanese dance (*buyō*), which places a premium on the sense of floating produced by the human body. Because the noh actor moves without altering the height at which his head moves, even slight vertical movements offer a stark contrast. A good example is when the actor leaps under the temple bell at the climax of the famous noh play *Dōjōji*, when a jealous woman turns into a serpent and dives under a bell suspended from the ceiling of the stage—an effective vertical use of the stage that subverts its basic horizontality. The action is all the more powerful because it undermines the expectations of audiences accustomed to horizontal movements.

The insight offered by Kanze Hisao on the enactment of space on the noh stage was distilled into one word: the kamae, the technique that enables the actor who stands on a stage open on all sides to transcend his physical self. The creation of a cosmic axis transcends his actual physical being, forming a universe just by standing there being pulled endlessly in all directions and radiating energy in all directions. In a sense, the noh space today described in those terms was already immanent in the rhetoric of pointing out famous places around Kyoto acted out in Zeami's famous play about Tōru the Minister.

NOTES

1. RELIGION AS THEATER: THE JISHŪ SECT

1. The Account of Dengaku in the Capital, *Rakuyō dengaku ki*, was written by Ōe no Masafusa (1041–1111), a nobleman and eminent scholar and poet. Hayashiya Tatsusaburō, ed., *Kodai chūsei geijutsuron*, Nihon Shisō Taikei 23 (Iwanami Shoten, 1973), 218. *Koshi-tsuzumi*, drums fastened at the hips or hung from the neck, are beaten on both sides. For a complete translation of the account see Jacob Raz, "Popular Entertainment and Politics: The Great *Dengaku* of 1096," *Monumenta Nipponica* 40, no. 3 (Autumn 1985): 283–298.
2. *Tengu sōshi*: Umezu Jirō, ed., *Tengu sōshi, Zegaibō-e*, Shinshū Nihon Emakimono Zenshū 27 (Kadokawa Shoten, 1978), 90. The fourteenth-century war tale *Taiheiki* offers a vivid description of *tengu*: "Some looked like kites with sharp angular beaks, others like mountain ascetics with wings on their backs." (See chap. 2 of this book.)
3. *Ippen Shōnin eden*, ed. Komatsu Shigemi, Nihon no emaki 20, 3rd edition (Chūō Kōronsha, 1997), 113. The dance at Ōi Tarō's residence is on 116–117; the scene at Katase, on 164–165. For the theory that the earthen mound represents the grave of Ippen's uncle, see Kurita Isamu, *Ippen Shōnin: Tabi no shisakusha* (Shinchōsha, 1977), 79.
4. Kanai Kiyomitsu, *Tenshō kyōgen-bon zenshaku* (Kazama Shobō, 1989), 512–514.
5. Yoshikawa Kiyoshi, *Jishū Ami kyōdan no kenkyū* (Geirinsha, 1956), 331–333.

6. Iwahashi Koyata, *Geinōshi sōsetsu* (Yoshikawa Kōbunkan, 1975), 268. His speculation about *kusemai* dances (280) draws on an entry for Tenbun 13 (1544) /7/18 in the diary of Cloistered Prince Sonchin, the head of Shōren'in temple in Kyoto, as referred to several lines later in the chapter.
7. *Taiheiki*, in Gotō Tanji and Kamada Kisaburō, eds., *Taiheiki*, 3 vols. Nihon Koten Bungaku Taikei 34–36 (Iwanami Shoten, 1960–1962), 2: 337.
8. *Kemmu shikimoku*: Satō Shin'ichi and Ikeuchi Yoshisuke, eds., *Chūsei hōsei shiryōshū* 2 (Iwanami Shoten, 1957), 4. A translation of the code is available in Kenneth A. Grossberg and Kanamoto Nobuhisa, trans., *Laws of the Muromachi Bakufu: Kenmu shiki and the Muromachi Tsuika-hō* (Tokyo: Monumenta Nipponica and Sophia University Press), 1981, 15–23.
9. See Yamaguchi Masao, "Nihon-teki baroque no genshō: Sasaki Dōyo to Oda Nobunaga," in *Rekishi, shukusai, shinwa* (Chūō Kōronsha, 1974), 55–77.
10. *Taiheiki* (chap. 37), vol. 3: 373–374.
11. For the possibility that Sasaki Dōyo began the practice of employing tonseisha, see Kōsai Tsutomu; "Dōbōshū zakkō," in *Zeami shinkō* (Wan'ya Shoten, 1962), 75.
12. *Daitō monogatari*, Zoku Gunsho ruijū 21:2 Kassen bu (619), rev. 3rd edition (1972), 357.

2. THE ARCHAEOLOGY OF PERFORMANCE IN AN AGE OF EXTRAVAGANCE

1. A local history of Harima Province (part of present-day Hyōgo Prefecture), *Mineaiki* can be found in Abe Takeshi and Ōta Junzō, ed., *Harima no kuni Ikaruga no shō shiryō* (Yagi Shoten, 1970), 328–329.
2. Tōin Kinkata, *Entairyaku*, Ōchō 1 (1311) / 3/2.
3. Takatoki's obsession with dengaku and fighting dogs is recounted in chapter 5, volume 1, of *Taiheiki*, in Gotō Tanji and Kamada Kisaburō, eds. *Taiheiki*, 3 vols. Nihon Koten Bungaku Taikei 34–36. Iwanami Shoten, 1960–1962, 1: 161–164. The banquet scene in which *tengu* appear (162) is translated later in this chapter. Also see Helen McCullough,

2. THE ARCHAEOLOGY OF PERFORMANCE ⊗ 233

comp. and ed., *Classical Japanese Prose* (Stanford, CA: Stanford University Press, 1990), 478–483.
4. Nijō-gawara lampoons: Kasamatsu Hiroshi et al., eds., *Chūsei seiji shakai shisō*, Nihon Shisō Taikei 22 (Iwanami Shoten, 1981), 345–348.
5. Fujiwara no Munetada, *Chūyūki* (Diary of the minister of the right), Chōshō 2 (1133) 5/8.
6. Hagiwara Izumi, "Nō ni itaru tsuzumi no hensen," pt. 1, *Kanze* (August 1979): 23–31; *Chōjū jinbutsu giga*, ed. Komatsu Shigemi, Nihon no Emaki 6 (Chūō Kōronsha, 1977), 102–103; *Nenjū gyōji emaki*, ed. Komatsu Shigemi. Nihon no Emaki 8 (Chūō Kōronsha, 1977), 44; *Urashima myōjin engi*, ed. Komatsu Shigemi, in *Hikohohodemi no mikoto emaki, Urashima myōjin engi*, Nihon Emaki Taisei 22 (Chūō Kōronsha, 1979), 72–73; and *Daisenji engi emaki*, ed. Sasaki Kazuo (Yonago: Inaba Shobō, 1971), 48–49.
7. Omote Akira and Katō Shūichi, eds., *Zeami, Zenchiku*, Nihon shisō taikei 24 (Iwanami Shoten, 1974), 261. (Hereafter cited as ZZ in the text.)
8. The next four block-quoted passages in this chapter come from *Taiheiki* (chap. 27), 3: 55–57.
9. *Taiheiki* (chap. 10), 1: 355; (chap. 15), 2: 102, 193. For a translation of Nagasaki's final battle see: McCullough, *Classical Japanese Prose*, 487–491.
10. The treatise *Kokon rendanshū* was written by the renga master Sōzei (d. 1455). See Takayama Sōzei, *Kokon rendanshū*, ed. Ikeda Tadashi, in *Sōzei rengaronshū*, Koten Bunko 85 (Koten Bunko, 1954), 17–19. The episode is discussed in greater detail in chapter 3.
11. Kaneko Kinjirō, *Tsukubashū no kenkyū*; *Tsukubashū* (Kazama Shobō, 1965). The verses are numbered in accordance with this edition.
12. Yamaguchi Masao's comment about renga was published in Yamaguchi Masao and Inui Hiroyuki, "Taidan: Bashō no shigaku (poetique)," *Kokubungaku: kaishaku to kyōzai no kenkyū* (January 1983): 21.
13. Yamada Yoshio, *Renga gaisetsu* (Iwanami Shoten, 1937), 174.
14. Yasuda Jirō, "Yamato no kuni higashi sanchū ikki," ed. Murata Shūzō, *Kinki daimyō no kenkyū* 5 (Yoshikawa Kobunkan, 1986): 358–382.
15. *Taiheiki* (chap. 32), 3: 207.
16. Kurita Isamu, "Za ni tsuite: utaawase, mono-awase to cha," *Chanoyu saijiki*, Autumn, Taiyō Collection 19 (Heibonsha, 1981): 29; *Renga*

hikyōshū: Okuda Isao et al., eds., *Rengaron shū, nōgakuron shū, hairon shū*. Shin Nihon Koten Bungaku Zenshū 88. (Shōgakukan, 2001), 184.

17. *Taiheiki* (chap. 36), 3: 356–358. The phrase "decorations in seven places" presumably referred to the latest fashion in decor, which consisted of lavishly displaying imported Chinese objects in seven places in a room.
18. *Taiheiki* (chap. 37), 3: 373–375.
19. *Taiheiki* (chap. 39), 3: 443–444. This passage (including the text appearing as a block quote below) is a paraphrase of Matsuoka's original.

3. THE ART OF COLLABORATION

1. Prince Sawara became crown prince upon his older brother's accession to the throne but was imprisoned following the assassination of the administrator of the new capital at Nagaoka in 785, and he died on his way into exile. Various misfortunes that subsequently befell the imperial house were attributed to his vengeful spirit, and he was posthumously awarded the title of emperor.

    Sugawara no Michizane was slandered by his political rival, Fujiwara no Tokihira, and banished to the southern island of Kyushu, where he died. The occurrence of various natural disasters in the capital after his death and the demise of Tokihira at a young age were attributed to him. In an effort to appease his vengeful spirit he was deified and enshrined as the god Tenjin (Heavenly Deity) at the Kitano shrine in Kyoto and elsewhere.

2. *Ryōjin hishō kudenshū* (book 14): see Sasaki Nobutsuna, ed., *Ryōjin hishō, Ryōjin hishō kudenshū* (Iwanami Bunko, 1933), 170–171. For the Zen monk's eighteenth-century travel diary see *Angya zuihitsu*, in Kokubun Tōhō Bukkyō Sōsho, ed., vol. 7, Kikōbun (Kokubun Tōhō Bukkyō Sōsho Kankōkai, 1925), 413–472.
3. Yanagita Kunio, "Shidare-zakura no mondai": see *Yanagita Kunio zenshū*, vol. 9 (Chikuma Shobō, 1998), 18–24; Okami Masao, "Mono: demono, monogi, hana no moto renga," *Kokugo kokubun* 24 (February 1955): 31–36. For the anthology, see: Kaneko Kinjirō, *Tsukubashū no kenkyū*; *Tsukubashū* (Kazama Shobō, 1965). The verses given here and further into the chapter are numbered in accordance with this edition.
4. *Saigyō zakura*: Yokomichi Mario and Omote Akira, eds., *Yōkyokushū*, 2 vols. Nihon Koten Bungaku Taikei, vols. 40 and 41 (Iwanami Shoten,

1960, 1963), 1: 293; *Saigyō's Cherry Tree*, Royall Tyler, trans., *Japanese Nō Dramas* (London: Penguin, 1992), 222.

5. Watanabe Tsunayo, ed., *Shasekishū*. Nihon Koten Bungaku Taikei, vol. 85 (Iwanami Shoten, 1966), 244; Robert Morrell, trans., *Sand and Pebbles: The Tales of Mujū Ichien* (Albany: State University of New York Press, 1985), 174–175. For the anecdote later in this chapter concerning Fujiwara no Takasuke see: Watanabe Tsunayo, *Shasekishū*, 246; and Morrell, *Sand and Pebbles*, 177–178.

6. Takayama Sōzei, *Kokon rendanshū*, ed. Ikeda Takashi, in *Sōzei rengaronshū*. Koten Bunko 85 (Koten Bunko, 1954), 17–19. The last line of Zenna's poem is slightly different in *Tsukubashū*.

7. For the reference to Yoshida Kenkō's *Essay on Idleness* given prior to this verse see *Tsurezuregusa*, Kanda Hideo et al., eds. *Hōjōki, Tsurezuregusa, Shōbōgenzō zuimonki, Tannishō*. Nihon Koten Bungaku Zenshū. Shōgakukan, 1971; *Taregami ōrai*, ed. Ishikawa Ken and Ishikawa Matsutarō, *Ōraimono hen*, Nihon kyōkasho taikei 2 (Kōdansha, 1967), 249; the verse I quote in chapter 6 is on 239.

8. *Ise Daijingū sankei-ki*, quoted in Gunji Masakatsu, *Furyu no zō, sōsakuin*, Gunji Masakatsu satteishū 6 (Hakusuisha, 1992), 218. Saku Jubitsu, "Account of a Pilgrimage to the Great Shrine of Ise," in *Travelers of a Hundred Ages: The Japanese as Revealed Through 1,000 Years of Diaries*, trans. Donald Keene (New York: Columbia University Press, 1999), 73–75.

9. Takeuchi Hideo, *Tenmangū*, Nihon rekishi sōsho 19 (Kōbunkan, 1968), 63–64; the quotation from Kitano shrine records regarding monthly renga performances is on 64. For the seventeenth-century account in the next paragraph, see: *Dekisai kyō miyage*, in *Kinsei bungaku ruijū. Kohan chishi hen*, vol. 6 (Benseisha, 1976).

10. The passage from *Zokusen kiyomasa ki* (Further records of Katō Kiyomasa [1562–1611]) is quoted in Gunji Masakatsu, *Fūryū no zō, sōsakuin*, 218–219.

11. *Taiheiki* (chap. 25), 2: 465. Quoted by Katsumata Shizuo, *Ikki*, Iwanami Shinsho 194 (Iwanami Shoten, 1982), 62–63. His comment about the disparity between leaders' fictive equality and their actual situation is on 74; the composite picture of monks' assemblies, on 46–47.

12. Yasuda Jirō, "Yamato no kuni higashi sanchū ikki," ed. Murata Shūzō, *Kinki daimyō no kenkyū* 5 (Yoshikawa Kobunkan, 1986), 369.

13. Yamada Yoshio, *Renga gaisetsu* (Iwanami Shoten, 1937), 174.
14. The thirty-six poetic immortals (*sanjūrokkasen*) were a group of superior poets selected by the critic Fujiwara no Kintō (966–1041) that became a popular motif in medieval art. A photo of the renga hall is available in Kumata Jinja, ed., *Hirano hōraku renga: kako kara genzai e* (Osaka: Izumi Shoin, 1993).
15. For an illustration see: *Boki ekotoba*, ed. Komatsu Shigemi, Zoku Nihon Emaki Taisei 4 (Chūō Kōronsha, 1985), 47; for illustrations of both *Boki ekotoba* and *Sairei sōshi* scrolls see *Sairei sōshi*, ed. Akai Tatsurō, Chanoyu kaiga shiryō shūsei (Heibonsha, 1992), 10–11 and 12–13, respectively.
16. Saitō Hidetoshi, "Kaisho no seiritsu to sono kenchikuteki tokushoku," ed. Murai Yasuhiko et al., in *Chanoyu no seiritsu*, ed. Nakamura Masao et al., Chadō shūkin 2 (Shōgakukan, 1984), 155–164. The Hōshin'in was founded by the monk Kenshun (1299–1357).
17. *Kanmon nikki*, (Fushimi no Miya Sadafusa [Gosukō-in]), 7 vols., ed. Kunaichō Shoryōbu. Zushoryō Sōkan 26: 1–7 (Kunaichō Shoryōbu, 2002–2014); Eikyō 4 (1432) / 7/7.
18. Yamaguchi Masao and Matsuoka Shinpei, "Taidan: Tōtaru media to shite no nō," *Kokubungaku kaishaku to kyōzai no kenkyū* 31 (September 1986): 26–27.

4. THE GENESIS OF PHANTASMAL NOH PLAYS

1. Paul Claudel, *L'oiseau noir dans le soleil levant*, in *Oeuvres en prose* (Éditions Gallimard, 1965), 1167.
2. *Konjaku monogatari shū* (14.7) *SNKBT* 3:2 99–301. "Kannon sutra" (*Kannon-gyō*) is a common name for chapter 25 of the Lotus Sutra, which extolls the saving grace of Kannon (Avalokiteśvara), the Bodhisattva of Mercy and Compassion.
3. *Nihon ryōiki* (3:16), 151–152. *SNKBT* 30. Kyoko Nakamura, *Miraculous Stories from the Japanese Buddhist Tradition* (Cambridge, MA: Harvard University Press, 1973), 242–243.
4. Sasaki Kōshō, "Nihon ryōiki ni arawareta hijiri to kanjin," in *Bukkyō minzokushi no kenkyū*, ed. Sasaki Kōshō. Sensei Chosaku Kankōkai (Meicho Shuppan, 1987), 33.

5. Nakanodō Kazunobu, "Chūsei-teki kanjin no tenkai," *Geinōshi kenkyū* 62 (1978): 27. Benkei's story was dramatized in the noh play *Ataka*, which was later adapted in kabuki as *Kanjinchō* (The subscription list).
6. For *Jinen Koji* see: Itō Masayoshi, ed., *Yōkyokushū*, 3 vols. Shinchō Nihon Koten Shūsei. (Shinchōsha, 1983, 1986, 1988), 2: 129–142 and 2: 448–451. (The *Enkyō sannen ki* passage quoted on 449 in the previous citation mentions Jinen Koji's performance in Nara.) For a translation of the play see Chifumi Shimazaki, *Troubled Souls from Japanese Noh Plays of the Fourth Group*. Cornell East Asia Series (Ithaca, NY: Cornell University, East Asia Program,1998), 195–247.
7. Umezu Jirō, ed., *Tengu sōshi, Zegaibō-e*, Shinshū Nihon Emakimono Zenshū 27 (Kadokawa Shoten, 1978), 90. Jinen Koji is depicted in color plate 8.
8. For *Genkō shakusho* see: Kuroita Katsumi, ed., *Shintei zōho Kokushi taikei* 31 (Yoshikawa Kōbunkan, 1932), 432ff.
9. For *Togan Koji* see: Sanari Kentarō, *Yōkyoku tuikun*, vol. 4 (Meiji Shoin, 1973), 2168. See Ishida Hisatoyo, ed., *Shokunin zukushi-e*, Nihon no bijutsu 132 (Shibundō, 1977), 50, for a discussion of the various functions of kanjin holy men.
10. *Sanjūniban shokunin utaawase emaki* [1494], in Mori Tōru, ed., *Ise Shin-Meisho-e uta-awase, Tōhokuin shokunin utaawase emaki, Tsurugaoka hōshōe shokunin utaawase emaki, Sanjūniban shokunin uta-awase emaki*. Shinshū Nihon emakimono zenshū 28 (Kadokawa Shoten, 1979), 45–52 (illustrations); 71–80 (text).
11. Ichiya (scroll 7): *Ippen shōnin eden*, ed. Komatsu Shigemi. Nihon no emaki 20. 3rd edition (Chūō Kōronsha, 1997), 194–195.
12. Kesa Tayū is first mentioned in *Kagenki* in Bunpo 1 (1317) 11/4. His performance at Tatsuta is cited in *Kagenki* in Gen'ō 2 (1320) /10/20; the one in front of the Sankyōin Hall at Hōryūji, in Enbun 4 (1359) /6/5. His remuneration on the fourth day of the Sixth Month of 1320 is listed in Annual Events Down Through the Ages (*Ōdai nenjū gyōji*); cited by Nose Asaji, *Nōgaku genryū kō* (Iwanami Shoten, 1938) 288–289.
13. Tomikura Tokujirō, ed., *Saikai yoteki shū narabi ni Tsuizō Heigo gūdan*. Koten Bunko 109 (Koten Bunko, 1956), 89–91.
14. For *Jinen Koji* see: Itō Masayoshi, *Yōkyokushū*, 2: 132.

15. Ōhashi Shunnō, *Ippen*, Jinbutsu Sōsho 183 (Yoshikawa Kōbunkan, 1983), 115–116. The dances at Sekidera (scroll 7) and Ueno in Yodo (scroll 9) are depicted in *Ippen shōnin eden*, 178–181 and 238–239, respectively.
16. Sasaki Kōshō, "Chūsei ni okeru chihō shaji no kanjin," 92.
17. The translation of the section on plays about hell (*Utage no shintai*, 102–105) reflects revisions in Matsuoka Shinpei, *Nō: chūsei kara no hibiki*, Kadokawa sōsho 2 (Kadokawa Shoten, 1998), 47–49, passim.
18. Ogasawara Kyōko, "Chūsei keiraku ni okeru kanjin kōgyō: Muromachi ki," *Bungaku* 48, no 9 (Iwanami Shoten 1980): 56–71. The story of the monk Manmai (Manbei) at Yatadera is recorded in the Yatadera Jizō engi. Nichizō's visit to hell is mentioned in various medieval texts; see Carmen Blacker, *The Catalpa Bow: A Study of Shamanistic Practices in Japan* (New York: Routledge, 2000), 166–167. The Urabon sutra tells how Buddha's disciple Moggallana (Mokuren Sonja) managed to save his late mother who was suffering in the realm of hungry ghosts. The Obon tradition in Japan of honoring one's ancestors grew out of the teachings of the Urabon (Ullambana) sutra.

The study of the relationship between kanjin hijiri and temple and shrine histories was published by Tokuda Kazuo in "Kanjin hijiri to shaji engi," *Kokubungaku Kenkyū Shiryōkan kiyō* 4 (1978): 44–59. For King Enma judging sinners in hell, see Helen Craig McCullough, trans., *The Tale of the Heike* (Stanford, CA: Stanford University Press, 1988), 213–215. The thirteenth-century tales about Tōru in hell discussed by Tokuda can be found in *Zoku kojidan* (4.24) and *Jikkinshō* (5.1), see Tokuda, "Kanjin hijiri," 49. For Tōru's confession see Satake Akihiro, ed. *Honchō monzui*. Shin Nihon Koten Bungaku Taikei 27. Iwanami Shoten, 1992.
19. A detailed discussion of Zeami's play *Tōru* can be found in chapter 7 of this book. For *Ukai* (Cormorant fishing), see Yokomichi Mario and Omote Akira, eds., *Yōkyokushū* 1: 174–80.
20. Nakamura Yasuo, "Nōmen izen," *Rekishi kōron* (October 1978): 88–89.
21. Amano Fumio, "Nō to bukkyō: shūra o megutte." *Kokubungaku kaishaku to kanshō* (December 1983): 135–137. For the *Taiheiki* passage see *Taiheiki*, 2: 395. The Ashura (Asura) realm inhabited by unruly warlike demigods was one of six paths (*rokudō*) of transmigration in which rebirth was governed by karma (good or bad deeds in a previous life:

hell (*jigoku*), hungry demons (*gaki*), ashura, humans, and devas or heavenly beings. Second-category noh plays, which cast warriors as the main character, are known as *shura mono*.

22. The sutra describing the demons cited by Amano is Kanbutsu zanmai kyō (Meditation on the Buddha). The theory that the play dealt with Kō no Moronao and his relatives was advanced by Takano Tatsuyuki, *Kabu ongyoku kōsetsu* (Rokugōkan, 1915), 42–46. Imagawa Ryōshun's treatises are published in Sasaki Nobutsuna, ed., *Nihon kagaku taikei* 5 (Kazama Shobō, 1957), 177–187.
23. The *Moromori ki* entry is dated Jōwa 5 (1349) /6/11. *Moromori ki* (Nakahara Moromori). In *Shiryō sanshū* [kokiroku hen] 2: 5. Zoku Gunsho Ruijū Kanseikai, 1968.
24. For *Funabashi* see: Itō Masayoshi, ed., *Yōkyokushū* 3: 189–199; Shimazaki, *The Boat Bridge*, in *Restless Spirits from Japanese Noh Plays of the Fourth Group: Parallel Translations with Running Commentary*. Cornell East Asia Series. Ithaca, NY: Cornell University, East Asia Program, 1995, 185–223.
25. For *Kayoi Komachi* see: Koyama Hiroshi, et al., eds., *Yōkyokushū*, 2 vols. Nihon Koten Bungaku zenshū. Vols. 33 and 34 (Shōgakukan, 1973, 1975), 2: 16, and 156n11; the confession is on 156–157. Eileen Kato, trans., "Komachi and the Hundred Nights," in *Twenty Plays of the Nō Theatre*, ed. Donald Keene (New York: Colombia University Press, 1970), 51–64.
26. Tokuda Kazuo, "Kanjin hijiri to shaji engi," 58.
27. For *Hyakuman* see: Itō Masayoshi, ed., *Yōkyokushū* 1: 149–159.
28. *Kanmon nikki*, Ōei 25 (1418) /3/12.
29. Sasaki Kōshō, "Chūsei ni okeru chihō shaji no kanjin," 85.

5. BEAUTIFUL TEMPLE BOYS AND THE EMPEROR SYSTEM

1. *Kinjiki*, in *Mishima Yukio zenshū: ketteiban* [hereafter *MYZ*], 44 vols. (Shinchōsha, 2000–2006), 3: 91–92; Mishima Yukio, *Forbidden Colors*, trans. Alfred H. Marks (New York: Knopf, 1968), 64–65. Eshin (Genshin; 942–1017), a Tendai monk who practiced austerities on Mount Hiei, is the author of *Ōjōyōshū* (The essentials of salvation),

an influential work outlining the six stages of rebirth (*Rokudō*) and promoting devotion to Amida Buddha and the recitation of the *nembutsu* as a means to attain rebirth in the Pure Land presided over by the Buddha.

2. Kon Tōkō, "Chigo," *Kon Tōkō daihyōsaku senshū* 5: 113–139 (Yomiuri Shinbunsha, 1973).
3. Mishima Yukio, "Chūsei ni okeru issatsujin jōshūsha no nokoseru tetsugakuteki nikki no bassui," in Saeki Shōichi et al., eds., *Mishima Yukio zenshū* 1 (Shinchōsha, 1975), 403–416. See also *MYZ* 16: 167–206.
4. *Reizei-ke ryū Ise monogatari shō*, a commentary on *Ise monogatari* connected to the Reizei-family lineage, dates from before 1300. Katagiri Yōichi, ed., *Ise monogatari no kenkyū shiryō hen* (Meiji Shoin, 1969), 293.
5. Tōno Haruyuki, "Nikki ni miru Fujiwara Yorinaga no danshoku kankei: ōchō kizoku no vita sexualis," *Historia*, no. 84 (1979): 15–29.

    The meaning of *bin o hasamu* (translated as "bound their sidelocks") in *Ama no mokuzu* is unclear.
6. *Tsurezuregusa* (section 225). Kanda Hideo et al., eds. *Hōjōki, Tsurezuregusa, Shōbōgenzō zuimonki, Tannishō*, Nihon Koten Bungaku Zenshū (Shōgakukan, 1971). Ō no Hisasuke was a court musician who died in 1295 at age 82.
7. Yoshimura Shigeki, "Jōkō seiji no jissō," Tennō no rekishi. *Shin Nihon rekishi* 7, 183–204 (Fukumura Shoten, 1955), 200.
8. Yamaori Tetsuo, *Tennō no shūkyōteki ken'i to wa nanika* (Kawade Shobō Shinsha. 1990), 58.
9. Kawai Hayao, "Kojiki shinwa ni okeru chūkū kōzō," *Bungaku* (April 1980): 62–71.
10. Kuroda Toshio, *Nihon chūsei no kokka to shūkyō* (Iwanami Shoten, 1975), 457.
11. Kuroda Toshio, *Jisha seiryoku: mō hitotsu no chūsei shakai* (Iwanami Shoten, 1980), 44–45.
12. Abe Yasurō, "Chūsei ōken to chūsei Nihongi: sokuihō to sanshu no jingi setsu o megurite," *Nihon bungaku* 34 (May 1985): 31–48.
13. A detailed examination of the connection between the Jidō legend and the origins of the medieval Tendai imperial accession protocol is offered by Itō Masayoshi, "Jidō setsuwa kō," *Kokugo kokubun* 49 (November 1980): 1–32; and Abe Yasurō, "Jidō setsuwa no keisei," pts. 1 and 2, *Kokugo kokubun* 53 (August–September 1984): 1–29 and 30–56.

14. *Taiheiki* (chap. 13), in Gotō Tanji and Kamada Kisaburō, eds. *Taiheiki*. 3 vols. Nihon Koten Bungaku Taikei 34–36 (Iwanami Shoten, 1960–1962), 2: 13–15. *Gāthā* are Buddhist chants or hymns. In "Jidō setsuwa kō" (11), Itō lists the eight verses from the Lotus Sutra as follows:

CHAPTER 2 "EXPEDIENT DEVICES" (P. 34)

Within the Buddha-lands of the ten directions
There is the Dharma of only One Vehicle.

CHAPTER 14 "COMFORTABLE CONDUCT" (P. 212)

Observing that all dharmas have nothing whatsoever,
Being quite like empty space. . . .

CHAPTER 16 "THE LIFE-SPAN OF THE THUS COME ONE" (P. 244)

For the Buddha's Word is not vain.
As a physician skilled in expedient devices. . . .

CHAPTER 25 "THE GATEWAY TO EVERYWHERE OF THE BODHISATTVA HE WHO OBSERVES THE SOUNDS OF THE WORLD" (P. 319)

His benevolent eye beholding the beings,
He is happiness accumulated, a sea incalculable.

Leon Hurvitz, trans., *Scripture of the Lotus Blossom of the Fine Dharma* (*The Lotus Sutra*) (New York: Columbia University Press, 1976). The Japanese title of chapter 25—Kanzeon bosatsu *fumonbon*—is commonly abbreviated to *Fumonbon* (translated in this chapter as "The Gateway to Everywhere").

15. *Shokoku ikken hijiri monogatari* (by Ryōkai), ed. Kyōto Daigaku Bungakubu Kokugogaku Kokubungaku Kenkyūshitsu. Kyōto Daigaku

Kokugo Kokubun shiryō sōsho 29 (Kyoto: Rinsen Shoten, 1981), 30–31. The Hiei shrine deity Jūzenji is an avatar of the bodhisattva Jizō.

16. Abe Yasurō, "Jidō setsuwa to chigo," pt. 1, *Kanze* (October 1985): 26–27.
17. For a discussion of the various texts and published excerpts see Komatsu Shigemi, "Kaisetsu: *Ashibiki-e* no ryūkō to kyōju," in *Ashibiki-e*, ed. Komatsu Shigemi. Zoku Nihon Emaki Taisei 20 (Chūō Kōronsha, 1983), 84–101, especially 90–96.
18. Nan-yüeh (Jp = Nangaku) was another name for Hui-ssu (515–577), the second patriarch of the T'ien-t'ai (Tendai) sect in China.
19. Komatsu Shigemi, "Kaisetsu," 87. The anecdote about *Tsunemasa* can be found in Takagi Ichinosuke et al., eds., *Heike monogatari*, 2 vols. Nihon Koten Bungaku Taikei 32 and 33 (Iwanami Shoten, 1959, 1960), 2: 105; see Helen Craig McCullough, trans., *The Tale of the Heike* (Stanford, CA: Stanford University Press, 1988), 247–249.
20. Komatsu's transcription of the passage from the 1450 manuscript *Chigo kanjō shi* (Private initiation of catamites) is located in Komatsu Shigemi, "Kaisetsu," 92.
21. *Honba*, *MYZ* 13: 607–608; Mishima Yukio, *Runaway Horses*, trans. Michael Gallagher (New York: Knopf, 1973), 213.
22. The passage from *Chigo kanjō shiki* (A private record of the initiation of chigo) quoted here is based on an unpublished transcription; see Komatsu Shigemi, "Kaisetsu," 94–96.
23. Mishima Yukio, "Seiteki henshitsu kara seijiteki henshitsu e [A picture of sexual transformation to political transformation]," *MYZ* 36: 100.

This editor's note provides context for the scene that Mishima describes, and on which Matsuoka bases his comparison in the following paragraph: *The Damned* (1969) takes place in Germany in 1934, as Hitler rises to power. The film's subtitle, *Götterdämmerung*, comes from the last cycle of *Der Ring* by Richard Wagner, whose fierce antisemitism is well documented. Visconti sets the scene Mishima describes here during the Night of the Long Knives massacre, a historical event that took place at the Bad Weissee resort hotel in Bavaria from June 30 to July 2, 1934, and during which key members of the Sturmabteilung (SA, or Brownshirts), and many others who were suspected of plotting to overthrow the Nazi regime, were killed. In Visconti's telling, the scene begins at a lakeside gathering of nude gay men. A young man in drag (Mishima's "half-naked youth in female attire") hears a procession of black sedans approaching, from which armed SS men emerge and make their way to the hotel. Visconti then stages a riotous male bacchanal that turns deadly when the SS men turn their machine-guns on all SA present, and an SA officer and a teenage boy found in bed together are immediately executed. See Christopher Sharrett, "Review of *The Damned*," *Cineaste* 47, no. 1 (Winter 2021): 63–65.

24. *Aki no yo no nagamonogatari* (Eisei bunko), Muromachi jidai monogatari taisei, [*MJMT*] 1: 313. For a translation of the story using a different text; see Margaret H. Childs, trans., "A Long Tale for an Autumn Night," in Margaret H. Childs, *Chigo Monogatari*: Love Stories or Buddhist Sermons?" *Monumenta Nipponica* 35, no. 2 (1980): 132–151, The allusion is to a poem by Bo Juyi in Hakushi monju (Boshi wenji) that is included in *Wakan rōeishū* (no. 115), an eleventh-century collection of Japanese and Chinese verses.

25. Mishima Yukio, "Chūsei ni okeru ichi satsujin jōshūsha," 406. The association of emperors with yūgen is expressed by Jien in the section of *Gukanshō* on Emperor Go-Sanjō: *Gukanshō*, ed. Okami Masao and Akamatsu Toshihide. Nihon Koten Bungaku Taikei 86 (Iwanami Shoten), 1964, 194.

26. *Kinjiki*, 254; Mishima Yukio, *Forbidden Colors*, 184. For the quotation from *Yama no oto*, see Kawabata Yasunari, *Kawabata Yasunari zenshū* 12 (Shinchōsha, 1980), 333–334; Kawabata Yasunari, *The Sound of the Mountain*, trans. Edward G. Seidensticker (New York: Knopf, 1970, Berkley Medallion Edition, 1971), 74–75. Mishima's comment was published in Shibusawa Tatsuhiko, *Mishima Yukio oboegaki* (Rippū Shobō, 1983), 196.

6. ZEAMI AND THE GRACEFUL AURA OF A BOY'S FIGURE

1. Kōsai Tsutomu, "Koshi yūfū," *Zeshi sankyū* (Wan'ya Shoten, 1979), 56–63. Kōsai's conclusion is based on a comparison between the sketch of the boy in *Nikyoku santai ningyō zu* and that of a chigo in the Buddhist text *Kenro seiyo*. Although Zeami's own copy of *Nikyoku santai*

ningyō zu has been lost, his vision of chigo can be grasped from his son-in-law Konparu Zenchiku's transcription, which is considered a faithful copy.

2. Fukuda Hideichi, "Zeami to Yoshimoto," *Geinōshi kenkyū* 10 (July 1965): 46–50; Nihon Bungaku Kenkyū Shiryō Kankōkai, ed. *Yōkyoku, kyogen* (Yūseidō, 1981), 33–40.

3. The fragmentary document was introduced by Ijichi Tetsuo, "Higashiyama Go-Bunkobon 'Fuchiki' o shōkai shite, chūsei no waka, renga, sarugaku no koto ni oyobu," *Kokubungaku kenkyū* 35 (March 1967): 32–48. The translation here has been changed using Matsuoka Shinpei's article "Zeami to Tōdaiji Kyōben," *Zeami: Chūsei no geijutsu to bunka* 1 (January 2002): 199–213.

4. See Omote Akira, "Yoshimoto shōsoku kotoba' shōkō," in *Nōgakushi shinkō* 2 (Wan'ya Shoten, 1986), 133–137.

5. Hidenaga's diary entries are quoted by Ōi Minobu in an essay on the relationship between flower arranging and the annual Tanabata festival. See Ōi Minobu, "Chūsei ni okeru tachibana rikka seiritsu no kiban—toku ni tanabata hana-awase ni tsuite," *Nihon Joshi Daigaku kiyō*, bungaku bu 11 (March 1962): 55–72.

6. Sanjō Kintada, *Gogumai ki*, Eiwa 4 (1378) /6/7.

7. See Ijichi Tetsuo, "Zeami to Nijō Yoshimoto to renga to sarugaku," in Nihon Bungaku Kenkyū Shiryō Kankōkai, ed., *Yōkyoku, kyōgen* (Yūseidō, 1981), 29.

8. *Tango monogurui*: Yokomichi Mario and Omote Akira, eds., *Yōkyokushū*, 2 vols., in Nihon Koten Bungaku Taikei, vols. 40 and 41 (Iwanami Shoten, 1960, 1963), 1: 203.

9. *Boki ekotoba*, ed. Komatsu Shigemi, Zoku Nihon Emaki Taisei 4: 70 (Chūō Kōronsha, 1985). For *Sendenshō*, see Kudō Masanobu, *Ikebana no seiritsu to hatten*, Nihon Ikebana Bunkashi, vol. 1 (Kyoto: Dōhōsha, 1992), 179 and 180. The *Kōyōki* diary entries are quoted in Ōi Minobu, "Chūsei ni okeru tachibana rikka seiritsu no kiban," 55–72.

10. Ōi Minobu, "Chūsei ni okeru tachibana rikka seiritsu no kiban" 69. Ōi also notes that the famous flower-arrangement master Bon'yū had once been a *kasshiki*. The *Kanmon nikki* diary entry is dated Ōei 32 (1425) / intercalary Sixth Month /22.

11. Nijō Yoshimoto, *Kyūshū mondō*, in Nose Asaji, *Renga kenkyū* 7 (Shibunkaku Shuppan, 1982), 340; for *Jūmon saihishō* see Kidō Saizō and

Imoto Nōichi, eds., *Renga ronshū, haironshū*, in Nihon Koten Bungaku Taikei 66 (Iwanami Shoten, 1969), 115.

12. For the description of young Murasaki and the passage likening her later in life to a mountain cherry tree see: Edward G. Seidensticker, trans., *The Tale of Genji*, 2 vols. (New York: Knopf, 1976), 1: 88 and 458, respectively; Abe Akio et al., eds., *Genji monogatari*, 6 vols., in Nihon Koten Bungaku Zenshū 12–17 (Shōgakukan, 1970–1976), 1: 281 and 3: 257.

13. Margaret H. Childs, trans., "The Story of Kannon's Manifestation as a Youth," in *Partings at Dawn: An Anthology of Japanese Gay Literature*, ed. Stephen D. Miller (San Francisco: Gay Sunshine Press, 1996), 31–35; *Chigo kannon engi*, in Komatsu Shigemi, ed., *Taima mandera emaki, Chigo kannon engi*, Nihon Emaki Taisei 24 (Chūō Kōronsha, 1979), plates 38–72; text, 156–159. The first meeting between the chigo and the monk is depicted in the color plates on 48–49. For the comment in *Toribeyama monogatari*, *MJMT* 10: 166–167.

14. Margaret H. Childs, trans., "The Tale of Genmu," in Margaret H. Childs, *Rethinking Sorrow: Revelatory Tales of Late Medieval Japan* (Ann Arbor: Center for Japanese Studies, University of Michigan, 1991), 34. *Genmu monogatari*, *MJMT* 4: 402.

15. *Bun'an dengaku nō ki* (Account of dengaku from the Bun'an era [1444–1449]): Ueki Yukinobu, ed., *Dengaku, sarugaku*, in Nihon Shomin Bunka Shūsei 2 (San'ichi Shobō, 1974), 154; the second quote is from 155.

16. According to *Enmai-za kabe-gaki* (The Enmai troupe's wall writings) members of the children's troupe who were chigo received special treatment comparable to members of the adult troupe. Omote Akira and Itō Masayoshi, eds., *Konparu kodensho shūsei* (Wan'ya Shoten, 1969), 312.

17. For a translation and discussion of *Izutsu* (*The Well-Cradle*) see Royall Tyler, ed. and trans., *Japanese Nō Dramas* (London: Penguin, 1992), 120–132.

18. Omote Akira, "Kadensho to hana no densho to motogi to," *Nōgakushi shinkō* 1: 326–329 (Wan'ya Shoten, 1979). The passage regarding flower arrangements in the early (*kohon*) *Fūshikaden* text is located in Okuda Isao et al., eds., *Rengaronshū, nōgakuronshū, haironshū*, in Nihon Koten Bungaku Zenshū 88 (Shōgakukan, 2001), 278, n5.

19. Nose Asaji, *Yūgenron*, 148 (Kawade Shobō, 1944). Yoshimoto, *Jūmon saihishō*, 111. The *Renga jūyō* passage can be found in Ijichi Tetsuo, ed, *Renga ronshū*, 2 vols. Iwanami Bunko (Iwanami Shoten, 1953, 1956), 1: 102.
20. The word *shiore* is the nominal form of the verb *shioreru* ("become moist or wilt"). The examples introduced in the text include the perfective verbal form (*shioretaru*), which functions as an adjective, and *uchi-shioretetaru* (the prefix "uchi" is an intensifier).
21. Konishi Jin'ichi, *Nōgakuron kenkyū*, Haniwa Sensho 10 (Haniwa Shobō, 1961), 99–100. The treatise by Yoshimoto's student is called *Bontōan hentōsho* (Bontōan's replies).
22. *Aki no yo no nagamonogatari* (Eiwa-bon) *MJMT* 1: 240–241. Margaret H. Childs, trans., "A Long Tale for an Autumn Nigh,." in Margaret H. Childs, "Chigo Monogatari: Love Stories or Buddhist Sermons?" *Monumenta Nipponica* 35, no. 2 (1980): 139.
23. *Tamura no sōshi*, *MJMT* 9, first and second examples on 82 and 89, respectively.

7. THE POETICS OF SPACE IN NOH

1. See Yokomichi Mario and Omote Akira, *Yōkyokushū*, 2 vols. Nihon Koten Bungaku Taikei, vols. 40 and 41 (Iwanami Shoten, 1960, 1963), 1: 456; and Kenneth Yasuda, trans., *Masterworks of the Nō Theater* (Bloomington: Indiana University Press, 1989), 339–340. *Ageuta* are rhythmical segments that begin in a high range and typically have a regular 7-5 rhythm following an initial 5-syllable line.
2. *Furu*: Zeami Motokiyo, *Zeami jihitsu nōhon shū: kōtei hen*, ed. Omote Akira (Wan'ya Shoten, 1997), 171–179; Royall Tyler, *To Hallow Genji: A Tribute to Noh* (Arthur Nettleton, 2013), 49–59.
3. *Tōru*: Yokomichi Mario and Omote Akira, *Yōkyokushū* 1: 299–300. The literal meaning of the Japanese place-names (translated in parentheses) is woven into the original narrative. See Yasuda, *Masterworks of the Nō Theater*, 470–475.
4. The first four lines of a poem by Ariwara no Motokata (*Kokinshū*, "Love," I, 473) have been woven into the text:

| Otowayama | Like Otowa (Rumor) Mountain, |
| oto ni kikitsutsu | I have heard about |

ausaka no	the Osaka (Meeting Slope)
seki no konata ni	Barrier, while living
toshi o furu ka na	on this side for many years.

5. An allusion to a poem by Fujiwara no Shunzei in the seventh imperial anthology Senzaishū ("Autumn," I: 259):

Yūsareba	When evening descends
nobe no akikaze	the autumn wind blowing across the fields
mi ni shimite	pierces the soul:
uzura naku nari	a quail plaintively cries
fukakusa no sato	in Fukakusa village.

The last line has been changed to Fukakusayama (Mount Fukakusa). An *uta* is a type of chant that does not have a fixed form. The following *rongi* is a rhythmical song consisting of a discussion between the shite and a secondary actor or the chorus, which sings the last part alone.

6. The first three lines of a poem by Ariwara no Narihira in the *Kokinshū* ("Miscellaneous I," 871) are woven into the text:

Ōhara ya	In Ōhara
Oshio no yama mo	Mount Oshio, too,
kyō koso wa	today must
kamiyo no koto mo	bring back memories
omoiizurame	of the age of the gods.

The headnote states that the poem was composed during a visit to Ōharano shrine by the Nijō empress while she still bore the title Mother of the Crown Prince.

7. *Hanjo*: Itō Masayoshi, ed., *Yōkyokushū*, 3 vols. Shinchō Nihon Koten Shūsei (Shinchōsha, 1983, 1986, 1988), 3: 119–120; Lady Han: Royall Tyler, trans., *Japanese Nō Dramas* (London: Penguin, 1992), 113. A *sashi* ("recitatives") is a segment consisting of unmetered poetry that is sung fluidly with a free rhythm.

8. *Hanagatami*: Itō Masayoshi, ed., *Yōkyokushū* 3: 106–107. A *kakeai* ("heightened exchange") is a series of lines that two actors share, which become increasing shorter before being taken over by the chorus.
9. *Ashikari*: Yokomichi Mario and Omote Akira, eds., *Yōkyokushū* 1: 360. James O'Brien, trans., *The Reed Cutter*, in *Twenty Plays of the Nō Theatre*, ed. Donald Keene (New York: Columbia University Press, 1970), 147–164.
10. *Akoya no matsu*: Yokomichi Mario and Omote Akira, eds., *Yōkyokushū* 1:149. *The Akoya Pine*: Tyler, *To Hallow Genji*, 23. The principal actor plays an old man who reappears in his true form as the God of Shiogama in act 2.
11. *Unrin'in*: Yokomichi Mario and Omote Akira, eds., *Yōkyokushū* 1: 149. Earl Jackson, Jr., trans., *Unrin'in*, in Karen Brazell, ed., *Twelve Plays of the Noh and Kyōgen Theaters*. Cornell University East Asia Papers (Ithaca, NY: Cornell University, 1988), 44.
12. Nishio Minoru equates *enken* with *kenpu* ("visual effect"): see Hisamatsu Sen'ichi and Nishio Minoru, eds., *Karonshū, nōgakuronshū*, Nihon Koten Bungaku Taikei 65 (Iwanami Shoten, 1961), 568, and suppl. n2. For Omote's remarks about enken see ZZ 126, 130, and 497.
13. Nakamura Yūjirō, "Watakushi no koten: nō butai no kūkan to Olympico gekijō," *Sōgetsu* 133 (December 1980): 28. The experiment by Jacques-Louis Barrault and Kanze Hisao took place at the Tessenkai Noh Theater in the Aoyama district of Tokyo in 1977. The symposium "Nō no butai kūkan ron" organized by the Hashi no Kai theater research group was held at the Tessenkai Noh Theater on November 21, 1980.

8. ZEAMI'S VISION OF THE ACTOR'S BODY AS A MEDIUM

1. Morisue Yoshiaki, "Tōgen Zuisen no *Shikishō* ni miru Zeami," in Nihon Bungaku Kenkyū Shiryō Sōsho Kenkyūkai, ed., *Yōkyoku, kyōgen*, Nihon bungaku kenkyū shiryō sōsho (Yūseidō, 1981), 41–46.
2. Kanze Hisao's remarks during a conversation with Watanabe Moriaki, a theater and French literature specialist, were published in Watanabe Moriaki, "Kamen no dramaturgy," in *Kamen to shintai: fukusū no kotoba*

(Asahi Shuppansha, 1978), 22. *Gigaku* was a masked dance-drama imported from the continent in the seventh century. The art form died out in the Edo period.
3. See Tsuchiya Keiichirō, "Omote: kamen, to shintai," in *Nō* (Shin'yōsha, 1989), 3–15.
4. Kanze Hisao, "Nōmen: sono uchi naru drama," in *Kamen no engi*, ed. Yokomichi Mario et al. Kanze Hisao chosakushū (Heibonsha, 1981), 2: 277–278. Zenchiku's play *Teika* is also still performed today.
5. The *kuse* section of noh plays typically consists of a short chant consisting of metered poetry in free rhythm sung by the chorus (*kuri*); a chant shared by the *shite* and the chorus (*sashi*); and the kuse.
6. Yoshimura Hitoshi, "Zeami nō geiron ni okeru kokoro to waza," *Rinrigaku nenpō* 38 (March 1989): 135–136.

9. THE ACTOR'S BASIC POSTURE AND THE ROOF-COVERED NOH STAGE

1. This chapter consists of a translation of chapter 10 from *Utage no shintai* combined with a more recent piece by Matsuoka on the history of the noh stage. See the translator's introduction.
2. See the discussion of the scenes at Odagiri, Saku, and Katase in chapter 1.
3. Kuroda Hideo, "Odori nenbutsu no gazō: shintairon no shiten kara," in Kuroda Hideo, ed., *Kaiga shiryō no yomikata*, Rekishi no yomikata 1, Shūkan Asahi hyakka Nihon no rekishi (Asahi Shinbun, July 30, 1988), 35. Dances were also performed on elevated stages at the Shijō Kyōgoku Shakadō (scroll 7; 186–187) and the aforementioned venues at Ichiya and Yodo, For the scenes at Kumi (scroll 8) and Ninomiya on the island of Awaji (scroll 11) see *Ippen shōnin eden*, ed. Komatsu Shigemi. Nihon no emaki 20, 3rd edition (Chūō Kōronsha, 1997), 211 and 294, respectively.
4. A similar attitude toward space can be found in sumo, whose roots also go back to magic to pacify earth spirits. The foot stamping of the sumo wrestler (*rikishi*) as a warm-up exercise at the start of a match harks back to the foot stamping of individuals with supernatural powers called *rikishi* who performed it to suppress evil spirits beneath the

ground. The pillar-supported roof covering the earthen ring (*dohyō*), an eighteenth-century innovation, creates a strong awareness of the earth beneath the ring. (In the Kokugikan National Sumo Hall in Tokyo, the roof is suspended from the ceiling of the arena.) The Jishū dance hut and the noh stage, however, focus more on the horizontal space created by the roof and the stage.

5. The entry in *Mansai jugō nikki* is dated Eikyō 3 (1431) /3/21. The comment in *Ōuchi mondō* about a roof over the bridgeway during the Bun'an era in the 1440s precedes the one cited later in this chapter from the Eikyō era (1429–1441); see *Ōuchi mondō*, Gunsho ruijū, v. 22 buke bu (no. 411), rev. 3rd ed., Zoku Gunsho Ruijū Kanseikai (1982): 445.
6. *Mansai jugō nikki*: Eikyō 1 (1429) /9/28, and Eikyō 2 (1430) /4/23.
7. The folding screens depicting scenes in and around the capital (*Rakuchū rakugai zu byōbu*) are in the National Museum of Japanese History. For a reproduction, see Koyama Hiroshi et al., *Nō kyōgen*, Zusetsu Nihon no Koten 12 (Shūeisha, 1980), color plate 209 (133).
8. Suda Atsuo, *Nihon gekijō shi no kenkyū* (Sagami Shobō, 1957), 194. Professor Matsuoka notes that another important consideration in the placement of the bridgeway presumably concerned the fact that most people are right-handed.
9. Hosokawa Yūsai, *Nō kuden no kikigaki*, in *Hosokawa gobu densho*, Hosokawa Shūsei 11 (Wan'ya Shoten, 1973), 35.
10. The *Kannō-zu byōbu* screen is owned by the Kobe City Museum. See Koyama Hiroshi et al., *Nō kyōgen*, plate 214 (138–139).
11. The noh flute can be heard once the noh stage is visible. The human voice is still inaudible when the sound of the *ōtsuzumi* hip drum can finally be heard.
12. Kanze Hisao, "Kokoro yori kokoro ni tsutauru hana" [The flower transmitted from heart to heart], in *Kamen no engi*, ed. Yokomichi Mario et al. Kanze Hisao chosakushū (Heibonsha, 1981), 150.
13. *Hachijō-bon kadensho:* see Hayashiya Tatsusaburō, ed., *Kodai chūsei geijutsuron*, Nihon Shisō Taikei 23 (Iwanami Shoten, 1973), 597. The comment about *Hyakuman* is on 600.
14. For the comment by Ōkura Toraakira see: *Waranbe-gusa*, Hayashiya Tatsusaburō, ed., *Kodai chūsei geijutsuron*, Nihon Shisō Taikei 23, 676. Sumo wrestlers (*rikishi*) also create the basic stance by lowering their

hips and use sliding steps (*suri-ashi*). The latter forms the foundation of the offensive and defensive moves.

15. *Zempō zōtan*, in Omote Akira and Itō Masayoshi, eds., *Konparu kodensho shūsei* (Wan'ya Shoten, 1969), 470 and 458. Zempō (b. 1454) was Zenchiku's grandson.
16. Omote Akira, "Nōgaku to budō," pt. 3, *Gekkan budō* (Nihon Budōkan, March 1976): 24–28. The martial arts guide *Shinkage-ryū heihō mokuroku no koto* (The new shadow tradition's catalogue of methods of war) was presented to Ujikatsu by the master swordsman Yagyū Muneyoshi (Sekishūsai).

GLOSSARY

ageuta (high range chant) A type of noh chant that begins in a high register. It generally consists of poetic lines divided into 7 and 5 syllables and is set to a congruent rhythm.

Amida Buddha Principal deity worshipped in Pure Land Buddhism, Amida Buddha presides over the Western Paradise.

Asura (*Ashura*) Sanskrit term for unruly warlike demigods, who ranked below heavenly beings and humans in the Six Realms of Transmigration. Second-category noh plays depicting the ghosts of warriors are referred to as *shura mono*. See *Rokudō*.

Avalokiteśvara See *Kannon*.

binzasara (rattle) Folk instrument made of short thin wooden strips tied together at one end with a cord. It is held in both hands and shaken to produce a sharp dry clacking sound.

chigo Child, temple attendant, catamite.

congruent rhythm (*Hyōshi au*) A style of noh singing in which the syllables of the text are sung in relationship to an eight-beat rhythm.

gāthā Buddhist chants or hymns.

Gongen (Incarnation) Avatar of a buddha in the form of an indigenous Japanese deity.

goryō-e Buddhist service for the repose of vengeful spirits.

Guse Kannon The World Savior Avalokiteśvara.

hakama Loose pleated ankle-length trousers. Very long ones that extend in back like a train are called *nagabakama*.

hijiri **(holy men or saints)** Religious figures unaffiliated with a religious establishment who traveled around the country practicing austerities and praying for the souls of the dead.

hisashi Aisle-like areas surrounding the center room in a temple building.

hokku **(opening verse)** A 5-7-5-syllable verse that begins a *renga* sequence.

issei **(entry song)** Short noh chant with a regular poetic meter that is set to a free rhythm. It is often performed by the *shite* when he first enters the stage.

Jishū (Time School) Branch of Pure Land Buddhism founded by the holy man Ippen who promoted the practice of invoking Amida Buddha's name while dancing in a circle.

Jizō Bodhisattva who relieves the suffering of sinners who have gone to hell.

jōza Fixed position nearest the bridgeway on a noh stage. See diagram of noh stage.

kaisho **(meeting place)**

kanjin Evangelism; public campaigns to raise funds to build and repair temples and shrines, make Buddhist statues, and the like.

Kannon (Avalokiteśvara) Bodhisattva of Compassion. Attendant of Amida Buddha.

kasa **(deep-brimmed hat)** Large low-brimmed hat woven out of straw or a similar material.

kasagi renga Linked verse performed while wearing a kasa to hide one's identity.

King Enma (ruler of hell) Judge who determines whether the dead should be punished in hell or rewarded for their deeds in the previous life.

koshi-tsuzumi Two-sided drum fastened at the hip or hung from around the neck.

Kūkai Buddhist monk, posthumously known as Kōbō Daishi, who founded the Shingon sect in Japan.

kuse The aural high point of a play, a kuse is a kind of narrative song. It is set to a congruent rhythm and is sung by the chorus except for a single line assigned to the *shite*.

Kusemai Popular medieval entertainment with a lively rhythm consisting of a narrative song sung rhythmically to the lively beat of a drum.

Monzeki Buddhist monk of imperial or aristocratic birth; also used to refer to the temple in which he lived.

Mount Hiei Headquarters of the Tendai Sect; located northeast of Kyoto.

naka-shōmen **(middle front)** Spectators' seats located between the *shōmen* (stage front) and *waki-shōmen* (seats facing the chorus). See diagram of noh stage.

Nambokuchō Age of the Northern and Southern Courts (1336–1392) Period when a schism between two imperial lineages led to the establishment of a Northern Court in Kyoto and a Southern Court to the south in Yoshino (Nara).

nenbutsu Invocation of Amida Buddha's name (*namu amida butsu*).

odori-nembutsu Dance performed while chanting Amida Buddha's name.

renga **(linked verse)** Poetry sequence made up alternating 5-7-5 and 7-7 syllable verses. Typically, each verse was composed by a different poet.

rokudō (six paths)   Six realms of existence in Buddhism arranged hierarchically: hell, hungry ghosts, beasts, warrior demons (ashura), humans, and heavenly beings. Rebirth in each realm is determined by one's deeds in the previous life.

rongi (discussion)   A noh segment in metered verse set to congruent rhythm, a rongi consists of an exchange between two characters, or a character and the chorus. The last part is sung by the chorus.

Saichō   Buddhist monk, posthumously known as Dengyō Daishi, who founded the Tendai sect in Japan.

Sannō Gongen (Mountain King)   Guardian deity of Mount Hiei, avatar of Shakyamuni Buddha, the Historical Buddha.

sasara   Folk instrument consisting of two bamboo sticks, one of which is rubbed against the other.

sashi (recitative)   Noh chant with a free rhythm often used during the shite's introductory scene, or before the kuse. It is sung in a clear flowing manner and may describe a scene or express inner feelings.

Shakyamuni   The Historical Buddha.

shiore   A word denoting moistness or a wilted state; acquired the meaning of gentle charm and grace in medieval aesthetics.

shite   Principal actor in a noh play.

shoin   Architectural style featuring elements such as an alcove (*tokonoma*), shelves, a desk, tatami flooring.

shōmen (stage front)   See diagram of noh stage.

taregami (flowing locks)   A child's hairstyle. Another name for a chigo in the middle ages.

tsure   Attendant of a principal or secondary actor in noh.

vajra (diamond or thunderbolt)   Buddhist ritual object.

waka   Thirty-one-syllable poems arranged in a sequence of 5, 7, 5, 7, and 7 syllables.

waki   Secondary actor in a noh play.

waki-shōmen   Spectators' seats on the side of the stage facing the chorus. See diagram of noh stage.

waki-za   Waki's fixed position near the pillar at stage front (left).

yūgen   Graceful beauty; refinement and grace.

BIBLIOGRAPHY

WORKS IN WESTERN LANGUAGES

Blacker, Carmen. *The Catalpa Bow: A Study of Shamanistic Practices in Japan*. New York: Routledge, 2000.

Brazell, Karen, ed. *Twelve Plays of the Noh and Kyōgen Theaters*. Cornell University East Asia Papers. Ithaca, NY: Cornell University, 1988.

Childs, Margaret, H. "The Story of Kannon's Manifestation as a Youth." In *Partings at Dawn: An Anthology of Japanese Gay Literature*, ed. Stephen D. Miller, 31–35. San Francisco: Gay Sunshine Press, 1996.

——, trans. "A Long Tale for an Autumn Night." In Margaret H. Childs, "*Chigo Monogatari*: Love Stories or Buddhist Sermons?" *Monumenta Nipponica* 35, no. 2 (1980): 127–151.

——, trans. "The Tale of Genmu." In Margaret H. Childs. *Rethinking Sorrow: Revelatory Tales of Late Medieval Japan*, 31–52. Ann Arbor: Center for Japanese Studies, University of Michigan, 1991.

Claudel, Paul. *L'oiseau noir dans le soleil levant*, in *Oeuvres en prose*. Éditions Gallimard, 1965.

De Poorter, Erika. *Zeami's Talks on Sarugaku*. Amsterdam: J. C. Gieben, 1986.

Hare, Thomas. *Zeami: Performance Notes*. New York: Columbia University Press, 2008.

Hurvitz, Leon, trans. *Scripture of the Lotus Blossom of the Fine Dharma*. New York: Columbia University Press, 1976.

Grossberg, Kenneth A., and Kanamoto Nobuhisa, trans. *Laws of the Muromachi Bakufu: Kenmu shiki and the Muromachi Tsuika-hō*. Tokyo: Monumenta Nipponica and Sophia University Press, 1981.

Kato, Eileen, trans. *Komachi and the Hundred Nights*. In *Twenty Plays of the Nō Theatre*. Ed. Donald Keene, 51–64. New York: Columbia University Press, 1970.

Kawabata Yasunari. *The Sound of the Mountain*. Trans. Edward G. Seidensticker. New York: Knopf, 1970, Berkley Medallion Edition, 1971.

Keene, Donald, ed. *Twenty Plays of the Nō Theatre*. New York: Columbia University Press, 1970.

Mishima Yukio. *Forbidden Colors*. Trans. Alfred H. Marks. New York: Knopf, 1968.

———. *Runaway Horses*. Trans. Michael Gallagher. New York: Knopf, 1973.

McCullough, Helen Craig, comp. and ed. *Classical Japanese Prose: An Anthology*. Stanford, CA: Stanford University Press, 1990.

McCullough, Helen Craig, trans. *The Tale of the Heike*. Stanford, CA: Stanford University Press, 1988.

Morrell, Robert, trans. *Sand and Pebbles: The Tales of Mujū Ichien*. Albany: State University of New York Press, 1985.

Kyoko Nakamura. *Miraculous Stories from the Japanese Buddhist Tradition*. Cambridge, MA: Harvard University Press, 1973.

O'Brien, James, trans. *The Reed Cutter*. In *Twenty Plays of the Nō Theatre*. Ed. Donald Keene, 147–164. New York: Columbia University Press, 1970.

Raz, Jacob. "Popular Entertainment and Politics: The Great *Dengaku* of 1096," *Monumenta Nipponica* 40, no. 3 (Autumn 1985): 283–298.

Saku Jubitsu, "Account of a Pilgrimage to the Great Shrine of Ise," in *Travelers of a Hundred Ages: The Japanese as Revealed Through 1,000 Years of Diaries*, trans. Donald Keene, 73–75. New York: Columbia University Press, 1999.

Sarugaku dangi. See De Poorter, Erika. *Zeami's Talks on Sarugaku*.

Shimazaki, Chifumi. *Troubled Souls from Japanese Noh Plays of the Fourth Group*. Cornell East Asia Series. Ithaca, NY: Cornell University, East Asia Program, 1998.

———. *Restless Spirits from Japanese Noh Plays of the Fourth Group: Parallel Translations with Running Commentary*. Cornell East Asia Series. Ithaca, NY: Cornell University East Asia Program, 1995.

Seidensticker, Edward G., trans. *The Tale of Genji*. 2 vols. New York: Knopf, 1976.
Tyler, Royall, ed. and trans. *Japanese Nō Dramas*. London: Penguin, 1992.
Tyler, Royall. *To Hallow Genji: A Tribute to Noh*. Arthur Nettleton, 2013.
Yasuda, Kenneth. *Masterworks of the Nō Theater*. Bloomington: Indiana University Press, 1989.

JAPANESE SOURCES

Unless otherwise noted, the place of publication is Tokyo.

The following abbreviations are used in parenthetical citations in the text (in lieu of citing the work in an endnote), or alternately in the endnotes themselves after the first full citation per chapter.

ZZ *Zeami, Zenchiku*. Ed. Katō Shūichi and Omote Akira. *Nihon shisō taikei*. Vol. 24. Iwanami Shoten, 1974.
MJMT *Muromachi jidai monogatari taisei*. Ed. Yokoyama Shigeru and Matsumoto Ryūshin. 13 vols. Kadokawa Shoten, 1981.
MYZ *Mishima Yukio zenshū: ketteiban*. 44 vols. Shinchōsha, 2000–2006.*
SNKBT *Konjaku monogatari shū*. Ed. Ikegami Jun'ichi. 5 vols. Shin Nihon Koten Bungaku Taikei 33–37. Iwanami Shoten, 1993–1999.

Abe Akio et al., eds. *Genji monogatari*. 6 vols. Nihon Koten Bungaku Zenshū 12–17. Shōgakukan, 1970–1976.
Abe Takeshi and Ōta Junzō, eds. *Harima no kuni Ikaruga no shō shiryō*. Yagi Shoten, 1970.
Abe Yasurō. "Chūsei ōken to chūsei Nihongi: sokui hō to sanshu no jingi setsu o megurite." *Nihon bungaku* 34 (May 1985): 31–48.
———. "Jidō setsuwa no keisei." Pts. 1 and 2. *Kokugo kokubun* 53 (August–September 1984): 1–29; 30–56.
———. "Jidō setsuwa to chigo." Pt. 1. *Kanze* (October 1985): 26–34.

---

*An older edition of *Mishima Yukio zenshū* is cited in the chapter 5 without abbreviation; see *Mishima Yukio zenshū*. Ed. Saeki Shōichi. 1: 403–416. Shinchōsha, 1975.

Amano Fumio. "Nō to bukkyō: shūra o megutte." *Kokubungaku kaishaku to kanshō* (Dec. 1983): 135–137
Angya zuihitsu. In Kokubun Tōhō Bukkyō Sōsho, ed. Vol. 7, 413–472. Kikōbun. Kokubun Tōhō Bukkyō Sōsho Kankōkai, 1925.
Boki ekotoba. Ed. Komatsu Shigemi. Zoku Nihon Emaki Taisei 4. Chūō Kōronsha, 1985.
Chigo kannon engi. In Komatsu Shigemi, ed. *Taima mandera emaki, Chigo kannon engi*, Nihon Emaki Taisei 24. Chūō Kōronsha, 1979.
Chōjū jinbutsu giga. Ed. Komatsu Shigemi. Nihon no Emaki 6. Chūō Kōronsha, 1977.
Daisenji engi emaki. Ed. Sasaki Kazuo. Yonago: Inaba Shobō, 1971.
Daitō monogatari. Zoku Gunsho ruijū 21: 2 Kassen bu (619), rev. 3rd ed. (1972).
Fukuda Hideichi. "Zeami to Yoshimoto." *Geinōshi kenkyū* 10 (July 1965): 46–50; reprinted in Nihon Bungaku Kenkyū Shiryō Kankōkai, ed. *Yōkyoku, kyogen*, 33–40. Yūseidō, 1981.
Genmu monogatari. In Yokoyama Shigeru and Matsumoto Ryūshin, ed. Muromachi jidai monogatari taisei 4, 398–416. Kadokawa Shoten, 1976.
Gukanshō (Jien). Ed. Okami Masao and Akamatsu Toshihide. Nihon Koten Bungaku Taikei 86. Iwanami Shoten, 1964.
Gunji Masakatsu. *Fūryū no zō, sōsakuin*. Gunji Masakatsu satteishū 6. Hakusuisha, 1992.
Hagiwara Izumi. "Nō ni itaru tsuzumi no hensen." Pt. 1. *Kanze* (August 1979): 23–31.
Hayashiya Tatsusaburō, ed., *Kodai chūsei geijutsuron*, Nihon Shisō Taikei 23. Iwanami Shoten, 1973.
Hisamatsu Sen'ichi and Nishio Minoru, eds. *Karonshū, nōgakuronshū*, Nihon Koten Bungaku Taikei 65. Iwanami Shoten, 1961.
Hosokawa Yūsai, *Nō kuden no kikigaki*. In *Hosokawa gobu densho*. Hosokawa Shūsei 11. Wan'ya Shoten, 1973.
Ijichi Tetsuo. "Higashiyama Go-Bunkobon 'Fuchiki' o shōkai shite, chūsei no waka, renga, sarugaku no koto ni oyobu." *Kokubungaku kenkyū* 35 (March 1967): 32–48.
———. "Zeami to Nijō Yoshimoto to renga to sarugaku." Nihon Bungaku Kenkyū Shiryō Kankōkai, ed., *Yōkyoku, kyogen*, 28–32. Yūseidō, 1981.
Ijichi Tetsuo, ed. *Renga ronshū*. 2 vols. Iwanami Bunko. Iwanami Shoten, 1953, 1956.

Ippen Shōnin eden. Ed. Komatsu Shigemi. Nihon no Emaki 20. 3rd edition. Chūō Kōronsha, 1997.

Ise monogatari, ed. Fukui Teisuke. In *Taketori monogatari, Ise monogatari, Yamato monogatari, Heichū monogatari*. Ed. Katagiri Yōichi et al. Nihon Koten Bungaku Zenshū 8: 133–244. Shōgakukan, 1972.

Ishida Hisatoyo, ed. *Shokunin zukushi-e*. Nihon no bijutsu 132. Shibundō, 1977.

Itō Masayoshi. "Jidō setsuwa kō." *Kokugo kokubun* 49 (November 1980): 1–32.

Itō Masayoshi, ed. *Yōkyokushū*. 3 vols. Shinchō Nihon Koten Shūsei. Shinchōsha, 1983, 1986, 1988.

Iwahashi Koyata. *Geinōshi sōsetsu*. Yoshikawa Kōbunkan, 1975.

Kanai Kiyomitsu. *Tenshō kyōgen-bon zenshaku*. Kazama Shobō, 1989.

Kaneko Kinjirō. *Tsukubashū no kenkyū*. Kazama Shobō, 1965.

Kanze Hisao. "Kokoro yori kokoro ni tsutauru hana." In *Kamen no engi*. Ed. Yokomichi Mario et al. Kanze Hisao chosakushū 2: 95–168. Heibonsha, 1981.

———. "Nō men: sono uchi naru dorama." In *Kamen no engi*. Ed. Yokomichi Mario et al. Kanze Hisao chosakushū 2: 270–291. Heibonsha, 1981.

Kasamatsu Hiroshi, et al., eds. *Chūsei seiji shakai shisō*. Nihon Shisō Taikei 22. Iwanami Shoten, 1981.

Kanmon nikki (Fushimi no Miya Sadafusa [Gosukō-in]). 7 vols. Ed. Kunaichō Shoryōbu. Zushoryō Sōkan 26: 1–7. Kunaichō Shoryōbu, 2002–2014.

Katagiri Yōichi, ed. *Ise monogatari no kenkyū shiryō hen*. Meiji Shoin, 1969.

Katsumata Shizuo. *Ikki*. Iwanami Shinsho 194. Iwanami Shoten, 1982.

Kawabata Yasunari. *Senbazuru, Nami chidori, Yama no oto*. In *Kawabata Yasunari zenshū* 12: 241–541. Shinchōsha, 1980.

Kawai Hayao. "Kojiki shinwa ni okeru chūkū kōzō." *Bungaku* (April 1980): 62–71.

Kidō Saizō and Imoto Nōichi, eds. *Renga ronshū, haironshū*. Nihon Koten Bungaku Taikei 66. Iwanami Shoten, 1969.

Komatsu Shigemi. "Kaisetsu: *Ashibiki-e* no ryūkō to kyōju." In *Ashibiki-e*. Ed. Komatsu Shigemi, 84–101. Zoku Nihon Emaki Taisei 20. Chūō Kōronsha, 1983.

Kon Tōkō. "Chigo." *Kon Tōkō daihyōsaku senshū* 5: 113–139. Yomiuri Shinbunsha, 1973.

Konishi Jin'ichi. *Nōgakuron kenkyū*. Haniwa Sensho 10. Haniwa Shobō, 1961.

Konjaku monogatari shū. Ed. Ikegami Jun'ichi. 5 vols. Shin Nihon Koten Bungaku Taikei 33–37. Iwanami Shoten, 1993–1999.

Kōsai Tsutomu. "Dōbōshū zakkō." In *Zeami shinkō*, 69–96. Wan'ya Shoten, 1962.

———. "Koshi yūfū," *Zeshi sankyū.* Wan'ya Shoten, 1979.

Koyama Hiroshi et al., eds., *Nō kyōgen.* Zusetsu Nihon no Koten 12. Shūeisha, 1980.

———, eds. *Yōkyokushū*, 2 vols. Nihon Koten Bungaku zenshū. Vols. 33 and 34. Shōgakukan, 1973, 1975.

Kudō Masanobu. *Ikebana no seiritsu to hatten.* Nihon Ikebana Bunkashi. Vol. 1 Kyoto: Dōhōsha, 1992.

Kumata Jinja, ed. *Hirano hōraku renga: kako kara genzai e.* Osaka: Izumi Shoin, 1993.

Kurita Isamu. *Ippen Shōnin: Tabi no shisakusha.* Shinchōsha, 1977.

———. "Za no shisō ni tsuite: uta-awase, mono-awase to cha." *Chanoyu saijiki*, Autumn, Taiyō Collection 19 (Heibonsha, 1981): 25–30.

Kuroda Hideo, "Odori nenbutsu no gazō: shintairon no shiten kara." In Kuroda Hideo, ed., *Kaiga shiryō no yomikata*, Rekishi no yomikata 1, Shūkan Asahi hyakka Nihon no rekishi (Asahi Shinbun, July 30, 1988): 35.

Kuroda Toshio. *Jisha seiryoku: mō hitotsu no chūsei shakai.* Iwanami Shoten, 1980.

———. *Nihon chūsei no kokka to shūkyō.* Iwanami Shoten, 1975.

Kuroita Katsumi, ed. *Shintei zōho Kokushi taikei* 31.Yoshikawa Kōbunkan, 1932.

Matsuoka Shinpei. *Nō: chūsei kara no hibiki.* Kadokawa sōsho 2. Kadokawa Shoten, 1998.

———. "Nō no kūkan: Yane no aru butai," *Chūsei no tachi to toshi: micro no kū*, Asahi Hyakka Nihon no rekishi: Rekishi o yominaosu, no. 7, Asahi Shinbunsha (March 1994): 30–37.

———. "Zeami to Tōdaiji Kyōben," *Zeami: Chūsei no geijutsu to bunka* 1 (January 2002): 199–213.

Mishima Yukio. "Chūsei ni okeru issatsujin jōshūsha no nokoseru tetsugakuteki nikki no bassui." In *Mishima Yukio zenshū.* Ed. Saeki Shōichi et al. 1: 403–416. Shinchōsha, 1975.

Mishima Yukio zenshū: ketteiban. 44 vols. Shinchōsha, 2000–2006.

Morisue Yoshiaki, "Tōgen Zuisen no *Shikishō* ni miru Zeami." In *Nihon Bungaku Kenkyū Shiryō Sōsho Kenkyūkai*. Ed. *Yōkyoku, kyōgen*, 41–46. Nihon bungaku kenkyū shiryō sōsho. Yūseidō, 1981.

Moromori ki (Nakahara Moromori). In *Shiryō sanshū* [kokiroku hen], 2:5 Zoku Gunsho Ruijū Kanseikai, 1968.

Nakamura Yasuo. "Nōmen izen." *Rekishi kōron* (October 1978): 87–91.

Nakamura Yūjirō. "Watakushi no koten: nō butai no kūkan to Olympico gekijō." *Sōgetsu* 133 (December 1980): 21–28.

Nakanodō Kazunobu. "Chūsei-teki kanjin no tenkai." *Geinōshi kenkyū* 62 (1978): 12–35.

Nenjū gyōji emaki. Ed. Komatsu Shigemi. Nihon no Emaki 8. Chūō Kōronsha, 1977.

Nihon ryōiki. Ed. Izumoji Osamu. Shin Nihon Koten Bungaku Taikei 30. Iwanami Shoten 1996.

Nose Asaji, *Nōgaku genryū kō*. Iwanami Shoten, 1938.

———. *Renga kenkyū*. In *Nose Asaji chosakushū* 7. Shibunkaku Shuppan, 1982.

———. *Yūgenron*. Kawade Shobō, 1944.

Ōi Minobu. "Chūsei ni okeru tachibana rikka seiritsu no kiban—toku ni tanabata hana-awase ni tsuite." *Nihon Joshi Daigaku kiyō*, bungaku bu 11 (March 1962): 55–72.

Ōuchi mondō. Gunsho ruijū, v. 22 buke bu (no. 411). Rev. 3rd ed. Zoku Gunsho Ruijū Kanseikai (1982): 440–458.

Ōhashi Shunnō. *Ippen*. Jinbutsu Sōsho 183. Yoshikawa Kōbunkan, 1983.

Ogasawara Kyōko. "Chūsei keiraku ni okeru kanjin kōgyō: Muromachi ki." *Bungaku* 48: no 9 (Iwanami Shoten 1980): 56–71.

Okami Masao. "Mono: demono, monogi, hana no moto renga." *Kokugo kokubun* 24 (February 1955): 31–36.

Okuda Isao et al., eds. *Rengaron shū, nōgakuron shū, hairon shū*. Shin Nihon Koten Bungaku Zenshū 88. Shōgakukan, 2001.

Omote Akira. "Kadensho to hana no densho to motogi to." *Nōgakushi shinkō* 1: 326–329. Wan'ya Shoten, 1979.

———. "Nōgaku to budō," pt. 3. *Gekkan budō* (Nihon Budōkan, March 1976): 24–28.

———. "Nō no dō(on) to ji(utai)." *Kokugo to kokubungaku* 62 (April 1985): 1–17.

———. "Yoshimoto shōsoku kotoba shōkō." *Nōgakushi shinkō* 2 (Wan'ya Shoten, 1986): 129–137.

Omote Akira and Amano Fumio, eds. *Nō no rekishi*. Vol. 1 of Iwanami Kōza Nō, kyōgen. 7 vols. Iwanami Shoten, 1987–1992.
Omote Akira and Itō Masayoshi, eds. *Konparu kodensho shūsei*. Wan'ya Shoten, 1969.
Omote Akira and Katō Shūichi, eds. *Zeami, Zenchiku*. Nihon shisō taikei 24. Iwanami Shoten, 1974.
Sairei sōshi. Ed. Akai Tatsurō. Chanoyu kaiga shiryō shūsei. Heibonsha, 1992.
Saitō Hidetoshi. "Kaisho no seiritsu to sono kenchikuteki tokushoku." Ed. Murai Yasuhiko et al. In *Chanoyu no seiritsu*, ed. Nakamura Masao et al. Chadō shūkin 2, 155–164. Shōgakukan, 1984.
Sanari Kentarō, ed. *Yōkyoku taikan*. Vol 4. Meiji Shoin, 1973.
Sanjūniban shokunin uta-awase. In Mori Tōru, ed. *Ise Shin-Meisho-e utaawase, Tōhokuin shokunin utaawase emaki, Tsurugaoka hōshōe shokunin utaawase emaki, Sanjūniban shokunin uta-awase emaki*. Shinshū Nihon Emakimono Zenshū 28: 45–52, 71–80. Kadokawa Shoten, 1979.
Sasaki Kōshō. "Chūsei ni okeru chihō shaji no kanjin: Ōmi kōhoku no shaji shiryō ni yoru." *Bukkyō minzokushi no kenkyū* (Meicho Shuppan, 1987): 53–99.
——. "Nihon ryōiki ni arawareta hijiri to kanjin." In *Bukkyō minzokushi no kenkyū*, ed. Sasaki Kōshō Sensei Chosaku Kankōkai. Meicho Shuppan, 1987.
Sasaki Nobutsuna, ed. *Nihon kagaku taikei* 5. Kazama Shobō, 1957.
——. *Ryōjin hishō, Ryōjin hishō kudenshū*. Iwanami Bunko, 1933.
Satake Akihiro, ed. *Honchō monzui*. Shin Nihon Koten Bungaku Taikei 27. Iwanami Shoten, 1992.
Satō Shin'ichi and Ikeuchi Yoshisuke, eds., *Chūsei hōsei shiryōshū* 2. Iwanami Shoten, 1957.
Shibusawa Tatsuhiko. *Mishima Yukio oboegaki*. Rippū Shobō, 1983.
Shokoku ikken hijiri monogatari (by Ryōkai). Ed. Kyōto Daigaku Bungakubu Kokugogaku Kokubungaku Kenkyūshitsu. Kyōto Daigaku Kokugo Kokubun shiryō sōsho 29. Kyoto: Rinsen Shoten, 1981.
Suda Atsuo, *Nihon gekijōshi no kenkyū*. Sagami shobō, 1957.
Taiheiki. In Gotō Tanji and Kamada Kisaburō, eds. *Taiheiki*. 3 vols. Nihon Koten Bungaku Taikei 34–36. Iwanami Shoten, 1960–1962.
Takagi Ichinosuke et al., eds. *Heike monogatari*. 2 vols. Nihon Koten Bungaku Taikei 32 and 33. Iwanami Shoten, 1959, 1960.

Takano Tatsuyuki. *Kabu ongyoku kōsetsu*. Rokugōkan, 1915.
Takayama Sōzei, *Kokon rendanshū*. Ed. Ikeda Takashi. In *Sōzei rengaronshū*. Koten Bunko 85. Koten Bunko, 1954.
Takeuchi Hideo. *Tenmangū*. Nihon rekishi sōsho 19. Yoshikawa Kōbunkan, 1968.
Tamura no sōshi. Yokoyama Shigeru and Matsumoto Ryūshin, eds. Muromachi jidai monogatari taisei 9. Kadokawa Shoten, 1981.
Taregami ōrai. Ed. Ishikawa Ken and Ishikawa Matsutarō, *Ōraimono hen*. Nihon kyōkasho taikei 2 (Kōdansha, 1967).
Tokuda Kazuo. "Kanjin hijiri to shaji engi." *Kokubungaku Kenkyū Shiryōkan kiyō* 4 (1978): 25–128.
Tomikura Tokujirō, ed. *Saikai yoteki shū narabi ni Tsuizō Heigo gūdan*. Koten Bunko 109. Koten Bunko, 1956.
Tōno Haruyuki. "Nikki ni miru Fujiwara no Yorinaga no danshoku kankei: ōchō kizoku no vita sexualis." *Historia*, no. 84 (1979): 15–29.
Toribeyama monogatari. Eds. Yokoyama Shigeru and Matsumoto Ryūshin. Muromachi jidai monogatari taisei 10. Kadokawa Shoten, 1982.
Tsuchiya Keiichirō. "Omote: kamen, to shintai." In *Nō*. Shin'yōsha, 1989.
Tsurezuregusa. Kanda Hideo et al., eds. *Hōjōki, Tsurezuregusa, Shōbōgenzō zuimonki, Tannishō*. Nihon Koten Bungaku Zenshū. Shōgakukan, 1971.
Ueki Yukinobu, ed., *Dengaku, sarugaku*. Nihon Shomin Bunka Shūsei 2. San'ichi Shobō, 1974.
Umezu Jirō, ed. *Tengu sōshi, Zegaibō-e*, Shinshū Nihon Emakimono Zenshū 27. Kadokawa Shoten, 1978.
Urashima myōjin engi. Ed. Komatsu Shigemi. In *Hikohohodemi no mikoto emaki, Urashima myōjin engi*. Nihon Emaki Taisei 22. Chūō Kōronsha, 1979.
Watanabe Moriaki. *Kamen to shintai: fukusū no kotoba*. Asahi Shuppansha, 1978.
Watanabe Tsunayo, ed. *Shasekishū*. Nihon Koten Bungaku Taikei. Vol 85. Iwanami Shoten, 1966.
Yamada Yoshio. *Renga gaisetsu*. Iwanami Shoten, 1937.
Yamaguchi Masao. "Nihon-teki baroque no genshō: Sasaki Dōyo to Oda Nobunaga." In *Rekishi, shukusai, shinwa*, 55–77. Chūō Kōronsha, 1974.
Yamaguchi Masao and Inui Hiroyuki, "Taidan: Bashō no shigaku (poetique)," *Kokubungaku: kaishaku to kyōzai no kenkyū* (January 1983): 15–37.
Yamaguchi Masao and Matsuoka Shinpei. "Taidan: Tōtaru media to shite no nō." *Kokubungaku kaishaku to kyōzai no kenkyū* 31 (September 1986): 6–31.

Yamaori Tetsuo. *Tennō no shūkyōteki ken'i to wa nanika*. Kawade Shobō Shinsha. 1990.

Yanagita Kunio. *Yanagita Kunio zenshū*. Vol. 9. Chikuma Shobō, 1998.

Yasuda Jirō. "Yamato no kuni higashi sanchū ikki." Ed. Murata Shūzō, *Kinki daimyō no kenkyū* 5 (Yoshikawa Kobunkan, 1986): 358–382.

Yokomichi Mario and Omote Akira, eds. *Yōkyokushū*. 2 vols. Nihon Koten Bungaku Taikei. Vols. 40 and 41. Iwanami Shoten, 1960, 1963.

Yokoyama Shigeru and Matsumoto Ryūshin, eds. *Muromachi jidai monogatari taisei*. 13 vols. Kadokawa Shoten, 1973–1985.

Yoshikawa Kiyoshi. *Jishū Ami kyōdan no kenkyū*. Geirinsha, 1956.

Yoshimura Hitoshi. "Zeami nō geiron ni okeru kokoro to waza." *Rinrigaku nenpō* 38 (March 1989): 125–139.

Yoshimura Shigeki. "Jōkō seiji no jissō." Tennō no rekishi. *Shin Nihon rekishi* 7, 183–204. Fukumura Shoten, 1955.

Zeami Motokiyo. *Zeami jihitsu nōhon shū: kōtei hen*. Ed. Omote Akira. Wan'ya Shoten, 1997.

SUGGESTED READINGS

REFERENCE AND CONTEXT

Lancashire, Terence. *An Introduction to Japanese Folk Performing Arts.* London: Routledge, 2016.

Leiter, Samuel L., ed. *Encyclopedia of Asian Theatre.* Westport, CT: Greenwood Press, 2007.

——. *Historical Dictionary of Japanese Traditional Theatre.* Lanham, MD: Scarecrow Press, 2006.

Liu, Siyuan, ed. *Routledge Handbook of Asian Theatre.* London: Routledge, 2016.

Marra, Michael F. *Representations of Power: The Literary Politics of Medieval Japan.* Honolulu: University of Hawai'i Press, 1993.

Mass, Jeffrey P., ed. *The Origins of Japan's Medieval World: Courtiers, Clerics, Warriors, and Peasants in the Fourteenth Century.* Stanford, CA: Stanford University Press, 1997.

Miner, Earl R. *The Princeton Companion to Classical Japanese Literature.* Princeton, NJ: Princeton University Press, 1985.

Salz, Jonah, ed. *A History of Japanese Theatre.* Cambridge: Cambridge University Press, 2016.

Shirane, Haruo, ed. *Traditional Japanese Literature: An Anthology, Beginnings to 1600.* New York: Columbia University Press, 2007.

Wiles, David, and Christine Dymkowski, eds. *The Cambridge Companion to Theatre History.* Cambridge: Cambridge University Press, 2013.

Yamamura, Kōzō, ed. *The Cambridge History of Japan.* Vol. 3, Medieval Japan. Cambridge: Cambridge University Press, 1990.

Zarrilli, Phillip B., and Gary Jay Williams, eds. *Theatre Histories: An Introduction.* New York: Routledge, 2006.

NOH

Atkins, Paul S. *Revealed Identity: The Noh Plays of Komparu Zenchiku.* Ann Arbor: Center for Japanese Studies, University of Michigan, 2006.

Bethe, Monica. *Dance in the Nō Theater.* Ed. Karen Brazell. Ithaca, NY: China-Japan Program, Cornell University, 1982.

Bethe, Monica, and Karen Brazell. "The Practice of Noh Theatre." In *By Means of Performance: Intercultural Studies of Theatre and Ritual.* Ed. Richard Schechner and Willa Appel, 167–193. Cambridge: Cambridge University Press, 1990.

Brazell, Karen. "Subversive Transformations: Atsumori and Tadanori at Suma." In *Currents in Japanese Culture: Translations and Transformations.* Ed. Amy Vladeck Heinrich. New York: Columbia University Press, 1997.

Brazell, Karen. "Citations on the Noh Stage." *Extrême-Orient Extrême-Occident,* no. 17 (1995): 91–110.

Brazell, Karen, and James T. Araki, eds. *Traditional Japanese Theater: An Anthology of Plays.* New York: Columbia University Press, 1998.

Brazell, Karen, and Richard Emmert. *Atsumori.* Tokyo: National Noh Theatre, 1995.

Brazell, Karen, Philip Gabriel, and Monica Bethe, eds. *Twelve Plays of the Noh and Kyōgen Theaters.* Ithaca, NY: East Asia Program, Cornell University, 1988.

Brown, Steven T. *Theatricalities of Power: The Cultural Politics of Noh.* Stanford, CA: Stanford University Press, 2001.

Choo, Lim Beng. "They Came to Party: An Examination of the Social Status of the Medieval Noh Theatre." *Japan Forum* 16, no. 1 (2004): 111–133.

Emmert, Richard. *The Guide to Noh of the National Noh Theatre: Play Summaries of the Traditional Repertory.* Tokyo: National Noh Theatre, 2012.

Foard, James H. "*Seiganji*: The Buddhist Orientation of a Noh Play." *Monumenta Nipponica* 35, no. 4 (1980): 437–56.

Goff, Janet E. "Noh and Its Antecedents: 'Journey to the Western Provinces.'" In *The Distant Isle: Studies and Translations of Japanese Literature in Honor of Robert H. Brower.* Ed. Robert H. Brower, Thomas Blenman

Hare, Robert Borgen, and Sharalyn Orbaugh. Ann Arbor: Center for Japanese Studies, University of Michigan, 1996.

———. *Noh Drama and The Tale of Genji: The Art of Allusion in Fifteen Classical Plays*. Princeton Library of Asian Translations. Princeton, NJ: Princeton University Press, 1991.

Hare, Thomas B. "A Separate Piece: Proprietary Claims and Intertextuality in the Rokujō Plays." In *The Distant Isle: Studies and Translations of Japanese Literature in Honor of Robert H. Brower*. Ed. Robert H. Brower, Thomas Blenman Hare, Robert Borgen, and Sharalyn Orbaugh. Ann Arbor: Center for Japanese Studies, University of Michigan, 1996.

———. *Zeami's Style: The Noh Plays of Zeami Motokiyo*. Stanford, CA: Stanford University Press, 1986.

Hare, Thomas B., trans. *Zeami, Performance Notes*. New York: Columbia University Press, 2008.

Keene, Donald. *Twenty Plays of the Nō Theatre*. Ed. Royall Tyler. New York: Columbia University Press, 1970.

Kenny, Don. *The Kyogen Book: An Anthology of Japanese Classical Comedies*. Tokyo: Japan Times, 1989.

Konparu, Kunio. *The Noh Theater: Principles and Perspectives*. Trans. Jane Corddry and Stephen B. Comee. Warren, CT: Floating World, 2005.

LaFleur, William R. "Zeami's Buddhism: Cosmology and Dialectic in Nō Drama." In *The Karma of Words: Buddhism and the Literary Arts in Medieval Japan*. Berkeley: University of California Press, 1983.

Lazarus, Ashton. "Folk Performance as Transgression: The Great *Dengaku* of 1096." *The Journal of Japanese Studies* 4, no. 1 (2018): 1–23.

Lim, Beng Choo. *Another Stage : Kanze Nobumitsu and the Late Muromachi Noh Theater*. Ithaca, NY: East Asia Program, Cornell University, 2012.

Marra, Michele. "Zeami and *No*: A Path Towards Enlightenment." *Journal of Asian Culture* 12 (1988): 37–65.

Morley, Carolyn A. *Transformation, Miracles, and Mischief: The Mountain Priest Plays of Kyōgen*. Ithaca, NY: Cornell University, East Asia Program, 1993.

Ortolani, Benito. *The Japanese Theatre: From Shamanistic Ritual to Contemporary Pluralism*. Princeton, NJ: Princeton University Press, 1995.

Pinnington, Noel. "Noh Drama." In *The Cambridge History of Japanese Literature*. Ed. David Lurie, Haruo Shirane, and Tomi Suzuki, 328–339. Cambridge: Cambridge University Press, 2015.

Pinnington, Noel J. *A New History of Medieval Japanese Theatre: Noh and Kyōgen from 1300 to 1600.* Palgrave Studies in Theatre and Performance History. Cham, Switzerland: Palgrave Macmillan, 2019.

Poorter, Erika de. *Zeami's Talks on Sarugaku: An Annotated Translation of the Sarugaku Dangi, with an Introduction to Zeami Motokiyo.* Amsterdam: J. C. Gieben, 1986.

Quinn, Shelley. *Developing Zeami: The Noh Actor's Attunement in Practice.* Honolulu: University of Hawai'i Press, 2005.

———. "How to Write a Noh Play: Zeami's Sando." *Monumenta Nipponica* 48, no. 1 (1993): 53–88.

Rath, Eric C. *The Ethos of Noh: Actors and Their Art.* Cambridge, MA: Harvard University Asia Center, 2004.

Raz, Jacob. *Audience and Actors: A Study of Their Interaction in the Japanese Traditional Theatre.* Leiden: E. J. Brill, 1983.

Shimazaki, Chifumi. *Restless Spirits from Japanese Noh Plays of the Fourth Group: Parallel Translations with Running Commentary.* Ithaca, NY: East Asia Program, Cornell University, 1995.

Shimazaki, Chifumi, ed. *The Noh.* 3 vols. Tokyo: Hinoki Shoten, 1972.

———, ed. *Troubled Souls from Japanese Noh Plays of the Fourth Group: Parallel Translations with Running Commentary.* Ithaca, NY: East Asia Program, Cornell University, 1998.

———, ed. *Warrior Ghost Plays from the Japanese Noh Theater: Parallel Translations with Running Commentary.* Ithaca, NY: East Asia Program, Cornell University, 1993.

Shimazaki, Chifumi, and Stephen Comee. *Supernatural Beings from Japanese Noh Plays of the Fifth Group: Parallel Translations with Running Commentary.* Ithaca, NY: Cornell University, East Asia Program, 2012.

Takeda, Sharon Sadako, Monica Bethe, and Hollis Goodall-Cristante. *Miracles & Mischief: Noh and Kyōgen Theater in Japan.* Los Angeles: Los Angeles County Museum of Art, 2002.

Teele, Rebecca, ed. *Nō/Kyōgen Masks and Performance: Essays and Interviews.* Claremont, CA: Pomona College Theater Department for the Claremont Colleges, 1984.

Terasaki, Etsuko. *Figures of Desire: Wordplay, Spirit Possession, Fantasy, Madness, and Mourning in Japanese Noh Plays.* Ann Arbor: Center for Japanese Studies, University of Michigan, 2002.

Thornhill, Arthur H. "Noh Drama Theory from Zeami to Zenchiku." In *The Cambridge History of Japanese Literature*. Ed. David Lurie, Haruo Shirane, and Tomi Suzuki, 340–346. Cambridge: Cambridge University Press, 2015.

Tyler, Royall. *To Hallow Genji: A Tribute to Noh*. Charleston, SC: CreateSpace, 2013.

Tyler, Royall, ed. *Japanese Nō Dramas*. London: Penguin, 1992.

Ueda, Makoto. "Zeami on the Art of the No Drama: Imitation, *Yugen*, and Sublimity." In *Japanese Aesthetics and Culture: A Reader*. Ed. Nancy G. Hume. SUNY Series in Asian Studies Development. Albany: State University of New York Press, 1995.

Waley, Arthur. *The Nō Plays of Japan*. New York: Knopf, 1922.

Yasuda, Kenneth, ed. *Masterworks of the Nō Theater*. Bloomington: Indiana University Press, 1989.

Yokota, Gerry. *The Formation of the Canon of Nō: The Literary Tradition of Divine Authority*. Osaka: Osaka University Press, 1997.

RELIGION

Blum, Mark L. *The Origins and Development of Pure Land Buddhism: A Study and Translation of Gyōnen's Jōdo Hōmon Genrushō*. Oxford: Oxford University Press, 2002.

Ippen, and Dennis Hirota. *No Abode: The Record of Ippen*. Honolulu: University of Hawai'i Press, 1997.

Law, Jane Marie, ed. *Religious Reflections on the Human Body*. Bloomington and Indianapolis: Indiana University Press, 1994.

Michio, Kamikawa. "Accession Rituals and Buddhism in Medieval Japan." *Japanese Journal of Religious Studies* 17, no. 2/3 (1990): 243–280.

Sanford, James H. *Flowing Traces: Buddhism in the Literary and Visual Arts of Japan*. Ed. William R. LaFleur and Masatoshi Nagatomi. Princeton. NJ: Princeton University Press, 2016.

POETICS

Carter, Steven D. "Chats with the Master: Selections from '*Kensai Zōdan*.'" *Monumenta Nipponica* 56, no. 3 (2001): 295–347.

——. *How to Read a Japanese Poem*. New York: Columbia University Press, 2019.

——. "Renga (Linked Verse)." In *The Cambridge History of Japanese Literature*. Ed. David Lurie, Haruo Shirane, and Tomi Suzuki, 317–327. Cambridge: Cambridge University Press, 2015.

——. *The Road to Komatsubara: A Classical Reading of the Renga Hyakuin*. Cambridge, MA: Council on East Asian Studies, Harvard University, 1987.

Carter, Steven D., ed. *Haiku Before Haiku: From the Renga Masters to Bashō*. New York: Columbia University Press, 2011.

Cranston, Edwin A. "'Mystery and Depth' in Japanese Poetry." In *The Distant Isle: Studies and Translations of Japanese Literature in Honor of Robert H. Brower*. Ed. Robert H. Brower, Thomas Blenman Hare, Robert Borgen, and Sharalyn Orbaugh. Ann Arbor: Center for Japanese Studies, University of Michigan, 1996.

Ebersole, Gary L. "The Buddhist Ritual Use of Linked Poetry in Medieval Japan." *The Eastern Buddhist* 16, no. 2 (1983): 50–71.

Hare, Thomas W. "Linked Verse at Imashinmei Shrine. *Anegakoji Imashinmei Hyakuin*, 1447." *Monumenta Nipponica* 34, no. 2 (1979): 169–208.

Horton, H. Mack. "*Renga* Unbound: Performative Aspects of Japanese Linked Verse." *Harvard Journal of Asiatic Studies* 53, no. 2 (1993): 443–512.

Konishi Jin'Ichi. "The Art of *Renga*." Trans. Karen Brazell and Lewis Cook. *Journal of Japanese Studies* 2, no. 1 (1975): 29–61.

Miner, Earl R. *Japanese Linked Poetry: An Account with Translations of Renga and Haikai Sequences*. Princeton, NJ: Princeton University Press, 1979.

Ramirez-Christensen, Esperanza U. *Emptiness and Temporality: Buddhism and Medieval Japanese Poetics*. Stanford, CA: Stanford University Press, 2008.

——. *Heart's Flower: The Life and Poetry of Shinkei*. Stanford, CA: Stanford University Press, 1994.

——. *Murmured Conversations: A Treatise on Poetry and Buddhism*. Stanford, CA: Stanford University Press, 2008.

Shirane, Haruo. "Visual Culture, Classical Poetry, and Linked Verse." In *Japan and the Culture of the Four Seasons: Nature, Literature, and the Arts*. New York: Columbia University Press, 2012.

CHIGO

Atkins, Paul S. "Chigo in the Medieval Japanese Imagination." *The Journal of Asian Studies* 67, no. 3 (2008): 947–970.

Childs, Margaret, H. "The Story of Kannon's Manifestation as a Youth." In *Partings at Dawn: An Anthology of Japanese Gay Literature*. Ed. Stephen D. Miller. 31–35. San Francisco: Gay Sunshine Press, 1996.

——. "The Tale of Genmu." In *Rethinking Sorrow: Revelatory Tales of Late Medieval Japan*, 31–52. Ann Arbor: Center for Japanese Studies, University of Michigan, 1991.

——. "*Chigo Monogatari*: Love Stories or Buddhist Sermons?" Monumenta Nipponica 35, no. 2 (1980), 127–151.

Faure, Bernard. "Boys to Men." In *The Red Thread: Buddhist Approaches to Sexuality*. Princeton, NJ: Princeton University Press, 1998.

Porath, Or. "Nasty Boys or Obedient Children?: Childhood and Relative Autonomy in Medieval Japanese Monasteries." In *Child's Play: Multi-Sensory Histories of Children and Childhood in Japan*. Ed. Sabine Frühstück and Anne Walthall, 17–40. Oakland: University of California Press, 2017.

——. "The Cosmology of Male-Male Love in Medieval Japan." *Journal of Religion in Japan* 4, no. 2–3 (2015): 241–271.

Schalow, Paul G. "Kūkai and the Tradition of Male Love in Japanese Buddhism." In *Buddhism, Sexuality, and Gender*. Ed. José Ignacio Cabezón, 215–230. Albany: State University of New York Press, 1992.

INDEX

Abe Yasurō, 122, 123, 128
acrobatics, xi, 5, 27, 31, 101; of *dengaku*, xvi, 24, 27, 32, 33, 158; intersection of acrobatic body and restrained body, xii; of *renga*, 33; *sangaku* and, 25
actors/acting, 95–96, 107; body reconstituted by the mask, 203; inner concentration of actor, 201–2, 203; *kamae* (actor's basic posture), xx, 212, 225–30; masks and, xx, 198–204; mode of walking (*hakobi*), 225; *saidōfū* performance, 192–93; three modes of acting, 159, 226; vigorous movements (*hataraki*), 208. *See also* Three Role Types; Two Arts
aesthetic terms, translation of, xxv
afterlife, nature of, xxi
aged mode (actor's role), 159, 186, 194, 196, 208, 212, 226. *See also* Three Role Types

Age of the Northern and Southern Courts (Nanbokuchō), xv, 19, 21, 34, 60, 93; *dengaku* craze during, 23; *renga* and, 37; *sarugaku* held in grandstand theater spaces, 28; subscription noh performances during, 109
ageuta (chant), 172, 246n1
Aki no yo no nagamonogatari [A long tale for an autumn night] (1377), 138–40
Akoya no matsu [The pine tree at Akoya] (noh play), 184, 248n10
akutō (outlaws), 20–21, 23
Amano Fumio, 100, 239n22
Ama no mokuzu (1420), 104
Amida Buddha, xv, xxii, 2, 89, 240n1; amulets inscribed with name of, 5; chanting name of, 4, 10, 83, 91, 216; *nenbutsu hijiri* holy men and, 50; statue on stage of *nenbutsu* performance, 8

Angya zuihitsu [Random notes of a pilgrim traveling on foot] (diary of Zen monk), 47
Ariwara no Motokata, 246n4
Ariwara no Narihira, 114, 161, 167, 206, 247n6
Ashikaga Takauji, 28, 33, 47
Ashikaga Yoshiakira, 40
Ashikaga Yoshihisa, 113
Ashikaga Yoshimasa, 71, 99, 113, 219
Ashikaga Yoshimitsu, xxv, 70, 113, 152, 192; discovery of Zeami and Kan'ami by, xviii, 150; on Zeami as beautiful boy, 153–54; Zeami as *chigo* and, 143, 158
Ashura realm of existence, 100, 238–39n21
Ataka (noh play), 237n5
audiences, xx, 4, 83; effect produced by actor's performance (*kenpū*), 190; laughter of, 23; performers directly facing, 109; Shijō grandstand collapse (1349) and, 31
Ayanokōji riverbed (Kyoto), 103, 104
azuma uta (eastern songs), 12

banquet songs (*sōka*), 5, 11–12, 13, 16
Barrault, Jean-Louis, 187, 248n13
basara (extravagance and excess), xi, xv, 16–17, 72; described in *Taiheiki*, 14; Kemmu code ban on, 19–20, 21; Sanskrit etymology of, 43
Benkei, 81, 237n5
beshimi masks, 99, 200
Bishamondō, 50–51, 52
Bishamonten (demon), 98
bodhisattvas, 12, 90, 107
Boki ekotoba (1351), 69, 152
Bontōan, 162, 166, 167
Bontōan hentōsho (Bentōan's replies), 246n21
bozushi (temple monks), 97
Brahma (deity), 12
Buddhism, xviii, xxi, 3, 29, 82, 108; architecture of, 175; Buddhas of Past, Present, and Future, 90; collections of Buddhist tales, 52, 53, 78; *gyōdō* ritual ceremony, 216–17; imperial system and, 121–22; Kegon sect, 147; oral recitations of *Heike monogatari* and, 88, 89; rituals to exorcise demons, 97; *sarugaku* and, 109; Shingon sect, 47, 114, 121, 123, 129; Tendai sect, 121, 123, 127, 129, 137. *See also* Jishū sect; Zen
bugaku court dances, 195, 215

calligraphy/calligraphers, 39, 135
cherry trees. *See* weeping cherry trees (*shidare zakura*)
chigo (beautiful temple boys), xxiii, 58, 111–13; adulation of boys in medieval Japan, 113–14, *115*, 116–19; aesthetics of, 153–61; age limit for, 161; depicted in medieval fiction, xix; English translation of, xxv; gender representation and, xi; initiation rite on Mount Hiei, xviii, xxii, 128–38; legend of immortal youth Jidō, 120–28; maskless

INDEX ❦ 279

performance and body of, 207–13; *shiore* (moistness) and, 165, 167–68; special training for, xvii, xviii; worship of, xiv. *See also* Fujiwaka (Zeami as *chigo*)
"Chigo" (Kon Tōkō, 1946), 112–13, 130
Chigo kanjō shi [Private initiation of catamites] (1450), 135
chigo monogatari genre, 114
Chihaya Castle, siege of (1333), 65
child emperors, xiv, xviii, 118, 126
China: arts imported from, 25; Chinese prose, 24; famous places (*meisho oshie*) in, 42; story of Jidō/Pengzu/Prince Shōtoku set in, 123–28, 134
Chinese characters, 57, 58, 112, 144
Chinese objects (*karamono*), 29, 40, 163, 234n17
Chin'ichi, 88
Chōgen, 80
Chōju jinbutsu giga (Scrolls of frolicking animals and humans), 24
Christianity, 72
chūmonguchi (musical opening piece), 102
"Chūsei" [The middle ages] (Mishima, 1946), 113
Claudel, Paul, 74
companions of the meeting hall (*go-kaisho no dōbō*), 70
court football, 144, .157, 159, 192, 229
"crazy Zen figures," 81
cross-dressing, xiv

Daianji temple (Nara), 94, 95
daigashira dances, 12
Daigoji temple, 103, 219, 220
Daijingū sankeiki [Account of a pilgrimage to the Grand Shrine of Ise] (Saka Jūbutsu, 1342), 57
Daijō'in temple complex [Kōfukuji] (Nara), 92
Daisenji engi emaki (Illustrated scroll of the legendary origins of Daisenji Temple), 24
Damned, The [*La caduta degli dei*] (film, dir. Visconti, 1969), 138, 140, 242–43n23
Danjō of Aida, 16
Danna school, 129
Dekisai Kyō miyuge (Dekisai's Kyoto souvenirs), 58–59
demons, plays about, 96–104
dengaku (field music-dance), xi, xii, xvii, 21–33; *chigo* and, 156–57, 158–59; *chūmonguchi* (musical opening piece), 102; downfall of Kamakura shogunate and, xvi; drums in performance of, 23, 24–25, 25; Great Dengaku (Kyoto, 1096), xiv, 1–2, 6, 21; guerrilla warfare compared to, 32, 33; Honza (original troupe), 22, 26, 29; Jishū sect and, 5; joint dances (*tachiai*), 102; at New Year's rites (1141), 23; opening musical pieces (*chūmonguchi*), 158; Shinza (New Troupe), 13–14, 22, 26, 29, 183; subscription performances, 28, 84–89, 99–104
de Poorter, Erika, xxvi

Deva Kings (Niō), 98
diabolo (*ryūgo*), 26
didactic stories (*sekkyō*), 5
Dōichi, 30
Dōjōji (noh play), 230
Dōshō, 34–35, 50, 51, 52
Dōyo (Sasaki Dōyo), xi, 69–70; cultural role of, 37–44; decorative spaces of, 39, 40, 234n17; flower-viewing party of, 41–44; interest in *renga*, 37–39; Jishū sect and, 14–17; outlandish tastes and behavior of, xv; tea party beneath cherry blossoms, xvi
dream plays (*mugen nō*), xxii, 76, 204–5
drums, 23, 46, 224; *koshi-tsuzumi* drum, 1, 24, 26, 231n1; *kotsuzumi* shoulder drum, 24–25, 106; *ōtsuzumi* hip drum, 250n11

Echi, 197
Edo period, 58, 62, 72, 73
Eichō era, 1
Eight Lectures on the Yuima (Skt: Vimalakīrti) sutra, 106
ekijin (gods of epidemics), 46
emperors, retired, xiv, 1, 21, 53, 122
Endō Gorōzaemon, 12
enken (distant view), xix, xxii, xxiv, 171, 179, 183, 189; bridgeway on noh stage and, 221; dancing figure merging with surrounding space, 189–90; kenpū ("visual effect") and, 186–87, 189; outside context of performance, 185; in Zeami's dramatic theories, 186

Enkyō sannen ki (1310), 27–28
Enma, King (ruler of hell), 48, 93, 96
Ennin (Jikaku Daishi), 130
Enryakuji temple, 63, 197
Eshin (Genshin), 129, 239n1
Eshin school, 129, 134
Essays in Idleness [*Tsurezuregusa*] (Yoshida Kenkō, 1330), 56, 116–17
etoki (visual explanations of shrine and temple origins), xvii
evangelism, transformed into performing art, 80–84
exorcism rituals, at New Year, xvii, 98
Extracts from the Philosophical Diary of a Murderer in the Middle Ages (Mishima), 140

famous places (*meisho oshie*), xix, 7, 42, 173–75, 230
female impersonators (*onnagata*), xvii
flower (flower-viewing) parties, 41, 147, 149
flower arranging, xii, xiii, 5, 40, 149, 244n5, 244n10; *chigo* trained in, xviii, 114, 152; earliest treatise on, 152; by *kasshiki*, 152–53, 244n10; Zeami's knowledge of, 162, 163
Flower Basket, The [*Hanagatami*] (Zeami play), 179, 180–81, 183
flower-pacification rites (*chinka-sai*), 3, 10, 36, 48; Dōyo (Sasaki Dōyo) and, 43; in Yasurai Hana festival, 46–47
foot stamping, 30, 193, 216, 218–19, 227, 249nn4 (chap 9)

Forbidden Colors [*Kinjiki*] (Mishima, 1951), 111–12, 113, 129, 138, 141
foundation story (*honzetsu*), 204
Fuchiki, 146
Fūgawakashū [Collection of elegant poems] (*waka* anthology), 51
Fujisawa, 6
Fujiwaka (Zeami as *chigo*), xi, 207; acting (singing and dancing) of, 158–59; Ashikaga Yoshimitsu and, 113; dancing aesthetics of, 155; Nijō Yoshimoto and, xviii, xix, 144, 146–47, 149–50, 151, 153, 161, 163; noh aesthetics and, 143–44; *shiore* (moistness) and, 169; *yūgen* concept and, 163–64. *See also* Zeami Motoyiko
Fujiwara clan, 117, 118
Fujiwara no Kintō, 236n14
Fujiwara no Kiyoskuke, 165
Fujiwara no Munetada, 23
Fujiwara no Shunzei, 247n5
Fujiwara no Tadamichi, 116
Fujiwara no Takasuke, 53
Fujiwara no Teika, 185
Fujiwara no Tokihira, 234n1
Fujiwara no Yorinaga, 116
Fukushōji (Settsu), 103
Fukuwaka-maru, 156–58, 169
Funabashi (noh play), 108
fundraising events, 91–92, 94, 108
Funi, 191
Furu (noh play), 173–74
Fūshikaden [Transmission of acting styles and the flower] (Zeami, ca. 1418), 143, 161, 193; on *chigo*'s training, 207–9; emphasis on role playing, 203; on *monomane*, 198; "Separate Secret Transmission" (Besshi kuden), 162–63; on *shiore*, 164–65, 170

Gaijashō [Notes on rectifying heresy] (1335), 15
gambling, xv, 20
Gangōji temple (Nara), 92
gāthā (Buddhist chants or hymns), 124, 241n14
Gekimoshō (Nijō Yoshimoto, 1358), 166, 167
gender representation, xi, xxiii
Genji Hikaru (fictional character), 55, 146
Genmu, 167
Genmu monogatari (The tale of Genmu, 15th century), 156
Genshi kimyōdan (Reception of secret teachings and pledge of faith before the altar), 129
ghosts, xxii, 47–48, 76, 94, 102
Gidarinji temple, 9
gigaku masks, 200, 249n2
Gion monastery (India), 94, 95
Gion shrine (Kyoto), 6, 7, 68, 100, 148; diary of Gion administrator, 11–12, 13; festival at, 25, 68, 150, 157, 158; *kusemai* dances at, 12
Giyō Hōshū, 191
Go-Daigo, Emperor, 19, 33
Gōdanshō (Ōe no Masafusa's conversations), 94
Goff, Janet, xii
Go-Hanazono, Emperor, 158

282 ~ INDEX

Gonjinshō (Shinto document, 1414), 127
Go on [Five types of singing] (Zeami), 173–74
Go ongyoku jōjō [Items concerning the five types of singing] (Zeami), 186
Go-Reizei, Emperor, 118
goryō (vengeful spirits), 3, 45, 46, 50; pacification of, 56; transcendent darkness of, 60, 64
goryō-e (festival for venerable spirits), 3, 25, 68, 113, 116
Go-Sanjō, Emperor, 116, 122, 123
Gozu Tennō [Ox-Headed King of Heaven] (deity), 68
Great Buddha Hall, Tōdaiji (Nara), 80, 81
Great Harvest Festival (Daijō-e), 122
Gukanshō (Jien's history of Japan, ca. 1220), 140, 243n25
Gusai, 37, 166

Hachijō kadenshō (Treatise on the transmission of the flower in eight books), 226–28, 228
haikai linked-verse, 73
haiku, xiii
hairstyles, xxiii
hana no moto no kushi (aesthetes beneath the blossoms), 56
hana no moto renga (renga composed beneath cherry blossoms), 10, 45, 49, 53, 56; connected to specific shrines and temples, 52; popularity among warriors, 65

Han Yu, 39
Hanzoku, Prince, 108
Harima Province, 232n1
Hasedera temple (Nara), 86, 155–56
Hashi no Kai (noh research association), xx–xxi
Hatagawa-dera temple (Zenriji), 87, 103
Heart of Perfect Wisdom Sutra, 90
Heian period, xxv, 9, 105, 114; court ladies of, 160, 169, 212; pacification ritual for souls of the dead in, 45, 51; peripatetic evangelists in, xxii
Heike clan, 89
heikyoku genre, 87
hell, 76, 101, 102, 108; Jizō statues' connection to, 60; liminal space linked to, 52; religious plays about, 93–96, 104–8; Tachiyama hell, 77
Hidenaga, 104
Hiei, Mount, 63, 76, 105, 140; analogous mountains in India and China, 127; *chigo* on, 126–27, 151–52, 167; guardian deity of, 99–100, 101, 127, 131; secret initiation of *chigo* on, 128–38; Tenkai Collection on Mount Hiei, 130, 135. *See also* Sannō Gongen [Mountain King]
Hie shrine, deity of, 30
Higashibōjō Hidenaga, 147–48, 152, 244n5
Hiko Yasha, 30
Hitler, Adolf, 242n23
Hōjō clan, 118

INDEX   283

Hōjō Takatoki, 22, 26–27, 28, 232n3
homosexuality, in court circles, xiv, 114, 143
Honba [Runaway horses] (Mishima), 136
Honchō monzui (Choice literature of this realm), 95
Hōryūji temple (Nara), 85, 86, 103, 116, 119
Hōsen, 92
Hōshin'in temple (Kyoto), 70, 71, 236n16
Hosokawa Kiyouji, 40
Hosokawa Yūsai, 221, 223
Hosshōji, 50, 51, 97
Hui-yuan, 82
Hyakuman (religious play), 107, 227

ichibu Heike (recitation of entire *Heike monogatari*), 87
Ichijō Fuyuyoshi (Fuyura), 122
Ichijōin subtemple (Nara), 220
Ichijō Kanera, 92
Ichijō Takenohana (Kyoto), 103
ichimi shinsui (water-drinking) ritual, 61, 63, 64
Ichiya (Kyoto), 83
Ikenobō Sen'ō, xii
ikki (military leagues/alliances), xvi, 36, 37; collaborative poetry sessions and, 45; formation of, 61–62; *ichimi shinsui* (water-drinking) ritual, 61, 63; *ikkō ikki* ("single-minded leagues"), 65; *karakasa renban* signatures on covenants of, 62–63; samurai leagues, 65; as socially unattached community, 64, 67
ikkō ikki ("single-minded leagues"), 65
Imagawa Ryōshun, 100
Imamiya shrine (Murasakino), 46
imayō (popular songs), 46
Imo-arai [Washing potatoes] (play), 7
Inagaki Taruho, 142
incense, 22, 42, 43
Indra (deity), 12
Initiation of Catamites, The (*Chigo kanjō*), *112*
Initiation of the Four Mandalas and Three Mysteries, 130
Institute of Eastern Culture [Tōhō Gakkai] (Tokyo), xxiv
Inuō, 103, 107
Ippen, xv, 4, 15, 85; dance of, 2, 3, 8; disciples/followers of, 6, 216; emergence of roof-covered dance hut and, 226; as founder of Jishū sect, 2; as fundraising entertainer, 89; itinerant group of dancers led by, 5; as *nenbutsu* performer, 83
Ippen hijiri-e [illustrated account of Ippen's life] (1299), 3–4, *84*, 91
Ise monogatari (Tales of Ise), 114, 205, 240n4
Ise shrine, 114
Iso no Zenji, 117
Itsukushima shrine, 215, 223–24
Iwanami Shoten, xxiv

Izumoji (the Izumo Road), 50, 52
Izutsu [The well-cradle] (Zeami), 161, 205–6, 212

Jakunin, 51
Jiami, 12
Jidō (Pengzu), legend of, 120–28, 131, 134, 136
Jien (Tendai abbot), 123
Jigenji temple, 47, 48
Jijū Shūami, 16
Jinbō, 12
Jinen Koji, 81–82, 83, 192, 237n6; as fundraising entertainer, 89; fundraising sermon in Nara, 85; memorial services for the dead and, 90–91
Jinen Koji (noh play), 107, 150
Jishinbō, 93
Jishū dance huts, xx, 218, 250n4
Jishū Gongen shrine, 49, 50
Jishū sect, of Pure Land Buddhism, xv, 2, 13, 50; dancers, xx; Dōyo (Sasaki Dōyo) and, 14–17; intrinsic ties with *renga*, 10; involvement in varied cultural phenomena, 5; main branch in Fujisawa, 6; *nembutsu* dancing, xxii; physicality and theatricality of, 5–6; roof-covered noh stage and, 218. *See also* Training Center, of Jishū sect
Jitsui, 156, 157–58
Jizō (bodhisattva), 4, 8, 93; as avatar of Enma, 96; Jūzenji as avatar of, 242n15; miracle involving, 108; pictorial account of miracles of, 9; statues of, 60; temples dedicated to, 9
Jizō bosatsu reigen ekotoba (1491), 9
Jizōdō hall, 4, 92
Jōa, 6–7, 9
Jōa II (Sakua), 11, 12, 13, 14
joint dances (*tachiai*), 102, 158
Jōkongō-in temple (Kyoto), 92
jugglers, 5, 26, 30, 102, 158
Jūichi, 88
Jūmon saihishō [Top secret treatise on ten questions] (Nijō Yoshimoto, 1383), 153, 163
Jūnenbō, Hana no Moto, 53, 54
Jūshin'in temple (Kyoto), 156
Jūzenji (Hiei shrine deity), 127, 242n15

kabuki theater, xvii, 160, 237n5
Kagenki (annals of Hōryūji temple), 85, 103, 237n12
kaisho (gathering places), xvi
Kajūji Uhyōe Gonza, 87–88
kakeai ("heightened exchange"), 181, 248n8
Kakinomoto no Hitomaro, 69
Kakunyo, 15, 69
Kakyō [Mirror of the flower] (Zeami, 1424), 188–90, 193–94, 201–2, 203, 226
kamae (actor's basic posture), xx, 212–13, 225–30
Kamakura period/shogunate, xiv, xxv, 20, 53, 98, 119, 215; *akutō* (outlaws) in, 21; breakdown in social norms during, xv; demise of shogunate, xv, 32; *dengaku*

craze and, 22; initiation of *chigo* during, 129
kami-sage (hair hanging down/descent of deity), 212
Kan'ami (father of Zeami Motoyiko), xvii–xviii, xxvi, 13, 76, 150, 158; acting style of, 95–96; noh plays performed in, 103; play about Tōru the Minister performed by, 95; plays by, 172; in role of Jinen Koji, 192; *yūgen* concept and, 204; Zeami's travels with, 159
Kanazawa (Hōjō) Sadaaki, 22
Kanbutsu zanmai kyō (Meditation on the Buddha), 100, 239n22
Kanchira (play), 174
Kanjinchō (kabuki play), 237n5
kanjin holy men, 79, 82, 83, 85, 99; itinerant monks and, 109; noh masks and, 106; religious plays and, 94, 95, 105, 107
Kanmon nikki [Diary of things seen and heard] (Prince Sadafusa), 71, 92, 152
Kannon [Avalokiteśvara] (bodhisattva), 48, 77, 236n2; as Amida Buddha's attendant, xxii; Guse Kannon the World Savior, 116, 119; initiation rite for *chigo* and, 130, 131, 132–34, 136–38, 140
"Kannon sutra," 236n2
Kanze Hisao, xxi, 187–88, 200–201, 230, 248n2, 248n13; on importance of story-telling, 206; on noh stage and actor's physical role, 225; on woman's mask and mugen noh, 204–5

Kanze Jūrō, 191
Kanze school, 178
Kanze Sōsetsu, 223
karakasa renban (joint Chinese-umbrella seals), 62–63
karma, 94, 133
kasa (deep-brimmed woven hat), xvi, 10, 57–58, 59
kasshiki (Zen temple attendants), 114, 152–53
Kasuga shrine (Nara), festival at, 97, 108, 116, 160, 163, 215, 224
Katase, 4, 216, 217
Katō Kiyomasa, 59
Katō Shūichi, xxvi
Katsumata Shizuo, 62, 63–64, 235n11
Kawabata Yasunari, 141–42
Kawachi Province, 20
Kawai Hayao, 120
Kayoi Komachi [Courting Komachi] (religious play), 105–6, 108, 110
Keigyo-maru, 152
Kemmu code, 19–20, 21, 34; regulation of drinking and carousing, 65; on *renga* parties, 38
Kenna of Suwa, 16
Kenro seiyo (Buddhist text, 16th century), 144
Kensen, 13
Kenshun, 103, 236n16
Kesa Tayū, 85, 86, 103, 237n12
Kiami (dengaku actor), 163, 183–84
Kiku Jidō [Ch. Ju Citong] (Chrysanthemum Boy), 123
Kikuwaka (*sarugaku* actor), 113
Kitano shrine (Kyoto), 58, 68, 234n1, 235n9

Kiyomizu temple, 49
Kōa, 12
ko-beshimi mask, 96
Kōfukuji temple complex (Nara), 36, 66, 215
Kokan Shiren, 82
Kokinshū (imperial waka anthology), 165, 167, 182, 246–47n4, 247n6
Kokon rendanshū [Conversations past and present on linked verse] (Sōzei, 1444–1448), 34, 233n10
kokujin ikki (samurai leagues), 65
Komparu Gonnokami, 103, 105
Komparu Zempō, 228–29
Kongō Gonnokami, 103, 197
Kongō noh school, 85
Konishi Jin'ichi, 165, 166–67
Konkōji temple, 10
Kō no Moronao, 100, 239n22
Kon Tōkō, 112–13, 130
ko-omote (woman's mask), 198–203, *199*
Kōsai Tsutomu, 144, 243n1
koshi-tsuzumi drums, 1, 24, 26, 231n1
kotsuzumi (shoulder drums), 24–25, 106, 224
Kōya, Mount, 92
Koyama Hiroshi, xxiii, xxiv, 105–6
Kōyōki, 103, 147
Kūkai (Kōbō Daishi), 114, *115*, 121
Kumano shrine complex, 68
Kumata shrine (Osaka), 68, 69
Kuniyaki, 13–14
kuri (short song sung by chorus), 205–6

Kurita Isamu, 37, 38
Kuroda Toshio, 120, 121
kuse/kusemai (narrative songs), 12, 13, 205–6, 232n6, 249n5
Kusunoki Masahige, 20, 65, 100
Kusunoki Masanori, 15, 40
Kyōben, 148
kyōgen (comic theater), xxiii, xxiv, 7, 227
kyōgen kigyo ("wild words and specious phrases"), 85
Kyōkō, 94
Kyūi [Nine levels] (Zeami), 185, 188
Kyūshū mondō [Kyūshū dialogues] (Nijō Yoshimoto, 1376), 153, 162, 166

Lady Han [Hanjo] (Zeami play), 179, 180, 182
Li Bo, 55, 145–46
lion dancers, fight with Shinza troupe, 13–14
"Long Tale for an Autumn Night, A," 167–68, *169*
Lotus Sutra, 77, 78, 85, 236n2; initiation of *chigo* and, 129, 131, 136; story of Kiku Jidō and, 124, 125, 127, 128

Mahāvairocana [Dainichi Nyorai] (the Cosmic Buddha), 123
Mandara (Mandala), 114
Manmai Shōnin, 238n18
Mansai jugō nikki, 250n5
Man'yōshū poetry, 69
martial arts, 229, 251n16

martial mode (actor's role), 159, 194, 196, 208, 212, 226. *See also* Three Role Types
masks: absence of mask in *chigo*'s performance, 207–13; acting system of three role types and, 194–98; actor's body and, 198–204; beshimi, 99, 200; composition of dream plays and, 204–7; demon, 98, 101, 195, 196, 200; emergence of new types of, xx; inner concentration of actor and, 201, 202, 213; *kasshiki* mask, 141; *ko-beshimi*, 96; Okina (Old man), 97, 106, 196, 197; tobide, 99, 200; visual sense limited by, xxii; for women's roles (*ko-omote*), 197, 198–203, *199*
matsubayashi ("pine music"), 224
Matsuoka Shinpei, xi–xiv, xxiv, 242n23; expansive view of performance, xvii; on history of noh stage, xx; noh teacher of, xxi, xxiii
Matsura (Zeami play), 174
Meiji era, 8
memorial services, 90–92, 108
Mibu no Tadamine, 182
Michinori, 117
"Middle Ages, The" (Mishima), 142
Miidera temple, 76, 78
mimesis, 211
Minamoto clan, 63, 80
Minamoto no Morofusa, 123
Minamoto no Tōru, 93–94
Minamoto no Yoritomo, xxv
Minamoto no Yoshiie, 94

Minamoto no Yoshitsune, 81
Minamoto Tōru, 175
mirror boards (*kagami ita*), 223, 224, 225
Misen, Mount, 224
Mishima Kage-yuzaemon, 12
Mishima Kōami, 12
Mishima Yukio, 111–13, 129, 136, 142; medieval *chigo* tales and, 141; on Visconti's *The Damned*, 138
Moggallana (MokurenSonja), 93, 238n18
Momori ki, 239n23
Monju [Mañjuśri] (bodhisattva), 114
monogurui ("mad-person") plays, 179, 194, 227
monomane (dramatic imitation; representational actions), 106, 159–60, 172, 198; character types and, 194–95; *chigo*'s training and, 209
monzeki (monks from elite families), 104
Moromori ki, 103
motogi ("main tree"), 162
Motoyoshi (son of Zeami Motoyiko), 27, 192
Mountain King. *See* Sannō Gongen
mugen noh plays, xxii, 204–5
Mumyōshō (poetry treatise, ca. 1200), 69
Muneharu, 148
Mu of Zhou, King, 123–28, 132, 134, 136
Muromachi period, xxi, xxiii, 114, 222, 229
Mushō, 51

musical instruments, 12; binzasara rattles, 24, 30; *biwa*, 87; flute, 23, 24, 30, 46, 250n11; gongs, 46. See also drums

Musōki (Record of a dream), 123

Myōhōin temple, 37, 219

Nagahama Hachiman shrine, 92

Nagasaki Takashige, 32

Nagashima Tadashi, xxi, xxiii, xxiv

Nakahara Moromori, 87, 101

Nakahara Yasutomi, 7, 87–88

Nakamura Yūjirō, 187–88, 189

Nakanodō Kazunobu, 80

Nanbokuchō. *See* Age of the Northern and Southern Courts

Nannaji temple (Kyoto), 135

natural disasters, xxi

nenbutsu dance, xvii, xxii, 4, 11, 216, 217; extreme physicality of, 8; as pacification ritual, 91; stages performed on, 8

nenbutsu hijiri (itinerant holy men), 10, 50, 54

Nenjū gyōji emaki (Picture scrolls of annual ceremonies and events), 24, 28

Nichizō, 93, 238n18

Nijō-gawara lampoons, 22–23

Nijō Yoshimoto, 28, 51, 103, 148, 149; aesthetics of, 161–62; attendance at *dengaku* event (1349), 104; court style of, 37; flower parties at mansion of, 147, 148, 161; letter describing boyish beauty of Fujiwaka/Zeami, xviii, 144, 146–47, 192, 211; on *shiore* (moistness), 166; *yūgen* concept and, 163–64; Zeami as *chigo* and, xix, 149–50, 158, 169

Nikyoku santai ningyō zu [Sketches of figures representing the two arts and three role types] (Zeami, 1421), 143, 144, 160, 186–87, 201, 243–44n1; on *chigo*'s training, 207–11; dancing *chigo* image in, *145*; on foot stamping, 193; as model for *Hachijō kadenshō*, 226; modes of dance in, 188; on woman's mode, 186, 198, 200

Nishi-Honganji temple (Kyoto), 220

Nitta Yoshisada, 33

noh theater, xxvi, 5, 75, 84; development of noh stage, 219–20; early development of, xvii; establishment of permanent stage with bridgeway, 221–30; folklore and, 110; Kongō school, 85; noh plays as literary texts, xxiii; receptivity to existing art forms, xvii; roof-covered stage, xx, 215–20; samurai elite patrons of, xi; *shura mono* (second-category plays), 239n21; spatial aspects of noh stage, 187–88; stage as empty space with cosmic directionality, 72; treatment of space in, xix; Zeami's theories on dramaturgy and performance, xiv, 160

"Nō no kūkan: Yane no aru butai"
[Noh space: The roof-covered stage] (Matsuoka, 1994), xx
Norinobu, 148
Northern Court (Kyoto), 6, 19, 61

Obasute [The discarded old woman] (play), 171–72
Obon tradition, 238n18
Odagiri, village of, 3, 4, 216
odori-nembutsu (ecstatic dance prayer), xi, 2, *84*
Ōe no Masafusa, 122, 123, 231n1
Ōhashi Shunnō, 91
Ōi Minobu, 244n5
Ōi Tarō, 4, 231n3
Ōjōyōshū [The essentials of salvation] (Eshin), 239–40n11
Okami Masao, 48, 50
Okina [Old man] (oldest noh play), 97, 218, 223
Ōkura Toraakira, 227–28
Ōmiwa shrine, 46
Ōmononushi (deity), 46
Omote Akira, xxvi, 147, 162
Ō no Hisasuke, 117, 240n6
Ono no Komachi, 105–6, 107, 165
Ono no Takamura, 93
oral narratives (*katari*), xvii
Oshio, Mount, 41
ōtsuzumi hip drum, 250n11
Ōuchi daimyo family, 219
Ōuchi mondō, 220, 250n5

pacification ritual, for souls of the dead, 8, 45, 46–47, 116

parties, xv, xvii; flower parties, 149; *renga* (linked verse), 36, 50; at Training Center, 9
Peach Blossom Festival, at Itsukushima shrine, 224
physicality, 17, 34; *dengaku* singing and, 27; of guerrilla warfare, 33; Jinen Koji's preaching and dancing, 83
poetry competitions, xvi, 9, 83
Private Record of the Initiation of Chigo, A (Chigo kanjō shiki), 130, 134, 137, 140, 242n22
prostitutes, 60
Pure Land Buddhism, xv, xxii, 2, 72

Rakusho roken (Imagawa Ryōshin), 100
rebirth, 77, 238n21; endless cycle of, xxii; in paradise, 5, 91, 92, 94; in realm of beasts, 3, 83; six stages of, 240n1; in the Three Evil Paths, 137
Record of Miraculous Events in Japan, A (Nihon ryōiki), 78–80
Records of the Grand Historian, Tōgen's commentary on, 191
Reed Cutter, The [Ashikari] (Zeami play), 180, 182, 183
Reizei Tamemasa, 162
renga (linked verse), xi, 5, 16, 33–37; *chigo* and, 151, 159; commoners' *renga*, 49; composed beneath weeping cherry trees, xxi, 45; *dengaku* and, 36; element of

renga (linked verse) (*continued*)
  chance in, 35, 67; first written anthology of (1356), xvi; as free, uninhibited art, 34, 35; *ikki* (military leagues/alliances) and, 60–67; at Ise shrine, 114; *jige renga* (commoners' *renga*), 10; *kasa*gi (hat wearing), 57, 59, 60, 64, 68; meeting places (*kaisho*) for, 68–73; *nenbutsu* dance and, 11; Nijō riverside graffiti and, 22, 65; opening verses (*hokku*), 49; peak of, 37; performed incognito, xvi, xvii; popular, xii; at Training Center, 9–10; trancelike state and, xx; transformation of, xiii. See also *hana no moto renga*

Renga hikyōshū [A collection of analogies to renga] (Sōchō, 1532), 37–38

Renga jūyō [Ten renga styles] (Nijō Yoshimoto, 1379), 163

renju poets, 52

Renri hishō [Secret notes on the principles of linking] (ca. 1349), 165–66

riken (detached viewing), xxii

Rikiami, 16

Rikka kuden daiji (work on flower-arranging etiquette), 152

Rinna, 12, 13

ritsuryō legal system, 117

Rokudō Chinmōji temple (Kyoto), 93

role playing, xvii, 203

Rozanji temple (Kyoto), 82

Ryō no gige commentary, 46

Ryūgen Sōjō nikki, 103

Ryūten (demon), 97, 98

Sadafusa, Prince, 71, 72, 92, 108, 152–53

Sadatsune, Prince, 157, 158

Sagami Lay Monk, 22, 26

saibara (ancient ballads), 12

Saichō (Dengyō Daishi), 127, 131

"Saigoku kudari" [Journey to the western provinces] (Rinna), 13

Saigyō-zakura [Saigyō's cherry tree] (Zeami play), 50

Saikai yoteki shū (Remnants from the western sea), 88

Sairei zōshi (picture scroll), 70

Sai shrine, 46

Saka Jūbutsu, 57, 58

Sakato troupe, 86

Sakua, 11

samurai, 60, 62, 65, 66, 69

Sanbōin subtemple (Daigoji), 104

Sandō [Three techniques] (Zeami, 1423), 160, 179, 180, 183

Sanjō Kintada, 150, 157

Sannō Gongen [Mountain King] (guardian deity of Mount Hiei), 99–100, 101, 127, 131, 211

Sano no Funabashi [The boat bridge of Sano] (noh play), 101–2

sarugaku (early noh), xvii, 27, 86–87, 191; comic skits, 75–76; demon plays, xvii–xviii, xxi, 102; *enken* (distant view) in, 172; in grandstand theater spaces, 28; Jishū sect and, 5; ritual sarugaku and plays about demons, 96–99;

subscription performances, 87, 89, 99; transformation of, 204; Yamato troupes, 103, 220
Sarugaku dangi [Zeami's talks on *sarugaku*] (1430), 27, 30, 95, 96, 192; aesthetics in, 163; on demon plays, 101–2; on development of noh stage, 221; on *enken*, 171–72, 179; on famous places, 174; on *Jinen Koji*, 150; on *Kayoi Komachi*, 105; on Kiami's performance, 183–84; on Komparu Gonnokami, 109; on masks, 196–97; on roof-covered noh stage, 215; on shogun with Zeami, 158; on *Suma Genji*, 114; on Zeami as actor, 96
Sasaki Dōyo, 152
Sasaki Kōshō, 92
Sasara Tarō, 82
sashi ("recitatives"), 180, 181, 247n7
Sawara, Prince, 46, 234n1
Secret Transmission of the Teachings on Catamites (*Kō chigo shōgyō hiden*), 112–13, 129
Seiryōji temple (Kyoto), 107
Sekidera temple, 91, 217, 238n15
sekkyō preachers, 82
Senbon Enmadō hall (Kyoto), 93
Sendenshō (Selections from an immortal's teachings), 152, 162
Sen no Rikyū, xii
Senzaishū (imperial waka anthology), 247n5
setsuwa (anecdotal tales), 76–80
Shakyamuni (the Historical Buddha), 90, 93, 107, 124, 126–28

Shasekishū [Collection of sand and pebbles] (1283), 52–53, 69
Shiba Takatsune, 41, 43
Shigehira (play), 174
Shii no Shōshō (religious play), 105–6
Shijō grandstand collapse (1349), 28–32
Shikadō [The path to achieving the flower] (Zeami, 1420), 143, 159, 160, 190; on boy's performance on stage, 212; on *chigo*'s training, 207, 208, 209, 210; on *enken*, 171; on Two Arts and Three Role Types, 195–96
Shiki sanban [Three ritual pieces] (*sarugaku* play), 97
Shimo Izumo-dera (temple), 51
Shimotsuma Shōshin, 221
Shinano Hōgen, 12
Shinano Province, 3, 4, 6, 16
Shinga, 114
Shinkage-ryū heihō moku-roku no koto [The new shadow tradition's catalogue of methods of war] (Sekishūsai), 251n16
Shinkokinshū (imperial waka anthology), 52–53, 165, 183, 185
Shinnyodō engi (An account of the origins of Shinnyodō temple), 107
Shin sarugaku ki (A new sarugaku record), 75–76
shintai (human body), xvii
Shinto, 88, 109, 122; architecture, 174–75; deities of, 195; Shinto songs (*kagura*), 12; shrines and shrine officials, 29, 98
Shin-Yakushiji temple, 81

shiore (moist or wilted state), 139, 155, 164–70, 246n20
shirabyōshi dance, 117, 158
shite (principal actor), xix, xxvi, 161, 173, 175; aura emanating from, xx; *enken* (distant view) and, 172, 179; in *The Flower Basket*, 180–81; in *Izutsu*, 205, 212; in *The Lady Han*, 180; mirror boards and, 224; in *The Reed Cutter*, 182; space physically generated by, 187–88; in *Tōru*, 175–76, 179
Shitennōji temple (Osaka), 215
shōdan (noh libretti), xxvi
shōdō (religious) plays, 93–96, 104–8
shōdō preaching, 89, 94
Shōgoin, 139, 157
Shokoku ikken hijiri monogatari [Tales of a holy man traveling around the country] (1387), 127
Shokumonyō wakashū (waka collection, 1305), 114
Shōren'in temple (Kyoto), 232n6
Shōtoku, Prince, 92, 114, 116, 119, 134. See also Jidō (Pengzu), legend of
Shu'ami of Koyama, 16
shugo daimyo (military governor), 14
Shūgyoku tokuka [Finding gems and attaining the flower] (Zeami, 1428), 185–86, 189, 198–99
Shukaku, Cloistered Prince, 135, 136, 152, 161
shura mono (second-category plays), 206
shushi (*jushi*) sarugaku, 96–97
shushi-bashiri rituals, 218, 228
Soa, 13

Sōanshū [Grass hut collection] (Tonna), 9
Sōchō, 37–38
Sokui hōmon no koto [Teaching on the imperial accession] (Sonkai), 134
Someda Tenjin renga society, 66, 69
Someda Tenjin shrine (Yamato Province), 36, 68
Sonchin, Cloistered Prince, 28, 232n6
Son'in, Cloistered Prince, 104
Sonshō'in subtemple, 146–49, 151, 158, 162, 210
Sōsetsu, 224–25
Sotoba Komachi [Komachi on the stupa] (early noh play), 107
Southern Court (Yoshino), 6, 15, 20, 33, 36, 66
Sōzei, 54–56, 233n10
stilts, 26, 102
Story of Kannon's manifestation as a youth (*Chigo kannon engi*), 137, 155–56, 167, 211
Style of Breadth and Detail (*kōshōfū*), 185
Style of the Correct Flower (*shōkafū*), 185
Style of the Wondrous Flower (*myōkafū*), 185, 188
subscription performances, 84–89, 93, 99, 219; *dengaku* events and demon plays, 99–104; memorial services for the dead and, 90–92; noh settings of, 108–10; noh stages and, 222, 223; *sarugaku* events, 102–4; at Tadasugawara (1464), 221

Sugawara no Michizane, 46, 58, 59, 66, 234n1
Suma Genji [Genji at Suma] (attrib. Zeami), 114
Sumiyaki [Charcoal burner] (*sarugaku* play), 163, 183
Sumiyoshi, battle of (1347), 61
Sumiyoshi no sengū no nō [The noh about moving the Sumiyoshi shrine] (Soa et al.), 13
sumo wrestlers (*rikishi*), 60, 249–50n4, 250–51n14
suri-ashi (noh technique), 218
Su Wu (Sobu), 181, 183
Suzuri-wari (Broken inkstone), 141

Taa, 6, 15
Taa Shōnin hōgo (collected teachings of Taa), 6
Tachikawa school, 129
Taiheiki (Chronicle of great peace), xv, xvi, 20, 43, 69, 231n2; *basara* daimyo depicted in, 21; *basara* extravagance illustrated in, 14; demon plays and, 100; on *dengaku* and fighting dogs, 22, 27, 232n3; on *dengaku* craze in Kamakura, 22; on *dengaku* performance, 26; on Dōyo and *tonseisha*, 15; on Dōyo as gambler, 40; on Dōyo's decorative spaces, 39; on Dōyo's flower-viewing party, 41–42; on *hana no moto renga*, 65; on Kiku Jidō, 124–28; on origins of *ikki*, 61–62; on Shijō grandstand collapse (1349), 28–32; on subscription plays, 84

Taira clan, xxi, 63, 80, 116
Taira no Tsunemasa, 135
Takakura Jizōdō hall (Kyoto), 103
Takamikura throne, 122, 123, 128, 131, 132
Takano Tatsuyuki, 239n22
Taka shrine (Yamashino Province), 98
Tale of Genji, The, xxiii, 114, 144–45, 153, 154
Tale of Mount Toribe, The, 211
Tale of the Heike (*Heike monogatari*), 63, 206; oral recitations of, xvii, xxi, 87–89, 108; Taira nobles wearing makeup in, 116
Tales of Times Now Past (*Konjaku monogatari shū*), 9, 76–78, 94
Tamura no sōshi (The tale of Tamura), 168–69
Tanabata flower festival, 71, 149, 152, 244n5
Tango monogatari [Madman of Tango] (Zeami), 151
Tanzan shrine (Tōnomine), 106
Taoism, 136
Taregami ōrai (13th-century textbook for boys), 56
Tatsuemon, 197
Tatsuta shrine, 86
tea ceremony, xii, xiii, 5, 72
Teika (Zenchiku), 205
tengu (mythical creatures), 3, 26, 231n2, 232n3; *dengaku* performance and, 26; *yamabushi* (mountain ascetics), 26, 32
Tengu sōshi picture scrolls, 2–3, 81, 83
Tenshō kyōgen bon (ca. 1578), 7

thirty-six poetic immortals (*sanjurokkasen*), 68, 236n14
Three Role Types, 159, 160, 210; as acting system based on masks, 194–98; boy's body and, 209, 212, 213; Woman's Mode and, 186, 212. See also *Nikyoku santai ningyō zu*
Toba, Retired Emperor, 116
tobide masks, 99, 200
Tōdaiji temple (Nara), 147, 210
Tōfukuji temple (Kyoto), 191
Tōgan Koji [The lay monk Tōgan] (noh play), 82
Tōgen Zuisen, 191
"Tōgoku kudari" ["Journey to the eastern provinces"] (Rinna), 13
Tōin Kinkata, 21–22, 28, 126
Tokuda Kazuo, 93, 95, 107
Tomono, marketplace of, 3
Tonna, 9, 11, 16–17
Tō no Nyūdō, 52, 53
tonseisha (semirecluses), 15–16, 40, 54, 70
Toribeyama monogatari (The tale of Mount Toribe), 155
Tōru (Zeami play about Tōru the Minister), 96, 108, 178–79, 246n3; famous places (*meisho oshie*) in, 174, 175, 178, 187, 230; *mondō* section, 175–76; *rongi* section, 176–78; *uta* chorus, 176, 178
Toshihito (shogun), 169
Toshisuke (shogun), 168
Toyotomi Hideyoshi, 221, 223
Training Center (Shijō dōjō), of Jishū sect, xv, 6–10, 93; Dōyo (Sasaki Dōyo) and, 14–15, 17; founding of (1311), 6; high-ranking patrons of, 7–8; mentioned in early theater texts, 7; second head of, 11–14
tsuchi ikki (debt-cancellation leagues), 65
Tsukuba mondō [Questions and answers on renga] (Nijō Yoshimoto), 51
Tsukubashū (Jōa II, 1356), 11, 34, 37, 38–39, 48–49, 54–55
tsure (attendant of principal or secondary actor), xxvi
Two Arts (singing and dancing), 37, 159, 160, 195, 210. See also *Nikyoku santai ningyō zu*

Uda, Retired Emperor, 94, 95
Uesugi Noriaki, 47–48
Ujikatsu, 229, 251n16
Uji Rikyū festival (1133), 23
Ukai [Cormorant fishing] (noh play), 96, 108
Uki [Notes on the right] (Cloistered Prince Shukaku, 1202), 135
Ukon (Zeami play), 174
Ullambana sutra, 93
Ungoji temple (Kyoto), 81, 90, 91, 140
Unrin'in [Unrin'in temple] (noh play), 184
Urabon sutra, 238n18
Urashima Myōjin engi (Legendary origins of the deity Urashima Myōjin), 24

Visconti, Luchino, 138, 140, 243n23
Vulture Peak (India), 124, 127

wabi-sabi (understatement), xi
Wagner, Richard, 242n23
Wakamiya festival (Nara), 116, 215, 224
Wakamiya shrine (Kasuga), 108
Wakan rōeishū, 243n24
waka poetry, 9, 45, 69; *chigo* and, 114, 151, 157; imperial anthologies of, 52–53, 165; *nenbutsu* dance and, 11
waki (secondary actor), xix, xxvi, 172, 173, 175; in *Izutsu*, 205; mirror boards and, 224; in *Tōru*, 175–76, 178
Wang Xizhi, 39
warriors, xvi, 20, 32, 67, 120, 216; as acting character-type (*shura*), 194–95, 239n21; actors as martial artists, 229; fear of hell among, xxi; ghosts of, xxi, 47, 206; Great Dengaku (Kyoto, 1096) and, 1; at Hidenaga's flower party, 147–48; *ikki* and, 61–62; lawlessness of, 21; pacification rite for souls of, 48; as *renga* enthusiasts, 65, 67; warrior tales, 5
Washinoo, 49–50, 54
Washinoo Takayasu, 7
Watanabe Moriaki, 248n2
weeping cherry trees (*shidare zakura*), xvi, 10, 42, 50; blossom-viewing parties, 15; at Hosshōji, 51; as passageway to underworld, xxi, 48; *renga* parties under, 50, 53, 54; sacred, 49; as space of social nonattachment and equality, 69
Wendi of Wei, Emperor, 125, 127–28

woman's mode (actor's role), 159, 160, 196, 200, 208, 212; *ko-omote* mask, 198, *199*; mad-woman roles, 227; *monomane* and, 194; *yūgen* concept and, 189. *See also* Three Role Types
Womb and Diamond Initiations (Abhiṣekas), 130

Xuanzong (Tang emperor), 145–46

Yagyū Shinkage, 229, 251n16
Yakuōji (Kyoto), 103
yamabushi (mountain ascetics), 26
Yamada Yoshio, 36, 67
Yamaguchi Masao, 35, 72, 233n12
Yamana Morouji, 37
Yama no oto [The sound of the mountain] (Kawabata), 141
Yamaori Tetsuo, 119
Yamashina Tokitsugu, 7–8
Yanagita Kunio, 48
Yang Guifei, 145–46
Yasuda Jirō, 36, 66
Yasurai Hana festival (Kyoto), 46–47, 56
Yata Jizōdō hall, 87, 88, 93
Yokoe no omi Narihito (legendary figure), 78, 79
Yorimasa (Zeami play), 174
Yōrō civil code, 46
Yoshida Kanetomo, 122
Yoshida-ke hinami ki, 103
Yoshida Kenkō, 56
Yōzei, Emperor, 118
Yuasa Jōji, 188, 189

Yūgaku shudōfū ken [Views on modes of training in the arts of entertainment] (Zeami), 185, 213, 226

yūgen (mystery), xi, 139–40, 153, 155; in actor's performance techniques, 195; as description of *chigo*, 158, 159, 160, 163–64, 207–9; flower arranging and, 152; woman's mode and, 212

Yūzū nenbutsu engi (An account of the origins of the Yūzū nenbutsu sect), 107

Zeami, Zenchiku (Katō and Omote, eds., 1974), xxvi

Zeami Motoyiko, xii, xxv, xxvi, 17, 76, 191–92, 218; as actor, 96, 103; aristocratic pursuits and, 150–51; as chief architect of noh theater, xiii; on demon plays, 101–2; on *dengaku*, 27; dream format in two-act plays, 109–10; early life and training of, xiv, xviii; on *enken*, 171–73, 189–90; on "figure of a boy," 143, 208, 209, 210; at flower parties, 162; masks and Zeami's theories, xx, 194–98; noh training of, 159; perfection of unique type of noh, 102–3; Rinna as influence on, 13; *saidōfū* performance and, 192–93; on *shiore* (moistness), 164–65, 170. See also Fujiwaka (Zeami as *chigo*)

Zeami Motoyiko, works of: *The Flower Basket*, 179, 180–81, 183; *Go ongyoku jōjō*, *186*; *Izutsu*, 161, 205–6, 212; *Kakyō* (1424), 188–90, 193–94, 201–2, 226; *Kyūi*, 185, 188; *Lady Han*, 179, 180, 182; *Matsura*, 174; *The Reed Cutter*, 180, 182, 183; *Saigyō-zakura*, 50; *Sandō* (1423), 160, 179, 180, 183; *Shikadō* (1420), 143, 159, 160, 171, 190; *Shūgyoku tokuka* (1428), 185–86, 189, 198–99; *Ukon*, 174; *Yorimasa*, 174; *Yūgaku shudōfū ken*, 185, 213, 226. See also *Nikyoku santai ningyō zu*; *Sarugaku dangi*; *Tōru*

Zeami's Talks on Sarugaku (de Poorter, 1986), xxvi

Zen, 114, 141, 152, 191, 229

Zenchiku (son-in-law of Zeami), 205, 210

Zenkōji temple, 16

Zenna, 10, 34, 49, 52, 54, 55–56

Zeshō, 49, 52

Zōami, 183

GPSR Authorized Representative: Easy Access System Europe, Mustamäe tee 50, 10621 Tallinn, Estonia, gpsr.requests@easproject.com